"This well-written and user-friendly workbook presents new ways of understanding and overcoming depression. Based on mindfulness, acceptance, self-compassion, positive psychology, and neuroscience, it combines solid research foundations with practical methods for climbing out of helplessness and self-blame, and building a satisfying life."

—**Ruth Baer, PhD**, author of *The Practicing Happiness Workbook*

"This book is a godsend for anyone struggling with depression. It is incredibly rich in terms of theoretical and scientific scope and depth, yet provides many practical, easy-to-do exercises for readers so they can start changing how they relate to themselves and their lives right away. I couldn't recommend this book more highly."

—**Kristin Neff, PhD**, associate professor of educational psychology at The University of Texas at Austin, pioneer in the field of self-compassion research, and author of *Self-Compassion*

"In this second edition of their classic self-help manual, Kirk Strosahl and Patricia Robinson bring two professional lifetimes' worth of wisdom and experience to help us better understand depression, and work with it both skillfully and compassionately. This well-written book presents us with cutting-edge strategies drawn from acceptance and commitment therapy (ACT), mindfulness, self-compassion, and neuroscience traditions in the service of building a life worth living. Perhaps what I like most about this book is that it isn't just about helping us cope with depression—it's a pragmatic guide to cultivating a life filled with meaning and purpose. Rarely does a self-help resource so skillfully capture so much of the best that psychology has to offer. Highly recommended!"

—**Russell L. Kolts, PhD**, professor of psychology at Eastern Washington University, and author of *CFT Made Simple* and *The Compassionate-Mind Guide to Managing Your Anger*

The
Mindfulness & Acceptance
Workbook for Depression

————— SECOND EDITION —————

Using Acceptance & Commitment Therapy to Move
Through Depression & Create a Life Worth Living

KIRK D. STROSAHL, PhD
PATRICIA J. ROBINSON, PhD

New Harbinger Publications, Inc.

Distributed in Canada by Raincoast Books

Copyright © 2017 by Kirk D. Strosahl and Patricia J. Robinson
New Harbinger Publications, Inc.
5674 Shattuck Avenue
Oakland, CA 94609
www.newharbinger.com

"Self-Assessment: Five-Facet Mindfulness Questionnaire," in chapter 4 of this book, is adapted from the Five-Facet Mindfulness Questionnaire (FFMQ) in R. A. Baer, G. T. Smith, J. Hopkins, J. Krietemeyer, and L. Toney. 2006. "Using Self-Report Assessment Methods to Explore Facets of Mindfulness." *Assessment* 13:27–45. Used by permission of the authors.

"How I Typically Act Toward Myself in Difficult Times" in chapter 11 is adapted with permission from the work of Kristin Neff.

Cover design by Amy Shoup; Acquired by Catharine Meyers; Edited by Marisa Solis

---

Library of Congress Cataloging-in-Publication Data

Names: Strosahl, Kirk, 1950- author. | Robinson, Patricia J., author.

Title: The mindfulness and acceptance workbook for depression : using acceptance and commitment therapy to move through depression and create a life worth living / Kirk D. Strosahl, PhD, and Patricia J. Robinson, PhD ; foreword by Steven C. Hayes.

Description: Second edition. | Oakland, CA : New Harbinger Publications, Inc., [2017] | Includes bibliographical references.

Identifiers: LCCN 2016050918 (print) | LCCN 2016051489 (ebook) | ISBN 9781626258457 (paperback) | ISBN 9781626258464 (pdf e-book) | ISBN 9781626258471 (epub) | ISBN 9781626258464 (PDF e-book) | ISBN 9781626258471 (ePub)

Subjects: LCSH: Depression, Mental. | Acceptance and commitment therapy. | BISAC: SELF-HELP / Depression. | BODY, MIND & SPIRIT / Meditation. | PSYCHOLOGY / Psychopathology / Depression.

Classification: LCC RC537 .S845 2017 (print) | LCC RC537 (ebook) | DDC 616.85/27--dc23

LC record available at https://lccn.loc.gov/2016050918

19   18   17

10   9   8   7   6   5   4   3   2   1   First Printing

To all the people I've worked with over the years who have taught me so much about the courage it takes to stare down and transcend depression. I'm privileged to have been a part of their unique life journeys. To my daughters, Regan, Frances, and Joanna: each of you brings a unique gift to the world and joy to my heart. To my life companion and writing partner, Patti: You have brought me alive inside in countless ways throughout our journey together. You are the love of my life. In memory of my beloved brother Mark Strosahl and best friend Greg Campbell: The Three Amigos ride no more, but I'm not done just yet!

—Kirk Strosahl

To our daughters, yours and ours: Let's raise them to be brave, not perfect.

—Patricia Robinson

Contents

Foreword:
Trading Illusions for Actions

Depression is not just a feeling. Depression is an action.

That simple insight will strike with a force as you read this book. It is an insight worth preparing for because as it dawns, it initially contains both good news and bad news. The bad news is that the human mind will often turn it into yet another source for blame: "If depression is an action, then I should not be doing it, but apparently I am, so it must be my fault." No surprise there. Judging and blaming are what our minds often do, particularly when we are depressed. But the actions that lead to depression—the actions that in a deep sense are depression—are nothing to be blamed for. After all, the human mind is far, far too tricky for anyone to untangle from it without help. Depression is not the fault of the depressed.

The empowering news inside this same insight is even more powerful and more sustaining than the illusion of helplessness or the habits of self-blame. As you read this book you will see that there is a concrete, active path forward. You are not a victim of your life. You are not doomed to endless suffering.

As you understand the actions that have kept you entangled, you will begin to see that there is another way. The alternative is not beyond you. It is available, with help to see it, right here, right now.

In this remarkable book, the husband-and-wife team of Kirk Strosahl and Patricia Robinson lay down an innovative, creative, and effective pathway out of depression and into your life. The book is like turning on a light inside darkened rooms of suffering. With the light comes greater understanding of what is in those rooms, where you are, and what has been in your way. It becomes easier to see how to navigate and how to come out into the warmth and freedom of a life without walls, directed toward your values.

From the first few pages of this book until the very last, the light of awareness that it casts is almost tangible. You can sense the gentleness, strength, and humanity of the people, two of my dearest friends, who have written this book. These authors are humble, centered, compassionate, and wise. They've been there. They are ready to walk you, step by step, through the actions that have created trouble and the actions needed to let go of depressed habits of mind. If you have patience with the process, self-compassion for the pain you are in, and a willingness to face the difficulties and fears of taking a fundamentally different pathway forward, this book can change your life.

I can say that without fear of contradiction, because the scientific evidence showing that the processes this book targets are central to depression has grown exponentially over the last decade. We now know a great deal about how cognitive entanglement works and how to help people become disentangled through mindfulness. We now know a lot about how avoidance of experience works, and how acceptance can dampen down the war within. And we know a lot about how openness to experience can help you get in touch with your values and begin to create a life with your moment-to-moment actions that resonates more with your deepest yearnings for meaning, wholeness, and connection with others.

You do not need to trust me or trust these authors for the benefits of this book to be felt. You do not need to believe anything or be convinced of anything. What you need is the willingness to look without blinking—to see what is true in your experience. As you try the methods in this book, your own experience will be your best teacher.

Depression is not just a feeling. Depression is an action. The "word machine" in between our ears may indeed fear what that means, but for human beings the message is hopeful, vital, and valid. You do not need to wait for life. It has begun and it is yours to live.

If you are ready to open up to that possibility, turn the page and begin.

—Steven C. Hayes
University of Nevada

A Mindful Approach to Depression

Our doubts are traitors, and make us lose the good we oft might win, by fearing to attempt.

—William Shakespeare

If you are battling depression right now, you are not alone. Depression is one of the most common emotional health issues in contemporary society. A conservative estimate is that 7 percent of the general public suffers from a clinical depression at any moment in time (Kessler et al. 2005). If we factor in depressions that are associated with other common problems such as posttraumatic stress, chronic anxiety, or drug or alcohol dependence, that figure can easily expand to 20 percent. If we further factor in acute depressions triggered by life stresses such as marital problems, parenting issues, money problems, unemployment, unsafe living conditions, and so forth, that figure could go much, much higher!

Depression is so common that it's hard to turn on the TV or browse the Internet without seeing some type of advertisement for a new drug, over-the-counter supplement, or other purported cure for depression. Moreover, news stories tend to sensationalize depression, for example, explaining the tragedy of a suicide by describing the victim's unsuccessful battle against depression. We also receive a grab bag of mixed messages about the causes of depression, ranging from it being heredity to a biological illness to a reaction to life stress or setbacks to the result of distorted thinking or major shifts in daily behaviors.

We also hear emotional appeals about what life is like when depression is treated successfully—that the formerly depressed person is now in a state of bliss, that his or her relationships have been restored and new ones formed. We see public service and commercial ads wherein a person who used to sit dejectedly with head in hands now walks gleefully with children, spouse, or pets and seems to be absolutely carefree. The message being given is that in order to get your life going again, you first must gain control over your depression.

We believe this portrayal of depression is not only misleading, but it also points depressed people seeking treatment in a direction that is unlikely to be of much lasting help. Depression is a far more complex mental process than these stereotypes suggest; no two depressed people are alike in the life circumstances that surround them or in how depression affects their life. What is needed is a different way of thinking about depression, a way that puts you back in the driver's seat and in control of your own destiny.

A NEW PERSPECTIVE ON DEPRESSION

There are many aspects of modern society that encourage us to live in a mindless kind of way. To keep up with the fast pace of living, our schedules are crammed with responsibilities and duties. We are taught that scheduling "me time" is a form of selfishness. Daily routines are so well practiced that we don't even think about what we're doing much of the time. We spend endless hours living in the past and the future rather than in the "here and now." The irony is that it is only in the here and now that we experience a true sense of being alive.

Unfortunately, the here and now is also where you make contact with emotional pain from current or past events in life. This pain might come from a trauma you experienced as a child or adult, a series of failed relationships or a divorce that left you doubting yourself, ongoing problems with children, a stressful and unrewarding job, and so forth. Whatever the source of your pain, you are faced with an ongoing quandary: in order to experience the vitality of life, you must also be willing to experience the emotional pain that life can give you.

Sadly, one of the rules we learn as children is to control our emotions or risk the social consequences of not doing so. We are taught that painful emotions are bad for us and that the goal is to control or eliminate them. The reality, though, is that emotions cannot be controlled in this way. When you try to control what you feel, your feelings just get bigger and more intrusive. And when you try to run from or avoid your feelings, you are robbed of the important information that your emotions have to offer you.

Your emotions, particularly the painful ones, provide the fuel that will propel you to make important changes that bring your life into better balance. If you avoid your pain, then it is very likely that those problems will just fester—and probably get worse. This is the trap that depressed people fall into. They unknowingly trade the vitality that comes from living in the present moment for the illusion of emotional safety.

Contrary to some other popular stereotypes, it is important to realize that depression is not something you *have*, it is something you *do*. Depression is the result of an organized set of behaviors that makes you emotionally numb and unable to act in ways that are consistent with your values. Depression is not an aberration, a fluke, or an accident of nature. It is a logical result of what you're putting into your life. Depression is a signal that you need to show up, be intentional, take an open and curious attitude toward your emotions, and engage in actions that reflect your values and principles.

So if you can't control your emotions or hide from them, what can you do? You can choose to experience your feelings and thoughts, both wanted and unwanted, and do what is meaningful to you. This is a *vital life*—a life worth living—and pursuing it is not a feel-good exercise, with one pleasant event leading to another. Rather, it is a commitment to living with whatever shows up on your life path.

We can become sad, anxious, or discouraged when the things that matter are not going well. It is what you do with these reactions that makes all the difference. Allowing yourself to feel what you feel, think what you think, and, at the same time, act according to your values is going to promote a sense of vitality, purpose, and meaning. If living life mindlessly and avoiding painful emotions is the way into depression, then living mindfully and accepting your pain is the way out. In this book, we are going to teach you how to do just that!

THE ACCEPTANCE AND COMMITMENT THERAPY APPROACH

The new perspectives, strategies, and skills we teach in this book come from a proven-effective therapeutic approach called *acceptance and commitment therapy* (ACT; pronounced like the word "act"). ACT is a cognitive behavioral therapy that has gained increasing prominence in both the popular press (Hayes and Smith 2005; Strosahl and Robinson 2014) and within the mental health and drug and alcohol treatment communities (Hayes, Strosahl, and Wilson 2011). ACT has proven to be a good treatment for depression in adults (Fledderus et al. 2012; Forman et al. 2012; Kohtala et al. 2015; Zettle and Hayes 1987; Zettle and Rains 1989) and adolescents (Hayes, Boyd, and Sewell 2011), and it seems to produce benefits that last long after treatment has stopped (Lappalainen et al. 2014).

One of the core goals of ACT is to teach you how to use mindfulness strategies to bolster present-moment awareness, foster emotional acceptance, and live your life based upon personal values. *Mindfulness* is a widely used term that means many different things to people, but, broadly speaking, we see it as the ability to pay attention to the present moment in a nonjudgmental, detached way; to practice compassion for self and others; and to behave with awareness, intention, and purpose in daily life. People who live according to these key principles may run into significant life challenges, as we all do, but they tend to be emotionally resilient and much less prone to depression.

Mindfulness and Depression

When we published the first edition of this book in 2008, research on the impact of mindfulness on mental health generally, and depression specifically, was just beginning to show up in the literature.

Now we now have an abundance of research studies showing that mindfulness is a very powerful treatment not just for depression but also for promoting long-term physical health and mental well-being (Sundquist et al. 2015).

Interestingly, even people who have experienced repeated episodes of depression (Teasdale et al. 2000; Teasdale et al. 2002) or have failed to respond to other treatments seem to benefit (Eisendrath et al. 2016). Thus, even if you have been experiencing depression for many years and have not responded to treatment, or you got better with treatment and now are in the midst of another depression, it is still quite likely you will benefit from the strategies presented in this book. Equally encouraging is that practicing mindfulness skills, at whatever level you currently possess, using the ACT approach is going to strengthen them and make them easier for you to use in daily life (Bohlmeijer et al. 2011). Further, changes in mindfulness abilities resulting from ACT have been associated with better treatment results (Arch et al. 2012; Forman et al. 2012; Zettle, Raines, and Hayes 2011).

Contemporary brain science tells us that mindfulness strategies literally snap the depressed person out of the mental fog of daydreaming, mind wandering, and rumination (Farb et al. 2010). Practicing mindfulness strategies isn't just a "feel good" strategy; it is actually a highly beneficial form of brain training (Levenson et al. 2014). Just like you exercise your body to strengthen your muscles and improve your circulation, exercising your brain strengthens your mindfulness muscle. We can say without reservation that, if you put the time into learning and practicing the mindfulness strategies we introduce in this workbook, you have a very good chance of getting on top of your depression.

BUT IS THIS APPROACH RIGHT FOR ME?

You might be wondering if the ACT approach is the right one for you. That's a good question, because no single approach works for everyone. To help you determine whether you might benefit from the skills we teach in this book, take a few moments to mentally complete the following brief quiz. See if any of the statements below describe you most of the time, or at least some of the time:

I often engage in daily activities without even being aware I'm doing them.

I find it difficult to slow down and just be in the moment.

I tend to be very judgmental of myself and the emotions I am experiencing.

I tend to replay past life setbacks or failures and try to figure out what is wrong with me.

My mind tends to wander when I am trying to pay attention.

I try to suppress or distract myself from any negative emotions I may be having.

I often end up becoming absorbed in my negative emotions.

I tend to be very self-critical and harsh with myself when I experience any kind of setback.

I find it hard to express what I am feeling inside.

I seldom let myself think about what matters to me most in life.

I tend to base my daily routines on controlling my depression rather than living according to my values.

I frequently feel like I'm just going through the motions in my life.

If one or more of these statements remind you of you, this book *can* help you! That's because all of these statements describe an important barrier to living mindfully. When you live mindfully, with awareness, you *can* better manage and overcome your depression. By learning and practicing the skills in this book, you *will* become more mindful. This book will teach you how to:

- Get into the "here and now," even during periods of emotional distress.

- Use a variety of words to describe and work effectively with distressing, unwanted thoughts, feelings, memories, and physical sensations.

- Detach from sources of emotional distress and not be judgmental about them.

- Be kind and affectionate toward yourself during those moments when you run into a personal flaw, setback, or failure.

- Make contact with what matters to you in life and then act with intention to head in that life direction.

A MANTRA: ACCEPT, CHOOSE, AND TAKE ACTION

Another way of thinking about ACT is as a prescription for healthy living:

A for Accept

C for Choose

T for Take action

"Accept, choose, and take action." Say this aloud several times now and really take it to heart. It may be helpful to you as you read and practice ACT strategies over the coming weeks. Write it on several pieces of paper and tape them to your refrigerator, your vanity mirror, your toilet seat, the edge of your computer screen, and wherever else you'll see it often. We want these three simple concepts to become your daily mantra. Say it to yourself twenty times a day or more! Sometimes we're accused of functioning more like cheerleaders than therapists, but heck, if cheerleading helps you build the life you've always wanted to live, we're sold on it.

ACCEPTING THE UNCERTAINTY OF CHANGE

Even if this program may seem like a perfect fit for you, you may be thinking, "I don't know if I'm ready to move out of my depression. I've tried different things to control my depression and they didn't work then. I'm worried. How do I know it'll work this time?" That's a very good question—and an important one. After all, doesn't our culture suggest that we should let sleeping dogs lie?

The reasons not to deal with your depression might seem clear: You could be exposed directly to more anxiety, fear, sadness, guilt, shame, anger, rejection, criticism, and disapproval from others. Things definitely could get worse before they get better. Being depressed is at least familiar. You know exactly what depression feels like, and you may have modified your daily life to fit depression in as part of your ongoing reality. You don't know exactly what will happen if you try something different. Things could get better or worse. But you do know exactly what will happen if you stay where you are: you'll probably get some of the same results in your life you've been getting up to now.

One reason you might want to explore the strategies we share in this book is the simple fact that you have an inherent desire as a human to have a say about how you live your life. It is in choosing that we bring purpose and deeper meaning to our life experiences and directions. This option is there for you. It's a birthright of all human beings, but that doesn't mean it's delivered to you on a silver platter—you have to seize it. Only you can do this, and it won't be easy. You need to be willing to fail sometimes, to feel sadness and loss, to experience guilt and shame, to think distressing thoughts, and to sometimes remember unpleasant and frightening experiences from your past. The choice to deal with difficult aspects of your life might require you to face a variety of unpleasant and painful experiences—and it offers you the opportunity to grow as a human being in the process.

In all honesty, you won't know how this turns out until you start trying some different behaviors. You might be thinking that you have absolutely no clue what the future will look like. You might even be predicting that you'll fail somehow, or that you'll be even more dissatisfied than you are now. That's completely understandable! In this book, we'll actually teach you how to say, "Hi there" to your mind when it starts to worry. It might sound silly now, but you'll soon discover that changing how you relate to your mind is a huge step toward overcoming depression!

HOW THIS BOOK IS ORGANIZED

This book is organized into three major sections to help you in your quest to transcend depression. Part 1 is called "Preparing for Radical Change." To begin, you need to understand what your depression experiences are, how they affect your current life, and the ways that depression might be preventing you (or protecting you) from dealing with personal problems you need to deal with. This will allow you to understand how your depression operates, both between your ears and in the outer world.

We will also introduce you to the ways that living mindfully can enhance your sense of vitality and well-being. We'll help you assess your mindfulness skills and develop a plan to begin improving them over time. Finally, we will introduce you to the key ACT concept of *workability*. This approach encourages you to shift from looking for strategies that *should* help your depression to looking for strategies that *will* help your depression. You will likely discover that although many of the strategies you use to cope with your depression might be working in the short run, they inevitably turn out to be unworkable in the long run and actually worsen your depression

Part 2, "9 Mindful Steps to Transcend Depression," is designed to help you clarify what you want your life to be about. We will teach you how to accept unpleasant realities, step back from them so they don't consume you, and then act in ways that promote better results for you. This part of your journey will sometimes be confusing, and involve thinking and behaving in ways opposite to those you might have used in the past. If you stick with it—and you can!—you'll begin to see the paradox that underlies depression and be able to do something about it. Each chapter in this section will expose you to several state-of-the-art brain training exercises, based on the results of neuroscience studies of depression, that are designed to help you strengthen the neural pathways in your brain that produce feelings of centeredness and well-being.

Part 3, "Creating the Life You Want to Live," will introduce you to some cutting-edge concepts from the field of positive psychology. We now know that your ability to engage in daily behaviors that produce a sense of relaxation or reward actually inoculates you from the stresses of daily living that can trigger depression. We will help you develop a positive daily living plan that will help you succeed at the daunting task of having some level of fun, relaxation, or reward every day! In the spirit of hoping for the best, while preparing for the worst, we will ask you to identify risk situations in your life that might pull you back into depression. Then, we will help you prepare a specific positive-action plan for those situations that might trigger a recurrence of depression.

Learning to stand up and make a commitment to promoting your sense of vitality in life requires you to be persistent, even when you have a bad day and don't live up to your promise. Persistence is everything when you want to develop a new way of living. This is why it is so important to connect to what matters to you most in life.

How to Use This Book

Like many people, you may be interested in a self-help book because of a desire to learn how to control your depression without bothering others or incurring the cost of professional help. This strategy can succeed to the extent that you stick with the program, so we've designed it to make this easier for you. Each chapter introduces one or two important ACT concepts and illustrates them with stories of real people who have struggled with depression. Each chapter includes exercises to help you develop your awareness of a particular issue and to practice skills that will help you succeed.

It's less important to be good at every strategy we discuss than to be good at using a few key strategies that fit your personal style. It's okay to jump around in the book, focusing on chapters that appeal to your interests and needs at the time. If you become adept with just a few ACT strategies, we are confident that you'll still notice an immediate effect on your quality of life.

To help you use this program over time, you can find accessory materials that support the strategies and activities described in this workbook on this book's website: http://www.newharbinger.com/38457. There you'll find free downloadable worksheets and guided audio versions of many mindfulness and experiential exercises. Look for the following icons in the text:

 This icon tells you that you can download a copy of the worksheet.

 This icon tells you that an audio version is available for download.

If you decide to move forward with this self-help program, we encourage you to download all of these materials ahead of time so that they are easily accessible to you. This will allow you to keep your focus on following along with the exercises in each chapter.

Ask Others to Support You

One strategy that will be useful right now is to mention what you're trying to do to a friend, intimate partner, sibling, or anyone who can hold your feet to the fire. Making a commitment to try something different in front of someone else is a powerful way to support your success.

You can do the same with your health care provider. Mention that you're trying to overcome depression and want to use this program. Ask your health care provider to check in with you about how you're doing with the program at each medical visit.

If you're working with a therapist, take this book with you to your next appointment and go over the structure of the program together. Then you can come up with a plan for integrating various sections of the book into the therapy process, perhaps using some of the chapters in part 2 as homework that you will complete between sessions.

A LITTLE STORY

Before we move on (and hopefully you move along with us!), there is a well-known Buddhist story that might help you find the boldness to commit to reading this book and following through with the ACT program. It's a story that speaks to having the courage to give life your best shot, despite the inevitable process of change that we all must learn to accept.

A young monk walks many miles, hoping to gain enlightenment from a renowned Zen master. When the student enters the master's chamber, the master is sitting on the floor drinking from a cup. The master explains to the student that the cup is very precious. The student agrees, and the master asks, "Why do you think this cup is so precious?" The student suggests it is the color and size of the cup and the slender quality of its handle. The master agrees that all of these aspects make it an attractive cup, but these are not its most precious properties. The student becomes confused and asks the master to answer his own question. The master sighs. "It is most precious because it is already broken and it has already held so many cups of tea."

Your life has a beginning and an end, with everything in between being an exercise in uncertainty and change. As the old saying goes, *The only constant in life is change.* This is the nature of pursuing your dream of a life worth living. The journey is perfectly made to teach you what you need to know, if you will only accept that everything is destined to change. Is this a reason to avoid starting the journey? We think not, especially as change is inevitable either way! We hope you agree, and we challenge you to keep reading.

Preparing for Radical Change

The unexamined life is not worth living.

—Plato

The main principle to follow in moving through your depression into a life worth living is to understand that you can only start from where you are, not from where you would like to be. To solve a complicated problem like depression, you must develop a boots-on-the-ground understanding of how your life is working *right now*. This requires you to take an honest look at several factors that might be contributing to your depression. And it compels you to begin thinking about developing new skills that will work better for you.

In part 1 of this book, we'll introduce you to several new ways of thinking about depression from the following viewpoints:

- Acceptance and commitment therapy

- Mindfulness

- Self-compassion

- Positive psychology

- Clinical neuroscience

We'll also introduce you to some core elements that drive depression:

- Following unworkable rules about dealing with painful emotions

- Living life on autopilot

- Using short-term avoidance strategies instead of long-term values-based approaches

Together, these elements keep you locked in a vicious cycle. But the good news is that you can easily escape this cycle once you learn to recognize it. We'll help you determine the extent to which these elements apply in your life by providing you with several self-inventories.

We'll also teach you about the qualities involved in being more mindful and flexible in your approach to challenging life moments. This includes being open to your personal experiences, being aware and in the present moment, and being engaged in what matters to you in life. You'll learn about the role that mindfulness plays in helping you move through depression, and we'll have you complete a self-assessment of your mindfulness skills and develop an initial plan for strengthening them.

Once you understand how depression works, you'll be in an excellent position to do something about it. The key is to learn to think about your depression in a new way and then get an accurate picture of the factors that are propelling you in unintended directions. This might be difficult at times because the truth doesn't always feel good—but the truth actually will set you free! So read each chapter carefully and try to complete all the exercises. Don't beat yourself up—just collect the results and get ready to embark on your quest to move through depression and into a life worth living!

Here's a worksheet to help you keep track of your confidence in your grasp of the material presented in each chapter. After reading each chapter, come back to this worksheet and rate your confidence level on a scale of 1 to 10, whereby 1 indicates that you need more help and 10 indicates that you've totally got it. Take your time with these initial chapters because they require you to go outside the box and rethink how depression is functioning for you, and against you, in your life right now. If you give yourself a chance to complete part 1, we promise that you'll understand depression—and what to do about it—in a new way that will give you a fresh start on creating the kind of life you want to live.

PART I CONFIDENCE WORKSHEET

Need More Help			Somewhat Confident			Confident			Got It!
1	2	3	4	5	6	7	8	9	10

Chapter		Confidence Level
1	New Perspectives on Depression	
2	Human Vulnerabilities in Depression	
3	It's All About Workability	
4	Understanding the Mind and Mindfulness	

If your confidence rating is 5 or less for any chapter, you might want to reread those sections of the chapter that were confusing to you. Or you might share the chapter with a friend and see if putting your heads together helps deepen your understanding of the material. Enlisting this type of support can often inspire you to keep working your way through the program. It takes patience to make changes in your life. Remember to be kind to yourself!

CHAPTER 1

New Perspectives on Depression

We cannot solve our problems with the same thinking we used when we created them.

—Albert Einstein

If you're looking at this self-help book, it's likely that you're struggling with serious issues in your life that you haven't been able to fix. You may be in a bad relationship, maybe even an abusive one. Maybe your job is at a dead end and you haven't mustered the courage to move on to something else because of the risks involved. You may simply be demoralized by the demands of life and the ongoing stress of it all. Perhaps you're trying to care for an aging parent while raising your children and pursuing a career. Perhaps you're having trouble with one or more of your children and can't find the right way to approach it. Or you might not be approaching it at all because you don't like conflict. You may be struggling with chronic health problems with no easy solution.

Perhaps you're fighting a secret or not-so-secret addiction to alcohol, drugs, sex, the Internet, or food—habits that help you escape from and numb personal pain in the short term but lead to more depression in the long run. It may be that you're so busy reliving your past that you've forgotten how to live in the present, or, worse, you're letting your past dictate the present. You may simply be living by the numbers, hoping that life will cut you a better deal if you follow all the rules. You might even be experiencing a lot of success in your life at the surface level, earning a good salary and having a nice home and lots of "toys" but feel unhappy and out of sorts nevertheless.

At first glance, none of these scenarios seems way out of the ordinary. These types of personal challenges are the bread and butter of everyday living. People fall in and out of love, get divorced, change or lose jobs, and grapple with unwanted events like health problems and the death of loved ones. But people often cope with challenging life moments in ways that don't work that well. There are almost 24 million people dependent on alcohol and other drugs in the United States alone (Grant et al. 2004), roughly 8.6 percent of the entire population. In particular, there has been a virtual nationwide epidemic of narcotic addiction, due in part to the ease with which narcotics can be legally procured. Narcotic overdose deaths are now the leading cause of accidental death in 29 states, surpassing automobile accident fatalities for the number one slot. The current annual rate of onset of mental disorders in the United States is 27 percent (Kessler et al. 2005; SAMHSA 2013), meaning that every year, one in four Americans will experience a serious emotional health problem.

The overall pervasiveness of mental health and substance abuse problems translates into a substantial lifetime risk of depression: approximately 20 percent for women and 10 percent for men (Kessler et al. 2005). This means that, during their lifetimes, one in five women will experience depression, and one in ten men. Do these numbers suggest that something is amiss in our basic human training? Is depression the common cold of modern living? If so, what's the pathogen responsible for this epidemic of suffering?

The purpose of this chapter is to present some new perspectives on depression that will help you see it in a different, more approachable way. We will examine depression in a way that is quite different from the traditional biomedical approach. First off, we will introduce you to a powerful, evidence-based treatment for depression called *acceptance and commitment therapy* (ACT; Hayes, Strosahl, and Wilson 2011). ACT works to promote the ability to:

- Be in the present moment in life

- Be accepting of and detached from unwanted, distressing experiences such as painful emotions, intrusive memories, or self-critical thoughts

- Act in ways that reflect personal values

Closely tied to ACT, but now a separate field of research in its own right, is the general role of *mindfulness* in the treatment of depression. In the introduction to this book, we mention that mindfulness is not a single skill but rather a group of skills, all of which are included in various ways within the ACT model. Mindfulness training has also been employed with success in other, non-ACT treatments for depression. The bottom line: You *can* reverse your depression if you learn how to apply mindfulness skills in your daily life.

We will also briefly examine the burgeoning field of *affective neuroscience*. In studying the nervous system as a basis for our emotions and mood, this area of science has led to a particular interest in identifying the neural mechanisms of depression, as well as in how mindfulness practice affects those mechanisms.

Another encouraging development in the last couple of years is the emerging role of self-compassion in the treatment of depression. We will examine the concept of self-compassion in more detail and show why learning to be self-compassionate is so central to moving through depression.

Next, we will look at depression from the perspective of *positive psychology*, a relatively new branch of psychology that studies human resilience and the ways that people create sustainable positive emotional experience in daily living. We now know that engaging in positive, emotionally rewarding behaviors on a daily basis creates a positive-emotion "savings account" that makes people more resilient when they run into life challenges or setbacks that, for some, might be a trigger for a descent into depression (Frederickson and Losada 2005).

Finally, we will examine the highly prevalent, somewhat simplified media account of depression as a genetically transmitted, biological illness that is best treated with antidepressant medications. Adhering to this viewpoint leads some people with depression to conclude that using medication is their only real hope of living a normal life. We will introduce you to an alternative way of thinking about depression: the *biopsychosocial model* (Schotte et al. 2006). This contemporary perspective does more justice to the complex biological, psychological, and social factors that contribute to depression.

After all, if you're going to focus your energy on getting on top of your depression, we want to help you zero in on the strategies that will give you the biggest bang for your buck. We think equipping you with a new, more complete point of view on what depression is—and what it isn't—will make moving through your depression seem eminently more doable. You can thus relax; take a slow, deep breath of fresh air; and attack the problem with a newfound sense of confidence and a clear sense of direction.

FIVE CONTEMPORARY PERSPECTIVES ON DEPRESSION

In order to understand depression in a new light, it is important to understand both contemporary theories about it and developments from different areas of psychological and brain research. When you combine these different perspectives, what emerges is a kind of user's manual for understanding depression and what to do about it. So let's take a look at depression from the following perspectives, which are the cornerstones of this book:

- ACT

- Mindfulness

- Self-compassion

- Positive psychology

- Neuroscience

The ACT Perspective

As we mentioned in the introduction, *acceptance and commitment therapy* (abbreviated and pronounced like the word "act") has been shown to be an effective treatment for depression in both adults and adolescents (Bohlmeijer et al. 2011; Hayes, Boyd, and Sewell 2011; Blarrina et al. 2016; Zettle and Rains 1989). ACT holds that depression is but one example of how people suffer when they follow culturally instilled rules about the necessity of feeling good as a major sign of health and well-being. From early childhood, we are trained to believe that natural, important human emotions—feeling sad, angry, rejected, grief stricken, lonely, ashamed, or anxious—are threats to our health and well-being. Therefore, they must be controlled or eliminated via any means possible.

Granted, painful emotions can be very unpleasant and can command our attention. But that doesn't mean that they are bad for you; they may in fact signal that something important to you is missing or underutilized in your life. At other times, painful feelings might signal the need for you to make a change in your life, like leaving a dysfunctional relationship. At still other times, painful emotions might help heal the wounds of loss, such as when someone close to you dies. Looked at logically, it would be difficult to see emotional experience as the "enemy within," but that's exactly what we learn as we grow up.

The other problem with this pervasive social rule is that private experiences such as painful emotions, disturbing thoughts, distressing memories, or unpleasant physical reactions cannot be controlled or eliminated by an "act of will." Paradoxically, when you attempt to control or eliminate them, they become even more intrusive in your awareness and seem even more out of control. When direct attempts to control or prevent unpleasant emotions don't work, people begin to hunt for other ways to get the job done, such as using alcohol or drugs to quell their feelings, or sleeping for hours on end to blunt their awareness of what is going on inside. Even more toxic in the long run, people figure out that avoiding situations, events, or interactions that trigger unpleasant emotional experiences is a way to control them.

For instance, you may have stopped participating in activities that trigger unpleasant feelings. You may be avoiding talking with your spouse or partner about painful issues in your relationship. You might be distancing yourself from friends because they seem to be doing better in life than you are, and it makes you feel out of place to get together with them because they are happy and you aren't. Put simply, you protect yourself from personal pain by withdrawing from or avoiding those things in your life that most matter to you. The reason these situations are emotionally painful is because they *do* matter to you.

Sadly, most of us don't even realize we are following rules like this—our behaviors are so well ingrained as to be almost automatic. So instead of trying something completely at odds with the rule, we follow it even more rigidly and forcefully. As we sink into the ooze of this unworkable, self-defeating approach, more and more extreme coping strategies seem warranted. These generally involve either quick-acting strategies designed to numb our awareness of distressing experiences (for example, drinking, drugging, overeating, binging and purging, cutting, or attempting suicide) or slower-acting strategies such as becoming withdrawn, disengaged, or emotionally numbed out (all typical symptoms of depression).

For a moment, think about your current life situation and the emotional challenges it brings. Perhaps you've been trained to believe that the goal is to be strong and not allow your emotions to surface. Worse yet, maybe you sincerely believe that having negative emotions such as sadness, anxiety, anger, or fear is a sign that there is something wrong with you. This type of message puts you at odds with your feelings in situation after situation. When you are at war with your own feelings, it will be almost impossible to use your emotions to help guide your behavior. Your instincts and intuitions will not enter into your decision-making process, and this leaves you prone to letting personal problems slide or, worse yet, avoiding dealing with them altogether.

In ACT, we view depression not as a problem to be solved but as an important signal that something isn't working quite right, that your life is out of balance in some important way We want to use the information contained in your depression to help you create a new life plan that doesn't involve suppressing how you feel or avoiding important life situations that can determine your overall quality of life. In ACT, we believe that *controlling your emotions, avoiding the situations that produce them, is the problem, not the solution.*

You don't get healthier by turning your back on how you feel—that only makes you more vulnerable to the very things you are trying to steer clear of. Avoiding problems in your marriage, family, job, or health doesn't make the problem go away—it actually makes the situation worse. For instance, if you don't address important problems in an intimate relationship, you may feel less connected to your partner and start to drift away. As things get worse, your depression will deepen and you may begin to avoid other problems, like the fact that you're feeling less romantic with your partner. Likewise, if your job is unfulfilling, and your approach is to not think about the fact that your work is losing its meaning, avoidance of the problem can make your work less interesting—and eventually you have to deal with burnout. Or if you have a risky health habit like smoking, drinking too much, or being too reliant on drugs, simply turning your back on the problem doesn't make it less risky.

And maybe, somewhere in the back of your mind, there's an intuition that depression is turning you into a person you don't want to be. Even if it's unintentional, falling into a pattern of avoiding unpleasant or painful feelings and the situations that trigger them is a major cause of depression.

The Mindfulness Perspective

ACT utilizes a wide range of mindfulness concepts and practices for good reason: because low levels of mindfulness are associated with high levels of depression (Williams 2010). Research has also shown that going through an ACT program like the one we present in this book hones mindfulness skills, like the ability to be present, detached, nonjudgmental, intentional, and values focused (Bohlmeijer et al. 2011). Even more important, positive changes in mindfulness skills are associated with improved treatment results in ACT (Arch et al. 2012; Forman et al. 2012; Zettle, Rains, and Hayes 2011).

One key process leading to depression is overidentifying with socially ingrained rules that emphasize controlling or eliminating distressing, unwanted emotions. The failed quest for emotional control is at the heart of depression. If you are depressed, you are often besieged by thoughts such as, "I shouldn't be as upset as I am. What's wrong with me? Why can't I feel good about myself? Everyone else seems to be happy and self-confident—why can't I be?" When you overidentify with rules and self-evaluations, they can seem like undisputed truths—and you might forget that they are just inner experiences.

Think about an alternative reality: What would happen if you could see thoughts as thoughts—not as undisputed truths that you must follow? If they produced an urge to act in an unhelpful way, what if you could simply experience an impulse as an impulse, without acting on it? What if you could reliably create a space between your thoughts and your actions, such that you don't have to do what your thoughts tell you to do?

The reason mindfulness skills work so well in depression is that they help you create a space between you and your thoughts and impulses. This allows you to pick *approach behaviors* instead of *avoidance behaviors*. Approach behaviors allow you to engage in important life activities, even if they are emotionally challenging (Barnhofer et al. 2009; Bihari and Mullen 2014; Williams 2008). Avoidance behaviors, while promising you emotional safety, actually remove you from the field of play, so to speak, putting you on the sidelines in your life. This can lead you to feel like your life is passing you by—and that feeling can be downright depressing to just about anyone!

If you get good at the mindfulness skills we will teach you, you could then hear the ongoing chatter of your "mental advisor"—the part of your brain that is constantly evaluating things and telling you what to do—without necessarily having to do what it says! So instead of trying to argue with your advisor, you could simply:

1. Be aware that the mental chatter is present,

2. Think about what is really important to you right now, and

3. Base your behavior on what matters.

How powerful are mindfulness skills in the treatment of depression? A recent study showed that mindfulness-based treatment is clearly superior to more conventional treatments in a sample of depressed primary care patients (Sundquist et al. 2014). An earlier study of depressed patients found that mindfulness training helped 72 percent of the patients significantly reduce their depression levels (Finucane and Mercer 2006). These patients reported that they enjoyed mindfulness exercises, and more than half continued to use these techniques after the study ended.

Another reason that mindfulness is so effective with depression is that it short-circuits *rumination* (Williams 2010). Rumination is a particularly unhealthy form of depressed thinking that involves replaying past or current life difficulties, excessively analyzing personal flaws and weaknesses, comparing oneself to others, and brooding about one's inability to "feel right" (Nolen-Hoeksema 2000). Indeed, British researchers have found that people who respond to treatment for depression are less likely to have *future* problems with depression if they receive training in mindfulness (Teasdale et al. 2000). These researchers also discovered that mindfulness training creates more detachment from and perspective on unproductive ways of thinking, such as rumination (Teasdale et al. 2002). With mindfulness skills in tow, you are far less likely to get drawn into the *rumination trap*. Specifically, the rumination trap occurs when you get entangled in ruminating, and then, to top things off, you begin to over-analyze why it is that you can't stop ruminating!

There is one last thing to consider: the benefits of mindfulness don't stop at helping you address depression. Indeed, a wide variety of other benefits have been associated with practicing mindfulness skills, including increased mental efficiency (Deshmukh 2006), better problem-solving skills (Hankey 2006), increased levels of compassion and altruistic feelings toward others (Weng et al. 2013), and increased levels of self-acceptance (Fennell 2004).

The Self-Compassion Perspective

Self-compassion is a powerful skill you'll want to acquire on your quest to transcend depression— and on your journey through life in general. Self-compassion involves taking an open, accepting, and nonjudgmental stance with respect to your personal flaws, inadequacies, and life disappointment.

As the old saying goes, "To err is human." Our hang-up, however, is that when we do mess up, our immediate emotional response is a feeling of alienation, as if we are on an island and are different from everyone else. To compound the problem, the painful feelings that come from failure or disappointment are real—they are not illusions. So how you treat yourself in your moment of pain will largely determine how much you suffer. If you are harsh with yourself, you will hurt even more. If you soften and treat yourself with kindness, and remember that you are part of humanity and are not alone, your emotional experience is likely to hurt far less.

The fact is, if you have been depressed for any length of time, you will likely suffer some negative real-life outcomes, like losing a primary relationship or a job, or being rejected by friends. Many times, depressions start with events that involve interpersonal loss, career setbacks, illness, death of a loved one, and so on. It turns out that how you treat yourself during these moments of suffering directly predicts your risk of depression. If you take a harsh, self-critical, self-rejecting stance, your risk of depression goes up steadily. If you treat yourself with kindness and acceptance, your risk of depression goes down steadily (Leary et al. 2007; Neff 2003; Neff, Rude, and Kirkpatrick 2007). When those inevitable moments of life disappointment or personal setback occur, you have a mindful alternative at your beck and call, in your moment of pain, when you are most tempted to beat up on yourself.

The Positive Psychology Perspective

Positive psychology is the study of how people cultivate an optimistic life outlook and positive mood states, even in the midst of challenging or difficult situations. Positive psychology researchers are finding that, just as depressed emotions are fueled by a downward spiral of isolation, withdrawal, and passive avoidance, positive mood states are produced by upward spirals of pleasant activities, social connections, and approach-oriented behaviors (Frederickson and Losada 2005; Garland et al. 2010).

Simply put, the emotional charge of your behavior (whether it be positive or negative) will tend to control your mood state. So one widely agreed upon, powerful remedy for depression is to persistently engage in positive, healthful activities in your daily life. This includes pursuing hobbies, exercising, doing relaxing leisure-time activities, and making casual as well as closer social connections. There is ample evidence in the depression-treatment literature that engaging in positive, healthy-emotion-producing behaviors has an immediate impact upon depression (Martell and Addis 2004).

The Neuroscience Perspective

Here we are going to put our science geek hats on for a bit and try to explain the important role that neuroscience is beginning to play in furthering our understanding of depression and what to do about it. The field of *affective neuroscience* studies the brain basis of human emotions, including how we develop emotions in the first place, where they are located in the brain, and how we regulate emotions and learn from emotional experience. Brain researchers investigate the possible neural roots of depression, hoping to locate areas of the brain implicated in depression that could be changed by brain training interventions.

A key concept in neuroscience is *neuroplasticity*. Neuroplasticity at the general level means that the brain is constantly adapting to environmental challenges and demands through a dynamic process of strengthening existing neural circuitry or, even more intriguing, creating new neural circuitry. Practically speaking, this means that you can strengthen and/or rewire your brain's neural pathways from the outside in. In other words, the behaviors you practice on a daily basis actually strengthen the neural connections in your brain that support those behaviors. So, for example, if you practice mindfulness and/or self-compassion skills on a regular basis, you will strengthen the neural circuitry in your brain that supports being mindful and self-compassionate (Lutz et al. 2008). For this reason, locating the areas of the brain that are responsible for promoting both positive and painful emotional states is critical if we are to capitalize on the potential benefits of neuroplasticity.

So far, the research on depression has yielded some very interesting results.

DEFAULT MODE NETWORK

The broadly distributed neural network in the brain that is implicated in depression is called the *default mode network* (DMN). Like the name implies, the DMN functions as a kind of "screen saver" for the brain when the brain is at rest. The DMN has been called the "dark energy of the mind" due to its tendency to encroach upon more task-oriented brain behaviors and to gobble up the brain's finite attention resources (Raichle et al. 2001). Activation of this network is associated with a variety of mental events that are linked to depression, including daydreaming, lapses of attention, reduction in sensitivity to sensory inputs from the body, and increased free-floating memory recall, to name a few (Buckner, Andrews-Hanna, and Schacter 2008; Spreng et al. 2013).

While it is tempting to think of the DMN as a nuisance, it actually plays a valuable role in maintaining our mental health. Accruing evidence suggests that DMN brain systems activated during rest are also important for active, internally focused mental processing, for example, when recalling personal memories, imagining the future, and feeling social emotions with moral connotations (Andrews-Hanna 2012).

TASK POSITIVE NETWORK

There's another major neural network in the brain called the *task positive network* (TPN). It is responsible for recruiting and applying brain resources needed to complete specific tasks, whether they are internally or externally focused, and whether they are negative or positive. The TPN actively competes with the DMN for the brain's resources and, in a perfect world, the TPN and DMN would exert natural checks and balances on each other. In other words, from a neuroscience perspective, healthy human functioning is achieved through a dynamic balance between task focus and the ability to rest, daydream, imagine, and reintegrate past memories and experiences (Spreng et al. 2013).

The problem arises when either network becomes chronically overactivated. In the case of depression, it is the overactivation of the DMN that is thought to be the main mechanism of concern. Current treatments generally require the depressed person to get present, pay attention, and engage in specific thinking or behaving tasks. This has the effect of reactivating the TPN so that it counteracts the dominance of the DMN.

EXECUTIVE CONTROL NETWORK

The *executive control network* (ECN) (Spreng et al. 2013), as the name implies, is a neural pathway that functions to protect the brain's limited resources and to distribute them in the most efficient way. It is responsible for managing what is called the brain's *working memory capacity*, or the ability to complete tasks even when there are conflicting tasks to attend to, such as sticking with a problem-solving strategy like deep breathing even as you are dealing with intense sadness (Marchetti et al. 2012). Mindfulness practices have been shown to strengthen areas of the brain that are known to be a part of the ECN (Lutz et al. 2008), and this is one mechanism through which mindfulness is beneficial in the treatment of depression.

A NEUROSCIENCE FRAMEWORK FOR INTERVENTION

What does all this mean for our understanding of depression? First, depression has been associated with overactivation of the DMN and underactivation of the TPN, which seems to be associated with underactivation of the ECN. In other words, depression puts the ECN to sleep, figuratively speaking, and this allows the DMN to gobble up a disproportionate share of brain resources. This explains the "inertia" problem in depression—that is, the way you have trouble starting a new behavior that would help you feel better. The motivation to do things just isn't there. This is due to the underactivation of the TPN. For instance, you know that you would feel better if you went outside and took a brisk walk in the park, but when you stand up to do it you feel like you're trudging through mud.

Second, underactivation of the ECN depletes working memory capacity very quickly. This leads to lapses in concentration and immediate memory when you are trying to multitask. In emotionally charged situations, you may feel confused and indecisive, and you might freeze instead of acting affirmatively.

Based upon what we now know, we can create new treatments and start to understand the brain impacts of existing ones (Sambataro et al. 2013; Singh and Gotlib 2014). For example, the ACT perspective holds that getting caught up in thoughts, feelings, or memories makes it very difficult to accept these private experiences for what they are. Instead, we physiologically and mentally react to them as if they were literally real, and we allow them to regulate our behavior. To offset this vulnerability in our hardwiring, ACT teaches us to detach from, or let go of, the impulse to overidentify with distressing, unwanted thoughts, emotions, or memories. Practicing this detached stance directly targets and strengthens areas of the brain responsible for regulating powerful emotions. For example, there is unique neural circuitry in the brain that supports *detachment*, or the opposite of being caught up in distressing experiences. This circuitry is controlled largely by the ECN—which as we know can be compromised when depression is present. And to make matters even more complicated, the neural pathways responsible for detachment regulate emotional arousal by dampening the amygdala, the part of the reptilian brain that produces emotional arousal (Shiota and Levenson 2012; Sheppes, Brady, and Samson 2014).

Let's take off the geek hats now and put this in plain English: When you are depressed, it is harder to pay attention to what is going on inside of you and, because of that, it is harder to stay detached when something painful shows up. This leads to becoming overidentified with what you're feeling, thinking, or remembering, particularly when the experience is painful and is identified as a threat to your safety and well-being. That primes the pump of your primitive emotion pathways, leading to a downward spiral of negative emotional experiences (Joorman and Vanderlind 2014). Taking a detached stance toward negative emotions in a moment of high arousal reverses this destructive process by downregulating the amygdala, thus short-circuiting the neural basis for any further downward spiraling.

If you are a neuroscientist thinking about what to do with this problem, you would likely say, "We need to do something to restore the depressed person's ability to focus attention and keep it focused." That is one of the main reasons why mindfulness training has entered the picture so dramatically in affective neuroscience. Recent studies show that mindfulness practices directly impact central neural pathways responsible for paying attention in a flexible, workable way. A recent study examined experienced meditators matched with naive control subjects who were asked to perform three different types of meditation. The results suggest that, for experienced meditators, each type of meditation resulted in reduced activity in the DMN and increased activity among several brain structures thought to be associated with the ECN. No such changes were observed in the naive control subjects (Brewer et al. 2011).

Neuroscience studies of compassion have shown two very compelling results that bear directly upon depression. Subjects in one study practiced compassion prayer thirty minutes daily for just two weeks, and pronounced brain changes were observed (Lutz et al. 2009). The other finding is that compassion training led to far more altruistic attitudes toward suffering in general (Weng et al. 2013). In other words, through compassion training you aren't just learning how to be compassionate toward someone, you are learning how to be compassionate to the human condition. This is the doorway to practicing self-compassion, because you are a part of humanity, not separate from it.

Neuroscience studies within the realm of positive psychology show that negative emotions have a distinct narrowing effect on attention. When you are depressed, what you pay attention to narrows such that what you are aware of is largely determined by your mood. You are aware of many more negative thoughts than positive thoughts; you remember many more negative events in your life; you experience more strings of negative emotions. When you engage positive emotions, your attention widens—and so does your ability to see your life in perspective. You'll recall both positive and negative memories with much more ease, and your emotions will tend to be more evenly distributed and restorative (Frederickson and Branigan 2005).

Throughout this book, we introduce you to different skills derived from these perspectives designed to help you move through depression. You can practice these skills at home in the way of brief *brain training exercises*. We use this term on purpose because you are literally training your brain's neural pathways to engage in activities that promote your sense of well-being. There is a simple truth associated with the concept of brain training: You are *always* training your brain to do something; the question is, what are you training it to do?

COMBINING PERSPECTIVES: A NEW START

When we combine the five perspectives into a unified biopsychosocial model of depression, what emerges is a completely different view of depression than you may have had when you started this book. Let's look at three important themes that each perspective has in common with the others:

Loss of Attention Control and Rule Following

Depression involves a disruption in the ability to control attention, preventing us from taking a nonreactive and nonjudgmental stance. In essence, depression interferes with our ability to be mindful. The biggest issue, from an ACT perspective, is that when depressed people lose control of their attention (which happens as a by-product of daydreaming, mind wandering, and rumination), they unknowingly get caught up in the web of their mind's judgments and evaluations. This leaves them vulnerable to socially instilled rules about dealing with emotions that lead to the use of avoidance strategies. They are then exposed to a steady barrage of messages that are just downright depressing: "You are a loser. You're destined to fail at the things in life that matter to you. Your mistakes in life are unforgivable. You have so many flaws that no one will ever love you. Even if you succeed at something in life, it is a fluke, and people will eventually see what a fake you are. You need to figure out what's wrong with you and fix it. Other people are happy and you aren't. Blah! Blah! Blah!"

Learning to be mindful, to pay attention, to be aware, and to react nonjudgmentally are key to overcoming the rule following that keeps us locked in a depressed state.

Avoidance Promotes Depression

Depression develops because of two types of avoidance that are practiced repeatedly over time. Both avoidant types become engrained in the brains' neural pathways and become habitual ways of responding to emotional distress.

- **Experiential avoidance:** refusing to make direct contact with unwanted distressing thoughts, emotions, memories, or physical symptoms. Experiential avoidance is done as a form of self-protection, based upon the mistaken belief that painful experiences are toxic or harmful.

- **Behavioral avoidance:** systematically avoiding, limiting time spent in, or escaping from situations, events, or interactions that could potentially trigger distressing, unwanted experiences.

You might be thinking, "If I am feeling really down, how is avoiding that feeling bad? Why is avoidance such a toxic process?" The short answer is that the life situations that trigger unpleasant emotional reactions in you are also likely to be the situations that matter to you. They might involve issues of intimacy, love, parenting, work, being part of a community of like-minded souls, and so on. These are the issues that come with being alive; they are not threats to your emotional health and well-being, however much they may seem to be. We know from research that life stressors are a trigger for depression at least half the time (Schotte et al. 2006). In fact, one highly publicized study found that at least 25 percent of all cases of clinical depression are really more likely a reaction to some form of interpersonal loss or setback (Wakefield et al. 2007).

Depression is like the "check engine" warning light on your car's dashboard. It is telling you that something is amiss and you need to take action. Engaging in emotional and behavioral avoidance during challenging life moments is like putting duct tape on the check engine light in your car, because you don't want to be upset by it. Doing so might keep you calm for a while, but eventually your car is going into the shop, probably with an even bigger problem than when the check engine light first came on. Similarly, if you don't listen to your body's warning light, your depression will likely get worse, and the original problem you were facing might escalate out of control. Worse yet, because you are not engaging in activities that matter to you, over time your sense of life direction just fades away. This further impairs your motivation to do things because there is no obvious purpose for doing so. *If you avoid the situations that matter in life or the emotional reactions they produce, you have little chance of addressing important growth-producing opportunities.*

Depressed Behavior Generates Depressed Mood

This theme is perhaps the most important for our purposes: *Depression is not something you have; it is something you do.* The behavioral theory of depression holds that people start engaging in actions that feed into depression long before they develop the disabling mental symptoms of depression (Carvalho and Hopko 2011). The neuroscience perspective shows us that many behaviors seen in depression—such as self-isolation, avoidance, passive problem solving, and a sedentary lifestyle—could be viewed as day-in, day-out forms of brain training. Without knowing it, you are actually training your brain to overactivate the DMN and create depressed mood and behaviors!

Similarly, positive psychology research is showing that the opposite is also true: Behaviors that produce positive emotions can spiral upward to create the motivation to perform more and different positive behaviors (Garland et al. 2010; Frederickson and Losada 2005). In other words, your behavior patterns determine your mood state, whether positive or negative. This is actually good news because, while it is very hard to dial up only the emotions you want to feel, you do have complete control over your behavior. Thus, you can choose to behave in healthy, productive ways even if you don't feel at the top of your game emotionally. It turns out your behavior is a superhighway to producing positive mood states!

The idea that behaviors produce depression is new to a lot of people. But let's look at an example that will show the commonsense aspect of this idea:

> You had a terrible night's sleep and feel out of energy when you wake up. You decide to cut back on your daily activities, including that walk you were going to take. You feel sluggish midday but power through with caffeine. At the end of the day you feel exhausted, and you also feel guilty for not doing all the things you planned. To feel better, you stay up very late watching TV. No big deal, right? The result is that you don't get caught up on sleep, and the next day you are even more tired. And so you cut back on activities again, and feel sluggish all day—and the cycle continues! It is the same with depression.

This example isn't meant to make you feel bad about your behavior patterns. Choosing to behave in healthy, productive ways on a day-in, day-out basis is a challenge for *everyone*. It is not a problem that is unique to depression. We just want you to understand that there *is* a way to move beyond depression that is under your immediate control! You can choose to experiment with new behaviors even when you are depressed.

FLAWS OF THE BIOMEDICAL PERSPECTIVE

Now that we have examined depression from the five contemporary perspectives, it might be useful to compare the comprehensive biopsychosocial approach with the traditional biomedical model of depression.

Is Depression a Biological Illness?

The message that depression is a biological illness is virtually everywhere. It has been actively promoted by the pharmaceutical industry, psychiatry, and some consumer advocacy groups. For the pharmaceutical industry, treating an everyday problem like depression as an illness converts into billions of dollars in drug sales. For consumer advocacy groups, calling depression an illness absolves people from responsibility for the problem and presumably reduces the stigma of having a mental health problem. For psychiatry, the belief simplifies the treatment approach to depression by making it a simple matter of finding the right medication.

We can say with confidence that current scientific evidence does not support defining depression as a biological disease. That's why the World Health Organization, the global body responsible for identifying and describing new disease entities, doesn't currently recognize depression as a clearly demarcated biological illness.

Is Depression the Result of a Chemical Imbalance?

The second assumption in the biomedical approach is that depression results from chemical imbalances in the brain, which in turn produce depressed mood, thinking, and behavior. This is sometimes referred to as the *serotonin hypothesis* because serotonin is the neurotransmitter that has been the object of much biologically based depression research over the years. Indeed, most modern antidepressants operate to alter the rate at which serotonin is produced and/or reabsorbed within the nervous system.

Whitaker (2010) reported on the result of an extensive review of all of the biological psychiatry literature pertinent to the serotonin hypothesis since the advent of modern antidepressant medications in the mid-1980s. He concluded that there is scant evidence for the theory that depression is caused by chemical imbalances. Of course, all human behavior ultimately comes down to a matter of biology and chemistry. But it isn't at all clear that differences in individual brain chemistry cause depression, nor is it clear that chemical imbalances cause the mood, thinking, and behavioral problems associated with depression.

A better way to think about the relationship among brain chemistry, mood, thinking, and behavior is that the arrows of causation point in both directions, not just one direction. Depressed behavior might exert as much influence on brain chemistry as brain chemistry exerts on depressed behavior, to cite one example. This biopsychosocial approach is cause for optimism if you are depressed, because it means there are many potential treatments available that could work, rather than relying on just the use of medication.

Are Medications the Best Treatment for Depression?

A natural result of the biomedical perspective is to regard medications as the first line of treatment for depression. Indeed, this country is awash in psychoactive medications of all kinds. The question is, how well do antidepressants work?

A recent review of the antidepressant medication treatment literature concluded that antidepressants are no more effective than placebos (sugar pills) in treating mild to moderate clinical depression, with mild evidence for the benefit of antidepressant therapy for patients with severe depression (Khin et al., 2011). Lending additional credibility to this review is the fact that it was sponsored by the U. S. Food and Drug Administration, the branch of government responsible for approving new drugs, in response to the growing controversy over how antidepressant drugs are approved in the first place. There is still an intense academic debate over the benefits of antidepressant therapy for severe depressions (Kirsch 2014).

If you suffer from mild to moderately severe depression, your response to an antidepressant likely will be about the same as if you took a placebo. In statistical terms, there is a 40 to 50 percent chance you will respond. And, as we often tell clients that are taking medications, don't ever underestimate the power of the placebo effect. In reality, it is the most powerful effect in all of medicine. The belief that you are taking something that is going to help you is even more powerful than what you are taking to help you.

There are, at the same time, other factors that go into determining how effective a treatment is for depression. One is what happens when you wean yourself off the medication, usually at about nine months to a year after initiating treatment. People who are treated using only antidepressant medication have very high rates of relapse, in the vicinity of 70 percent. Interestingly, many studies suggest that behavioral therapy is actually *more* effective over time in terms of preventing future episodes of depression (Paykel 2006). This is important because depression tends to be a recurrent problem. Many people who experience depression have a pattern of recovering and then relapsing again. Often this pattern continues throughout a person's life. Any approach that reduces the chances of being depressed again is definitely worth exploring.

Do Medications Work Faster?

Another factor worth exploring is how long it takes the treatment to start working. A popular belief is that medications work faster than therapy or self-help programs. However, studies suggest that behavioral and cognitive therapies may actually work faster than antidepressants (Kelly, Roberts, and

Ciesla 2005; Mynors-Wallis et al. 2000). Recent studies of behavioral treatments have shown that a significant number of patients show sudden large improvements in their symptoms within the first one to three treatment sessions (Cape et al. 2010; Lutz, Stulz, and Kock 2009).

What Role Do Medications Play?

This leaves us with two very important questions, which you are no doubt asking if you're already taking antidepressants or considering taking them: *What role does the medication play in my recovery? And what roles do the concepts and strategies in this book play?*

Our answer (admittedly biased!) is a simple one: Even if you've benefited from antidepressants, it's still wise to practice the strategies we teach in this book. They could help you avoid a relapse into depression in the future.

If you're currently taking antidepressants, think about them this way: Medications, if they work, might help reduce some of your symptoms, including overwhelming fatigue, loss of energy, lack of sleep, and problems with concentration, any of which can keep you from making positive changes in your life. In this sense, medication can be helpful for some people. It might reduce some of the overwhelming symptoms you experience that make it hard for you to get in gear.

But medications can't make those positive changes for you—only you can do that. The skills and strategies suggested in this book can serve as a kind of map for when, where, and how to make these life changes. We want to be very clear that we are not opposed to people using antidepressants. Rather, we want you to have the information you need to judge the risks and benefits of using medications. Our intention is to help you take a balanced view of what drugs can do for you, and what you must do for yourself.

TRADING ILLUSIONS FOR ACTIONS

Once you understand depression for what it is, rather than what it seems to be, you're in an excellent position to begin to do something about it. Depression is really a signal that something is out of balance in your approach to living. It is never simply an accident of nature; it is perfectly designed to tell you something important about how your life is going. Rather than rejecting your depression as a blight or just resigning yourself to having it, you can learn to accept where you are at in your life and view depression as a natural consequence of living in very complicated circumstances.

Right here, right now, you can stop beating up on yourself for being depressed and treat yourself with kindness and affection instead. You can redirect your energy toward solving the dilemmas that have you stuck—right now. There is a solution to this problem at your fingertips, and in the remainder of this book we'll show you how to transcend depression and develop a vital, purposeful life.

IDEAS TO CULTIVATE

- Depression is not abnormal—nearly 20 percent of all people experience it!

- Depression is the natural result of avoiding painful life issues, instead of facing them. And it's cunning—depression tricks you into behaving in ways that only feed your depression.

- Depression is something you *do*, not something you *have*. It's based in your behavior patterns—something that you can change.

- Depression results from three specific patterns that you can correct: avoidance, loss of attention control, and behaviors that produce downward negative emotion spirals.

- Depression is a signal that your life is out of balance. It's a call to action and, as such, can help you create a better life.

- Mindfulness strategies appear to have a very positive impact on depression and affect neural pathways in the brain that have been linked to depression.

- Learning to be mindful and self-compassionate can short-circuit patterns of avoidance that lead to depression.

- Cultivating a positive-emotion lifestyle can help you reverse the downward spiral of depression.

CHAPTER 2

Human Vulnerabilities in Depression

I hope that in this year to come, you make mistakes. Because if you are making mistakes, then you are making new things, trying new things, learning, living, pushing yourself, changing yourself, changing your world. You're doing things you've never done before, and more importantly, you're doing something.

—Neil Gaiman

Living in modern times requires us to respond to an array of personal challenges that life offers up, whether we feel ready for them or not. These challenges include big life events (divorce, loss, trauma, chronic pain) and the ongoing, moment-to-moment hassles that create stress in daily life (next-door neighbors that yell at each other, traffic jams, the indigestion from having eaten an unhealthy meal quickly, not having money to pay bills). Your job is to somehow navigate these challenges and live a vital, meaningful, purposeful life.

To borrow from a famous saying: *Life is one damn thing after another; your job is to make sure it isn't the same damn thing over and over again.* When you run into a barrier in life, the goal is to soften into it and roll with it so that you can continue on…until the next barrier. This is somewhat like floating down a river on an inner tube. You have to relax as you make contact with boulders and stretches of rapid water, and then allow the water to carry you downstream, trusting there will probably be a stretch of calm water somewhere ahead. Unfortunately, this message is not commonplace in our society. We are taught something very different: to resist the experience of pain and to show how strong we are by conquering our emotions. This notion makes us vulnerable to all kinds of problems, including depression.

One major area of vulnerability in depression comes from dealing with the cascade of daily life stressors that are a part of modern living. Ongoing life stressors, large and small, serve to challenge our problem-solving abilities and resiliency. On your journey out of depression, you will benefit greatly from learning to identify risky situations in your daily life that can trigger a depression. The better you become at recognizing and anticipating life events that make you vulnerable, the more adept you will be at short-circuiting the mental sequence that leads to unworkable coping strategies. As we laid out earlier, normal living consists of lots of challenging situations, events, and interactions. In this chapter, we will ask you to look around and see where the triggers are in your life right now.

Most life challenges require us to come up with creative solutions, even while experiencing some level of emotional discomfort. The potential for making mistakes is certainly there. But the potential for learning more about yourself in the process is huge—especially if you cultivate a sense of curiosity, openness, and acceptance of your inner experiences while focusing most of your energy on coping with and/or solving the problem at hand.

A second major vulnerability in depression is that we are all socially programmed to avoid emotional discomfort. This is partly the result of early learning experiences that influenced us without our necessarily being aware of them. From a young age, we receive lots of social messages encouraging us to control our emotions and behavioral impulses. If we failed to do so, we might even be punished. A frustrated parent might have chided you with the threat, "Stop crying, or I'll give you something to cry about!" Even if you had a good reason for crying, the message suggests that there is something wrong with your crying and you must stop it if you don't want to be punished. This type of emotional-control training occurs throughout childhood.

Some of your early role models may not have been much help in teaching you how to take an accepting, open stance toward your emotions. They may have tired of battling their own emotions and resorted to using alcohol or drugs, or isolated themselves from others, or taken to overeating. Maybe they came to suffer from chronic depression, relying on medication and dealing with challenges by pretending problems weren't there.

Another way we learn to use avoidance is by trial and error. We might notice that a certain response (avoiding phone calls that we know will make us upset, for example) seems to help, so we use that response again. What we don't necessarily realize is that *while a response may have worked in one situation, there's no guarantee it will work in a different situation, or work the next time, even in a similar situation.* Or, more important for our purposes, *we don't realize that emotional avoidance might work for a short period of time but eventually backfires in the long run.* This is not necessarily a conscious choice on our part, because we quickly internalize all kinds of rules as we acquire the ability to use language, both overtly (speaking) and covertly (thinking). In fact, most of these socially trained rules are incredibly resistant to change, even when following them leads to disastrous results.

To implement a flexible stance in the presence of challenging life moments requires that you be able to step back from mental rules, see them as rules, and not allow them to dictate your behavior. Then, and only then, will you be in a position to choose the problem-solving strategies that are most likely to work. A favorite analogy we use with depressed clients is this: if life stressors and daily hassles are the match, then following socially instilled rules that encourage emotional and behavioral avoidance is the gasoline.

In this chapter, we give you the opportunity to examine the risk situations you are facing in your life right now, and then to examine and better understand the forces inside of you that might tempt you to avoid dealing with them. To transcend depression, it's important to practice skills that let you quickly identify and bypass strategies that promise short-term relief but guarantee long-term grief.

THE MATCH: COPING WITH LIFE STRESS AND DAILY HASSLES

It is not at all uncommon for people to experience distressing symptoms in reponse to big life events or to the impact of smaller daily stresses. A term often used for these short-term symptoms is *dysphoria*. Nearly everyone goes through periods of dysphoria in response to something challenging in life.

It is what you *do* when you get dysphoric that is all important in determining the direction in which your mood will go. One common knee-jerk response is to follow the emotional avoidance rule. This will lead you to focus your energy on controlling or eliminating painful thoughts, feelings, memories, or physical symptoms. However, a cornerstone of the ACT approach is to recognize that you cannot control or eliminate painful experiences simply by avoiding them or pretending they aren't there. They not only don't go away, but they come back with a vengeance! And as you keep failing in your quest for control, you gradually slip into the numbness of depression. This state of emotional numbness is the only place left to retreat to when you've exhausted your brain's finite resources.

An alternative way to respond to emotional distress is to "suit up and show up." This way involves getting yourself up and "back into the game," doing what matters to you in life. You could say that this is an approach-oriented problem-solving strategy. You feel what is there to be felt, and you do what matters to you in that same moment. The goal is no longer to control or get rid of your feelings; instead it is to use your feelings as a guide to discover what matters to you. The reason you are feeling emotional pain is not because you are broken or defective, but because there is something that matters to you in this situation. If you are willing to go for what matters to you, your pain can be your ally rather than your enemy. Of course, this is easier said than done. Indeed, the "suit up and show up" way of responding requires a significant amount of skill in mindfully accepting distressing and unwanted private events, and acting in a way that is consistent with your personal values. But it is the way a vulnerable human can transcend depression!

The first step is to simply notice that you are at a *choice point*, or a fork in the road, where what you do next will be a major factor in determining how you feel in the long run. Some choice points will be big, like the loss of a job, a breakup with a partner, being a victim of crime or abuse, the death of a loved one, or the loss of a home to foreclosure. Other choice points are more insidious because they are smaller and happen often. We call these *daily hassles* and, as the name suggests, they are the little annoyances that keep popping up in daily life: burned toast, a child's temper tantrum, the snide remark from a coworker, the forgotten lunch, an overdraft notice, and the flat tire that makes you late for an appointment.

Daily hassles can grind us down, particularly if we try to continually avoid or suppress our emotional reactions to them. Taking the "soldier on" approach can result in unexpected consequences, such as increased irritability and a higher level of emotional reactivity in general. It can also lead to a growing sense of numbness and withdrawal from immediate experiences. Both of these consequences can exert a toll on our personal relationships and our problem-solving abilities as well. Let's look at three common life events that offer important choice points: loss, traumatic stress, and health problems.

Dealing with Interpersonal Loss

Sometimes it is a bitter disappointment in a relationship that launches a person into depression. Let's look at how this happened to Bob, in order to understand how easily one can make the wrong turn in life.

BOB'S STORY

Bob, a forty-seven-year-old physician, first experienced symptoms of depression while in medical school. His training was rigorous, and he often went long periods without adequate sleep. He managed to pass his classes but began to lose his enthusiasm for medicine. Although he had reservations, he went ahead with a plan to marry his long-term girlfriend after graduation from medical school. His wife was a very positive person and loved him a great deal, so life seemed better for several years. Bob graduated from his residency program and then joined a practice in a small town. He was committed to serving patients in a rural area, where there were fewer medical resources. He didn't anticipate that this commitment would have him working longer hours than ever.

He and his wife had two children, and she often complained about his seeming lack of interest in improving their marriage. Bob felt defensive and that there was no way to win, and so he withdrew from her and the children. He took to drinking wine in the evenings because he felt more relaxed. At first, the wine seemed to give him a little energy for talking with his wife and playing with his kids. But then it just seemed to make it hard for him to focus, so he turned to watching sports on TV nonstop.

It took all of his focus just to get up and go to work and make it through the day. Bob was actually surprised when his wife left and took their children to live with her parents in a nearby city. A few months later, a colleague expressed concern, telling him, "You're not yourself. You look tired and maybe hungover. Maybe you should see someone." This put Bob at a choice point, and this time he made a different choice—he sought help for his problems.

Coping with Trauma

Life is full of challenges, and experiences of traumatic events starting in childhood add up and increase human vulnerability to depression. One large study looked at how adverse events in childhood—parental divorce, domestic violence in the home, physical abuse, emotional abuse, sexual abuse, substance abuse by a parent, incarceration of a parent, and mental illness of a parent, among others—impacted mental and physical health in the adult years. (Felliti et al. 1998; Dong et al. 2004). The authors were surprised by how common these events were for people and by the fact that most people had never received any help in coping with them. Anna's story provides an example of how difficult it can be to survive the emotional aftereffects of trauma.

ANNA'S STORY

Anna was the first person in her family to go to college. She was bright and hardworking, and completed her undergraduate studies in three years by going to school during the summers. Her childhood and teen years had been tough: Her parents divorced when she was a child, and her mother died when she was ten. When she was a teenager, her grandfather was murdered, and during her freshman year in college, she was a victim of date rape. Graduate school was an opportunity to get herself into a new setting with more career opportunities, so she enrolled without taking even a short break.

Anna wanted to have friends, but she felt so different from other people her age. And her time for socializing was limited. She told no one about her troubled history and sensed that all of the bad stuff was somehow her fault. She worked hard in her graduate classes, took extra hours at her job in child welfare, and sent money to her father, who was disabled from a work injury. At night, she surfed the Internet, watched horror movies, and played online video games until she was so exhausted that she fell asleep at her desk. Anna's sleep was disturbed by nightmares. And when she woke up, she felt pain in her chest, which she worried about. Also, tension in her shoulders and neck annoyed her throughout the day.

Over time, she found it hard to concentrate on her studies and began to skip lectures and an occasional exam. Anna's grades dropped, and her major professor called her in for a conference. This put Anna at a choice point, and she chose to do something proactive about her growing symptoms of depression. She decided to read a self-help book recommended by her professor and promised that she would see a counselor at Student Health Services in a month if she wasn't feeling better.

Lifestyle Choices and Depression

Another common pathway into depression involves falling into patterns of behavior that lead to poor health. A common misconception in our culture is that health comes naturally, that there is no real need to work to preserve it, and that doctors can find ways to eliminate health problems when they do occur.

Actually, it is behavioral and social factors that are the heavy hitters in health outcomes, rather than access to medical treatment. It is the hard stuff—eating well, exercising, getting restful sleep, and cultivating good relationships—that helps us feel good physically and mentally. Engaging in unhealthy behaviors is a common way to avoid or control distressing emotions, and Joe's story illustrates the long term cost of using this strategy.

JOE'S STORY

Joe had always struggled with the feeling that he didn't fit in with his peers, that he was an oddball. When Joe was in social situations during his teen years, he would play with his phone or hang out at the food table until he could make an excuse to leave. Joe liked cooking and considered himself a "foodie," so a pattern of eating to avoid his feelings spread to other contexts in his life, such as when he was studying, playing video games, or feeling lonely.

By the time he enrolled in college, he weighed more than three hundred pounds. In his senior year, he met a delightful woman and lost quite a bit of weight to please her. They married, and within the first year of their marriage he gained all the weight back plus some. His wife was critical of his weight and his eating habits, particularly his eating ice cream out of the carton at night after dinner. Eventually, she had an affair, and Joe fought off devastating feelings of rejection by moving to a separate bedroom, snacking, and listening to music in his room at night.

When his doctor diagnosed high blood pressure and high cholesterol, Joe felt even worse about himself. He made excuses for not attending church and avoided family gatherings except on big holidays. He preferred to stay home, where he could watch movies, listen to music, and enjoy his favorite junk foods. Joe didn't want to feel the pain of being rejected by his wife, and he didn't want to hear any more bad news from his doctor. He didn't want to have the worries he had about his body, which seemed to be failing him.

Late one night, Joe experienced severe chest pain, and his wife took him to the emergency room. He was diagnosed with angina and told to lose weight and change his eating habits or he might end up suffering a heart attack. That day Joe found himself at a choice point. The next day he told his wife that he needed to see a therapist to help him turn his life around.

Bob, Anna, and Joe each avoided painful personal problems in order to function—until they realized that their solutions did not help them function, at least not in ways that really mattered to them. Their values regarding health, relationships, work, and play were alive and well, but their behaviors were driven by avoidance rather than passion. As is typical with most people who suffer from symptoms of depression, all three made a decision to seek professional assistance to improve their lives. With help, they learned to use many of the skills we teach in this book. They learned how to turn around and face their depression one small peak at a time.

Risky Business: Depression Triggers

Remember the old saying, *An ounce of prevention is worth a pound of cure?* This saying speaks volumes about how depressions get started as well as how to get out of them. As we mentioned earlier, stressful life situations can act as triggers for depression or, if allowed to fester, can create chronic depression. These risky situations can be found in any domain of your life: your relationships, work/ study, leisure/play, and health. There is no benefit in trying to ignore these risky situations, hoping they won't materialize or that they will somehow get resolved on their own. If you find yourself taking that approach, it might be a signal that you are unknowingly following the emotional avoidance rule. A far more productive approach is to look these problems squarely in the eye so that they don't sneak up on you.

IDENTIFY YOUR DEPRESSION TRIGGERS

To help you better understand the smoldering problems that might increase your vulnerability, read through the list of depression-risk situations below, and for any that might apply to you, rate how big of a problem it is on a scale of 1 to 10, whereby 1 is not a big problem at all and 10 is an extremely big problem. In the right-hand column, indicate whether the risky situation has developed recently or has been around for a long time.

Depression Risk Inventory

Risky Situation or Trigger	Rating (1 to 10)	Problem (recent or long term)
My relationship with my life partner is not satisfying.		
I don't enjoy myself when I have free time.		
I have a lot of physical pain or poor health.		
I'm not really inspired by what I do for a living.		
I am in a time-consuming caretaker role for someone with chronic health problems.		
I don't feel good about how I'm taking care of my body.		
I have regrets about things I did earlier in my life.		
I don't get enough sleep and feel tired often.		
I don't have a spiritual practice.		
I believe that my friends have let me down or used me.		
I'm alienated from or have frequent conflicts with my children, siblings, or parents.		
I'm struggling with memories of childhood abuse or trauma.		
I use drugs, alcohol, or tobacco more frequently than I should.		
I'm under a lot of pressure at home or at work.		
I worry about money a lot.		
My partner is physically or emotionally abusive.		
Other (describe):		

Further Exploration. What did you discover as you completed this risk assessment? Did you mark a lot of areas or just one or two? How much emotional turmoil does each risk factor cause? Some of these problems might be chronic or long-standing issues, and others may have surfaced only recently. Here are two basic rules of thumb for calculating your level of depression risk:

- The more problems you have that create painful feelings for you, the greater your risk.

- The longer these problems have festered in your life, the greater your risk.

THE GASOLINE: RULE FOLLOWING

Most depressed people don't deliberately avoid dealing with their pressing problems. At some level, they know that avoiding personal problems doesn't help their situation and that tiptoeing around painful thoughts, feelings, or memories doesn't solve anything. So why is it that intelligent, insightful people can know in their hearts and minds that a particular strategy isn't helping, but still use it anyway?

It all comes down to the two toxic processes we mentioned in chapter 1: rule following and avoidance behavior. Together, they form a powerful one-two punch that makes it very hard for people to get out of the harmful cycle of avoidance that feeds depression.

If a strategy is systematically making a depressed individual feel worse, then the commonsense solution is to stop using it and look for something else that might work better. But this usually doesn't happen in depression—or in a lot of other situations that cause suffering. There must be some mental process that is overriding a depressed person's ability to objectively assess the results of ineffective strategies and then make needed changes in the approach. Right? The culprit appears to be the very makeup of the mind itself, which makes us insensitive to the direct results of our behaviors, particularly those behaviors that are under the influence of rule following.

We'll try not to be too abstract about this, but we'd like to share a bit of science to help you understand how language and thought actually create what we affectionately call the "mind" and how the mind, in turn, controls our behavior. This is a little tricky because most of us aren't used to looking at our mind as a scientific oddity; rather, we're used to *being* our mind and doing what it says. Let's start by delving into a relatively new approach to human language called *relational frame theory* (RFT; Hayes, Barnes-Holmes, and Roche 2001). RFT has had a huge impact on the development of ACT; indeed, many ACT interventions are based on the principles of RFT.

How Language Controls Behavior

The basic goals of RFT are to discover how the various capabilities of human language are acquired over the life span and to decipher the complex process by which language functions to regulate our behavior. Two important functions of language are to both organize and regulate the behavior of each member of the clan. These regulatory functions are embedded in language itself, so we might not even be aware that our behavior is controlled by hidden forces within the mind.

Basic to the RFT approach is the idea that spoken and unspoken language (what we know as thought) are essentially the same thing. They are symbolic activities that allow us to both express ourselves to others and silently reason within ourselves. As far as we know, humans are the only species that have this capacity, which is sometimes referred to as *self-reflexivity*. This means that we can engage in internal dialogues with our minds. This is a terrifically useful evolutionary development and is clearly the reason we are at the top of the food chain, but there is also a dark side to this fantastic ability. When it is turned inward and applied in the wrong way, it can produce enormous suffering. While we are at the top of the evolutionary pyramid, humans are also the only species known to commit suicide. For present purposes, we want to zero in on how it is that language can invisibly move us in the wrong direction when it comes to making contact with, understanding, and utilizing our emotional experience.

Rule-Governed Behavior

In RFT, the term *rule-governed behavior* is used to describe behavior that's under the direct control of *arbitrarily derived symbolic relations*. (That term is a mouthful for anyone. Try to say it twenty times really fast if you dare!) Arbitrarily derived relations allow us to form mental rules about how to behave without actually coming into direct contact with the consequence the rule refers to. Their evolutionary importance cannot be overstated. If you think of language as the operating system that has put us at the top of the food chain, then think of rule-governed behavior as the main cog of that system. We can teach children hundreds if not thousands of important facts about life just by giving them a mental rule. This means the child doesn't have to learn the rule via firsthand experience. For example, a mother tells her child, "Never, never touch the burner on the stove when it is hot or you'll hurt yourself!" The child doesn't have to go over to the stove and learn this simple, painful truth by putting his or her hand on the burner. Rule-governed behavior is such a powerful way to transmit knowledge that this is the dominant way that human knowledge is being advanced.

Rule governance also extends to the organization of social and cooperative behaviors. Many of these socially oriented rules also contain a promised reward for compliance, for example, "Smile and the world will smile with you, cry and you cry alone." If the rule says, "Feeling sad is unhealthy for you, and when you get rid of being sad you will be healthy again," following that rule will be more important than being aware of whether the rule actually works in real life. This is a basic principle of RFT known as *augmentation*. An *augmental* promises additional rewards for following the programmed rule (for example, if you just get rid of your sadness, then you will live a healthy and happy life).

Augmentation is such a potent form of behavioral control that it pretty much overwhelms our ability to change behaviors based upon the actual results of following the rule. This means that once a rule is established in your language system, it will continue to be followed even if the objective results of doing so are dismal. Sound familiar? You've probably been in life situations in which you used the same strategies over and over without much in the way of results. Maybe you argued repeatedly with a spouse, partner, child, or parent about the same basic issue with no sign of progress. Or you snacked on some junk food at night to help you chill out even though it leads to heartburn and difficulties with sleeping later.

In order to exert their regulatory influence on behavior, you have to *buy* rules and then follow them—sometimes consciously but often without awareness that you are doing so. Buying a rule means that you attach to it and allow it to direct your behavior. For example, let's imagine that it's your birthday and your partner hasn't said anything about cooking a special dinner or taking you out to dinner. You might run into a rule such as, "If my partner really loved me, I shouldn't have to even mention that it's my birthday and that I'd like to do something special." This rule encourages you to keep quiet and see if your partner shows you the behavior that demonstrates love and caring. Because most rules actually originate within language, we have a hard time seeing them for what they are, and so most of the time we are not conscious that the rule is controlling our actions. In ACT, the term used to describe this process of overidentifying with rules is *fusion*. Like the term implies, fusion involves melding yourself within your experience in the moment, such that you lose the distinction between yourself and what you are experiencing. In a fused state, people become very susceptible to rule following.

For example, it isn't unusual for a depressed person to think something like, "I know drinking is only going to make my depression worse" on the way home from work. Once at home, this same person may think, "I feel angry, my life is going nowhere, and I can't allow myself to feel this way. The only way I'm going to feel better is to have a drink." Minutes after recognizing, again, that drinking will only worsen the problem of depression, this person may attach to other rules that propel him to drink to excess. These rules suggest that to feel healthy he must immediately eliminate "bad" feelings, such as anger and emptiness, and "bad" thoughts, like "My life isn't going anywhere." Unfortunately, the solution of drinking leads to more depression in the long run.

The tricky thing about fusion and rule following is that they are both essential to our ability to operate in a social context. You don't want to be questioning your mind when it gives you a rule not to enter the crosswalk when the stoplight is red. When you hold hands with someone you love and say, "I love you," you don't want to be thinking that "I love you" is just a thought. You want to fuse with that thought and experience the full force of your intimacy in the moment.

So the real challenge you will face in your quest to transcend depression is learning when it pays to fuse with and follow rules, and when it is destructive to do so. The first step in this process is to simply become aware that there is a distinction between you and your thoughts, feelings, memories, and physical sensations. You are not the same as your experiences. Think about your relationship to your thoughts, emotions, and memories like this: If you have a thought or emotion, *you can be the owner of it or you can be owned by it.* When you're the owner, you would say something like, "I'm having the thought that life is pointless" or "I'm aware of feeling sad right now." The ability to simply be aware of thoughts, feelings, or memories—without buying into them—is a cornerstone of mindfulness.

Rule Following and Living on Autopilot

Nowhere is the impact of rule following more evident than in the steady stream of automatic, habitual behaviors that have come to characterize modern life. We have exchanged intentional living for a life organized by social rules that require us to perform activities that have little or no connection to our values. If you think about your current daily activities (brushing your teeth, commuting to work or school, eating a meal, interacting with your partner), how much of the time are you aware of being in the moment and being intentional in your actions? If you're like most people, the answer will be, "Not very much of the time." In ACT, we call this *living on autopilot*. We tend to go through the motions of daily life with limited awareness and intentionality.

For years, it has been an accepted scientific fact that as little as 5 percent of our behavior is intentional and purposeful. The other 95 percent of the time, our behavior is controlled by environmental cues (alarm clocks, text notifications, calendar alerts) and social cues (doing what others are doing, dressing to imitate others; Baumeister et al. 1998). Neuroscience studies have demonstrated that we are hardwired to observe, integrate, and copy the behavior of others (Gazzola and Keysers 2009). The brain's architecture is designed to help us do the same thing as other members of the tribe.

To make matters worse, neuroscience research shows that we do things automatically as part of the brain's attempt to protect problem-solving and attention resources. So, to a limited extent, automatic behavior serves a protective function. There are literally hundreds, if not thousands, of activities that we must perform every day just to be human. Research shows that when you pass a certain threshold of doing activities on only a voluntary basis, you'll quickly have trouble maintaining the same level of intention and awareness from moment to moment (Galliet et al. 2007).

From the ACT perspective, *being on autopilot isn't the problem; it is being on autopilot most all of the time that is dangerous.* Extended time spent on autopilot allows rule-governed behaviors to occupy areas of life where rules don't work very well. Particularly if you are depressed, one likely result of a lot of time on autopilot is that you will habitually engage in a steady succession of small-scale emotional and behavioral avoidance behaviors. In this sense, daily challenges of living can function somewhat like the ancient Chinese practice of water torture: One drop of water on your head doesn't seem like much until you've spent days experiencing one drop of water at a time. One little act of emotional avoidance doesn't seem like a big deal, but what's to stop it from becoming a hundred?

Rule following is rule following, and unless you consciously break the pattern of avoidance by getting present and intentional, your vulnerability to depression can quickly get out of hand. To develop resistance to autopilot rule following in everyday life, it's important for you to develop a reliable set of go-to strategies that help you get present and intentional. And the first step in doing that is to look at your vulnerabilities toward running on autopilot. Those areas will tend to reflect the rules you're following. The exercise that follows will help you do just that.

INVENTORY OF AUTOMATIC LIVING

The following survey will help you identify tendencies toward automatic living in your current lifestyle. Read each item and circle an item number if it applies to you.

1. I feel bored much of the time.

2. I spend a lot of time watching TV or surfing the Internet.

3. I have trouble doing things at a slower pace than what I'm used to.

4. I'm always looking ahead and planning ahead.

5. I like to zone out when I have free time.

6. I often feel disconnected from my body's senses.

7. I often notice that I'm not paying attention to what I'm doing.

8. I often forget to stop and take relaxation breaks during the day.

9. I find it difficult to relax even when I have free time.

10. I prefer activities that distract me when I have free time.

11. I have trouble following through on tasks that require close attention.

12. I feel numb inside much of the time.

13. I feel rushed and like I'm always running behind.

14. I notice that I stop paying attention when I'm talking with someone.

15. I have trouble spending quality time with my partner or children.

16. I tend to see my day as full of duties to perform.

17. I tend to put off doing activities that I might enjoy.

18. I get irritated if my daily routine is interrupted.

19. I don't like to sit still and will try to keep myself busy.

20. I feel like I'm not cut out to relax and chill out.

Further Exploration. Now take a minute to notice the statements that you circled. These are the daily experiences that contribute to autopilot behavior and that may set you up for depression. Now that you've identified them, you can work toward creating a more mindful and meaningful lifestyle. You can get there by daily engaging in specific new practices, which you'll learn in part 2.

THE GASOLINE: AVOIDANCE

Many behaviors that are typically associated with depression—such as isolating at home; daydreaming; sleeping a lot; avoiding social interactions with a spouse, children, or friends; watching excessive TV; texting or being on social media for hours on end; and mindlessly surfing the Internet often—are better thought of as avoidance behaviors. Some of them keep us out of touch with unpleasant emotions; others steers us away from life situations, events, or interactions that are likely to trigger painful experiences inside.

While many of these behaviors may temporarily buffer depressed individuals from painful private experiences, in the long run they generate more depression. This is because when you disengage from people and the other things that matter to you, you also remove the potential rewards that might be waiting for you in those same activities. Thus, habitually engaging in emotional and behavioral avoidance behaviors can put you into a vicious downward spiral that is very hard to get out of. Because of this, it is very important that you identify both current and potential patterns of emotional and behavioral avoidance in your life.

Why Avoidance Doesn't Work

What if it is impossible to gain control over thoughts, feelings, memories, or physical symptoms simply by willing them away? What if the end result of avoidance strategies is that you actually have *more* distressing, unwanted private experiences, not less? Let's examine these two powerful ideas in more detail.

PRIVATE EXPERIENCES ARE AUTOMATIC

As far as we know, it's impossible to prevent emotions, thoughts, memories, and sensations from occurring in the first place. They are part of your learning as a human being. And the nervous system doesn't work by subtraction. This means you can't unlearn thoughts, feelings, or memories once they're stored in your experience. They can show up at any time, in any situation, and you have no say as to when, where, and how they will make an appearance. Your thoughts, emotions, memories, and physical responses are historically learned and are conditioned to appear whenever a situation triggers them. You can't keep a memory from making an appearance. You can't prevent an emotional reaction from showing up. You can't prevent yourself from thinking an unpleasant thought. The grand illusion contained in the emotional avoidance rule is that we somehow possess these abilities, when in fact we don't.

AVOIDANCE LEADS TO A REBOUND EFFECT

Suppression, a common form of avoidance, is the conscious attempt to squash a private experience out of awareness. Here is a little exercise to show why suppression doesn't work. Try this for a moment:

Think of a campfire. Imagine the flames, smell the burning wood, and feel the warmth of the air. Now stop. Stop having this image or memory, stop smelling the smoke, and stop the perception of warmth. Stop them completely. You are not to think of any of this from this moment on. What happens when you prohibit yourself from thinking about the campfire?

Now let's try something different. Think back to being in school, and recall something unkind that a teacher said or did to you. How old were you at the time? What were your teacher's exact words and tone of voice? Try to recall the room, your teacher's appearance, and all the other aspects of the experience in as much detail as possible. Now stop thinking about this unpleasant experience. Put all thoughts, memories, and feelings about it completely out of your mind.

How did you do? If you found the image of the campfire or your memories of your teacher's unkindness hard to get rid of, you are by no means alone. Research shows us that conscious attempts to suppress or avoid our private experiences will actually increase their intensity. This holds true not only for unpleasant thoughts or memories (Marcks and Woods 2005) but also for negative feelings (Campbell-Sills et al. 2006). So if you try to suppress an emotion, memory, or thought that you don't like, it will just come back to you in spades. It's another paradox: You can't control which private experiences show up, but you can make them much worse by trying to suppress them.

INVENTORY OF EMOTIONAL AND BEHAVIORAL AVOIDANCE

Pick a recent life situation, event, or interaction that didn't go well and left you feeling even more depressed. Take your time to write a few sentences about the situation. Then write down four specific actions you took in that situation. Finally, analyze what function that behavior might have had.

Situation: _____

_____

_____

Action 1: _____

Action 2: _____

Action 3: _____

Action 4. _____

Now, look at the function of the actions you took. Did one or more of your actions serve one of the following purposes?

    a.   Avoiding the situation or interaction that might trigger emotional pain

b. Treating unpleasant emotions, thoughts, or memories as threats to my well-being

c. Distracting myself from negative emotions

d. Numbing myself to negative feelings

e. Trying to control my emotions in order to not feel worse

Further Exploration. Did you identify one or more actions that involved rule following and avoidance in an effort to control your feelings? We all do this to some extent. However, we can come to rely too much on these strategies. Once you begin to understand how rule following and avoidance work, you can anticipate and look for the situations, events, or interactions that tend to trigger those responses in you and practice "just noticing" the urge to follow the rule or avoid the situation.

MOVING MINDFULLY THROUGH DEPRESSION: DARE TO IMAGINE

From the ACT perspective, the way through depression involves learning to pay attention to the patterns of rule following and avoidance that can end up fueling your depression, rather than helping you feel better. Depression is essentially a signal that you are having a difficult time detecting and accepting your emotions, and making choices that help you pursue the life you want. If you think of it this way, you will realize that learning to deal with your depression is more of a means to an end than an end itself. The end we have in mind is helping you create a life worth living, one in which you are doing life-enhancing things that support your values.

IMAGINE A BETTER FUTURE

This guided exercise offers a glimpse of what you'd be doing right now if your depression was no longer a barrier to you having a better future. Sit down in a comfortable position, close your eyes, and take several long deep breaths.

> *See if you can focus on where your life is right now—the things in life you feel good about as well as things that are causing you to suffer. Now, imagine that your depression miraculously disappeared overnight and is no longer a factor in your life. Because this miracle happened while you were sleeping, you don't actually know what made your depression disappear. All you know is that you are now free to choose to do the things in life that really matter to you.*

First, imagine what steps you would take to protect and improve your health. *This might involve cutting back on your use of chemicals or improving your diet or exercising more. It can be anything that comes to mind.*

Next, imagine what you would like to do to improve the number or quality of your social connections *and* close relationships, *be it through working to grow your relationship with your life partner, children, friends, or siblings, or being more involved at the community or volunteer level. Just let whatever comes to mind show up without evaluation.*

Now think about what would matter to you in your work, career, or education *pursuits. Just see if there is some action that you would like to take to move yourself forward in this area of life.*

Finally, think about how you would like to spend your leisure time—*the time when you get to play in life. What would playing look like for you? It might involve improving yourself as a spiritual being or challenging yourself with a new hobby or pastime. Just see what shows up when you let yourself imagine a better future in this area of life.*

And now, just allow yourself to savor the moment of having a better future ahead of you. Breathe into that better future. See it as a distinct possibility for you. And, when you are ready, come back into the moment and take some time to complete the written portion of this exercise.

A Better Future for Me...

For each of the areas listed below, write one important thing you would be doing if the barrier of depression evaporated while you slept.

In my pursuit of personal health (including exercise, spirituality, diet, and alcohol or drug use), I would

_____.

In my relationships (partner, family members, friends), I would _____.

In my work activities (including as a homemaker, volunteer, or student), I would _____.

In my leisure life (including play, hobbies, recreation, creative pursuits), I would _____.

Further Exploration. Don't worry. We aren't going to ask you to do all of these things—just yet. For now, just pat yourself on the back for being willing to imagine! Whenever you return to this list, think about your progress and whether you're getting closer to realizing any of these visions for your life. If you start to address emotionally difficult personal issues and situations, you can radically transform your life. It takes commitment, time, practice, and accepting that you won't always feel good. But we guarantee you that this is something you can do!

IDEAS TO CULTIVATE

- The life events, situations, and interactions that can trigger depression are as numerous and varied as the people who experience depression.

- Small, repeated daily life hassles can be as depressing as big life events.

- Rule following involves having your behavior regulated by social rules that are hidden in your language system.

- A habitual pattern of living on autopilot can set you up for depression, because it makes you prone to rule following.

- Emotional avoidance is a particularly toxic form of rule following that involves refusing to make direct contact with distressing thoughts, feelings, memories, or physical sensations.

- Behavioral avoidance involves steering away from life situations that might trigger painful emotions.

- Learning to recognize patterns of avoidance in your life is a big step forward in your quest to transcend depression.

- Acceptance and mindfulness skills will allow you to approach distressing private experiences with an attitude of openness and curiosity.

CHAPTER 3

It's All About Workability

It is a risk to love. What if it doesn't work out? Ah, but what if it does?

—Unknown

As we have mentioned, we don't want you to think of depression as a problem to be solved as much as a signal that something in your life is not working. That aspect of your life that is not working is the problem that needs to be solved. And it's not getting rid of your depression that's going to do it; it's finding those things that aren't working and fixing them that will. And you can't do that very well if you are preoccupied with trying to control your depression or the other feelings that lurk close by.

Chances are, if you are going through this self-help program, you are already knee-high in at least one challenging life situation. To achieve lasting change, you must first be brutally honest with yourself and take inventory of where you are right now. This can be really difficult—it can feel uncomfortable, even scary—but it is a healthy and essential move toward healing. As we like to say: *Start from where you are, not from where you'd like to be!*

At the end of the previous chapter, we dared you to imagine a better future, a life in which you are able to do what really matters to you in four key areas of living: relationships, work/study, leisure/ play, and health. In this chapter, we will help you take stock of how your life is actually working in those same areas of living. We are not doing this to bum you out. We want you to keep that image of a better future in mind as you examine the strategies you are currently using to move your life forward.

As we help you go through this personal inventory, you will learn about *workability*, a key ACT strategy that you can use to short-circuit rule following. Remember: Most of the avoidance rules you follow are also being followed by other people, and this makes it even more difficult to walk away from these rules. Indeed, avoidance might even seem sensible on some level. But if what the emotional avoidance rule promises (freedom from emotional pain, resulting in health and happiness) could actually materialize, we wouldn't be having this discussion. Because therein lies the rub: Following the rule, no matter what its promises are, doesn't actually deliver the goods!

To see through rules, you not only have to be aware that they are there but also understand what they are promising. Workability helps you analyze whether your methods of responding to your depression are actually working. The rule you are heeding promises positive results if you just follow it. The questions you must answer include: *Are these strategies working to promote my best interests in life? Or are they driving me deeper into depression?*

In this chapter we'll also look at possible depression risk factors in your life right now, along with ones that might appear in the immediate future. Finally, we will work with you to identify life domains where you can try intentional, mindful strategies that are likely to produce better results.

THE FOUR CORNERSTONES OF HEALTH

Keep in mind that "Health is a state characterized by anatomical, physiological, and psychological integrity; ability to perform personally valued family, work, and community roles; ability to deal with physical, biological, psychological, and social stress; a feeling of well-being; and freedom from the risk of disease and untimely death" (Last 1988, 57). We like this definition because it acknowledges that health isn't simply a physical state; it's also a psychological and social state. This definition also suggests that health is a dynamic relationship between positive coping and stress-inducing behaviors. Simply put, either your behaviors can restore you and buffer you from depression, or they can tear you down and make you more vulnerable to depression.

In keeping with the philosophy that depression is not something you *have* but is something you *do*, we want you to begin taking a closer look at vitality-producing and depression-producing behaviors in the four main domains of life. The exercise that follows provides an opportunity for you to evaluate behaviors in each major life domain.

BEHAVIORAL RISK AND VITALITY ASSESSMENT

Use the following four worksheets to reflect on your behavior patterns as they relate to the fundamentally important life domains of relationships, work/study, leisure/play, and health.

Read through each statement and place a checkmark next to those that ring true for you most of the time. At the end of each worksheet, count the number of checkmarks placed in both shaded and unshaded boxes, and record the totals. Note that there are no right or wrong answers. These surveys are designed to provide you with a baseline for your experience. Later, say a month from now, you can repeat this assessment and check your progress.

Today's date: _____

Relationship Behaviors	✓
I seek emotional support from friends or family, even if I worry about being a burden to them.	
I tend to avoid friends or family because I don't want them to see how depressed I am.	
I often notice that people are nice to me, and this helps a lot with what I'm going through.	
Even with the disappointments I've gone through, I still try to nourish my relationships with those around me.	
Much of the time, I find it hard to just be present with my intimate partner, children, or other people I'm close to.	
I avoid my friends because it makes me anxious to hear about how their lives are going compared with mine.	
I often snap at people and then withdraw into my shell to avoid dealing with them.	
I take pride in the fact that I have been a good friend to people in my past.	
I avoid acting on a problem if it might involve conflict with my partner, children, parents, or other people I'm close to.	
Total checkmarks (unshaded and shaded)	

Work/Study Behaviors	✓
I avoid putting myself in a position where I might fail at something at work, even if it means I won't advance in my job.	
I go to work or school, even on my bad days.	
When a peer, teacher, or supervisor criticizes my work, I get mad or worry about it a lot.	
I don't really like my work, but I do it the best I can because it pays the bills.	
I've failed to finish projects at work or school because I procrastinate too long.	
When I find myself daydreaming at work or school, I can get myself refocused on the task at hand.	
The more important a project or assignment is, the more likely I am to work on it—it's the boring stuff that slows me down.	
It seems like I'm just going through the motions at school or at work.	
When I have a conflict with a teacher or supervisor, I get really upset and often can't sleep that night.	
I might ask for a raise, promotion, or new job assignment at work, even if I thought I might not get it.	
Total checkmarks (unshaded and shaded)	

Leisure/Play Behaviors	✓
I have things I enjoy doing alone.	
When I have free time, I feel better because I can take my time and do something I want to.	
I tend to worry about my problems when I have free time.	
I can usually make myself try something fun on the weekends, even with limited energy.	
Boredom is a big problem for me.	
When I try to do something fun or relaxing, I focus on how I'm feeling and not on what I'm doing.	
I join in enjoyable activities with other people because I may start having fun too.	
Even a little obstacle can stop me from following through on an activity that might be enjoyable for me.	
I have hobbies that I take pride in doing or talents that I try to develop.	
Total checkmarks (unshaded and shaded)	

Health Behaviors	✓
I exercise on a regular basis, even when I am not motivated and have low energy.	
I spend a lot of time trying to put negative thoughts, images, emotions, or memories out of my mind.	
I set goals for improving my health, such as getting more exercise or cutting down on smoking.	
I tend to drink alcohol or take drugs to help me control my feelings.	
I am a spiritual person and have a spiritual practice (yoga, prayer, meditation, journaling).	
I spend a lot of time watching TV, surfing the Internet, playing video games, or engaging in other types of low-energy behavior.	
I do things to help me relax and slow down (take a walk, stretch my body, watch a sunset, sit in a garden).	
I have a bedtime routine that allows me to relax and prepare for restful sleep.	
I don't eat in ways that might improve my health, even when I have the choice.	
Total checkmarks (unshaded and shaded)	

Further Exploration. Now let's look at your scores. Did you check more shaded than unshaded boxes? If so, it's probably not going to surprise you that the shaded boxes represent behaviors that might put you at an elevated risk for depression, whereas the unshaded boxes represent behaviors that could produce a sense of vitality and reduce or counterbalance your risk. As we said, there are no right or wrong answers, and we all have an assortment of coping behaviors that we apply across varying life situations.

Did you identify some vitality behaviors? If so, great—keep them going. Perhaps you found some vitality behaviors that you have done in the past—or might like to try in the future. Keep these in mind to explore later; the goal is to find workable solutions.

What did you learn about your risk behaviors? Did you endorse more risk behaviors in one life domain than in others? Did any of the risk behaviors you endorsed surprise you? Remember that the purpose of taking a fearless inventory is to get your feet on the ground and see things accurately. It is neither good nor bad. It just is. In preparing for radical change, you first have to know where you are starting from before you can form a plan for getting to where you would like to be.

WORKABILITY: THE NEMESIS OF RULE FOLLOWING

Workability is a central concept in the ACT approach. It conditions how you look at your behavioral options in life. The goal of course is to use behaviors that promote the kind of life you would like to live. The reference point is just as important as applying the workability test, because you can only assess how something is working by being clear about what "working" would look like. This is why we invited you to dare to imagine a better future at the end of chapter 2. That future is your reference point. You gauge the workability of any particular life strategy you are using in terms of whether it is moving you toward that reference point. If the strategy is moving you in the direction of a better future, then it is working; if the strategy is moving you away from the life you want to live, then it is not working.

Another benefit of workability is that it shifts your focus to the *actual results* of your actions, not what you think *should* happen. For example, if you decide that you will feel better if you stay home and don't hang out with your friends, because then you won't be a burden on them, test it out! Did you actually feel better in the end? Or did you feel worse? Using the workability yardstick calls out your rule following behaviors and puts the rule to a test by an interested party: you. The goal is to determine whether following the rule produces the results that are promised in the rule. In other words: *It isn't about what SHOULD work; it is about what IS working and what isn't!*

LES'S STORY

Les is a forty-nine-year-old divorced mailman who loves dogs. He hoped to own a dog, but he put this plan on hold in order to focus on his other work and family obligations. He not only worked full-time and took on extra shifts to help pay for his kids' college tuitions, he also cared for his mother, who struggled with advancing dementia.

For many years, he would pause on his mail route to watch someone with a dog, and he'd imagine that he had one too. Then he made himself stop looking because it made him feel sad, and he didn't want to feel sad. He stopped talking about dogs too, because that made him sad. He even tried to pretend that he was annoyed by other people and their pets; but in his heart, he loved dogs and he still wanted one.

Over time, his work and caregiving duties increased to the point that they pretty much consumed all of his time. His mood began to decline. He secretly blamed his mother for making it impossible for him to own and care for a dog, and he became increasingly short-tempered with her. He began to turn down chances to spend time with his kids in order to preserve his declining energy for work and taking care of his mom. Pretty soon, they stopped calling to invite him out, and Les was hurt and felt that they had rejected him.

Workability and Values Go Hand in Hand

Les's story demonstrates a core principle of workability, namely, that it is closely tied to what matters to you in life. The issue is not about whether it's right or wrong to have a dog; it's a matter of what Les is seeking in his specific life context and whether his strategies are *workable*, or helping him succeed.

When Les looked at dogs and imagined having one, he was making contact with what mattered to him—sharing his life with a dog. When Les turned away from what mattered, he began dealing with the emotional consequences through emotional and behavioral avoidance. These strategies, in turn, created problems of their own. His suppressed sadness resurfaced as irritability toward his mother. His avoidance strategies also depleted his mental energy, which resulted in him pulling away from his kids.

Workability Is About Results, Not Promises

Workability focuses on the direct results of strategies you're using in life. No matter how fond you are of avoiding personal pain, if doing so makes our situation materially worse, you must be willing to go in another direction and face the pain. In general, emotional and behavioral avoidance strategies can't stand the test of workability, no matter how ingrained or automatic they may be. You are either getting the results you want in life or you're not. And if you're not, it's time to try something different!

When Jill fused with this rule—"I must meet all of his needs now, when life is so hard for him"—she could not see that following it was exhausting her and robbing her of the joy she might experience in caring for her husband were her life activities more balanced among work, play, and love. Trying to address all of her husband's needs without help from others was not producing feelings of love and closeness. Quite the contrary, it was leaving her tired, sad, hopeless, and irritable. Only when she was able to stop and see the rule was she able to realize that her actions were not working to produce the assumed results. Despite all her efforts, her good-wife behaviors were not resulting in a good-relationship experience for her husband or herself.

JILL'S STORY

Let's take the example of Jill, an older woman who struggled with negotiating the challenges of retirement when her husband became ill. Prior to retirement, Jill had a full life. Although she disliked her long commute, she liked her job. She also enjoyed reading and going to book club meetings with her friends. She also loved knitting and listening to music. She planned to do more knitting and to attend more music events after retirement, but her husband suffered a stroke shortly after her retirement, and she devoted most of her time to caring for him.

When not caring for him, Jill worried about him and distracted herself from her growing sense of disappointment and frustration by watching mindless television shows and eating comfort foods that only made her feel worse. Her husband's health continued to decline, and she told herself she had to stay the course and be available to him around the clock. Any attempt to see friends or even do enjoyable things at home seemed to be out of the question, given the demands of the care her partner needed at this point in his life.

Workability in Daily Life: The Yardstick

Since life is dynamic, workability in one's life moves up and down. This is a basic truth of living a vital life. Behavior that pays off for you in one situation might result in problems in another. When life workability is high, your sense of vitality in relationships, work, and leisure pursuits is strong. This doesn't mean you have peak life experiences every day, but it does mean that you know what's important to you and that you are moving toward it. Remember: as hard as it may be to keep this truth in mind now, a life worth living isn't defined by the absence of pain; rather, it's a path on which pain is accepted and experienced in a healthy way. To keep yourself focused on workability, we recommend that you end each day by rating its workability using the yardstick below!

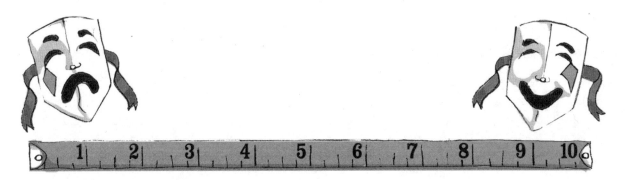

A WORKABILITY MOMENT

This exercise will help you understand from firsthand experience that workability isn't so much about the absence of pain as it is about approaching pain in a way that produces a sense of showing up and living according to what matters.

Begin by recalling an emotionally challenging situation, event, or interaction when you showed up and did what you believed in, even while you were in pain. Describe the situation in the lines provided, then write down the actions you took that were workable.

Next, think a little deeper. What showed up in your body or mind that told you that your approach was working? Did you feel proud of yourself? Did you notice a more relaxed feeling in your body? Did you have the sense of growing as a person? Just look around in your memory of the situation and see what is there in a positive vein. Write this down as well.

Challenging event, situation, or interaction:

_____

_____

_____

Workable actions I took:

1. _____

_____

2. _____

_____

3. _____

_____

Mental experiences of workability:

1. _____

_____

2. _____

_____

Bodily experiences of workability:

1. _____

_____

2. _____

_____

Further Exploration. What happened when you really immersed yourself in this workability moment? What kinds of feelings showed up? Was there a mixture of difficult feelings and more-gratifying feelings? That is often the case when we deal in a workable way with a challenging situation. Some of the painful emotions are there right along with the more rewarding ones.

Did you experience the workability of the moment anywhere in your body? Sometimes we carry a lot of physical tension into a painful situation. Then, when we engage in workable actions, the tension gives way to other bodily experiences like excitement or a sense of relaxation.

Hopefully you discovered that you don't have to engage in avoidance to feel better. The kind of "feeling better" derived from avoidance is just the absence of pain. The rewards that come from workable responses go far deeper than that. They often involve not just the reduction of pain but, more important, the appearance of positive emotional experience, positive self-regard, and optimism.

THE CHOICE POINT: SHORT-TERM RELIEF, LONG-TERM GRIEF

Before we proceed with the next step of your fearless self-inventory, we want you to learn the difference between *short-term coping strategies* and *long-term coping strategies*. A lot of the risk behaviors listed in the Depression Risk and Vitality Assessment are short-term coping strategies designed to help you deal with your depression in the moment. When you are depressed, it is easy to make decisions based on how you are feeling and the rules that pop up in your mind. This often occurs with limited awareness and intention, such that you don't realize you are at a *choice point*. A choice point is a moment of truth that can be small or large in scope. It involves choosing to move in the direction of your better future or in the opposite direction, toward depression. The question is: What are you going to choose at this moment in time?

If you move in the direction of avoidance, it will likely take you away from the life you would like to live, even if the impact is ever so small. As we pointed out in chapter 2, avoidance behaviors can function like Chinese water torture. Each avoidance behavior looks small in magnitude, but when you add them up, they have the power of a freight train.

For example, if you decide to have a couple of drinks to help you feel better, you're using a short-term strategy to manage your depression; alcohol might help you relax in the here and now, but it creates problems in the future—even the near future. Note that there's nothing inherently wrong with having a couple of drinks, and this is the tricky part. The question is: Did the drinking result in behaviors that support or oppose your values? For instance, if you value your family, and drinking weakened your connection to them, that strategy did not work for you.

Many coping decisions make sense because they are a familiar part of the autopilot lifestyle. This is the paradox of depression. It seems as though what you're doing would be beneficial, but it turns out that it isn't. Again, this is usually because a short-term strategy is being implemented.

On the other hand, many of the vitality behaviors listed in the Depression Risk and Vitality Assessment are examples of long-term coping strategies. They're done to promote your health and well-being over time. They're much less concerned with addressing how you feel *right now*—although you can see immediate results with some behaviors—they're more concerned with long-term vitality and wellness.

For example, to escape the depressed feeling you get from having to tidy your kitchen, you decide to go through your Netflix queue. You watch a movie, and when it's over, you discover that little has changed, that you're still as depressed as when you first sat down to watch the show—and the kitchen is still a mess. Instead, at the choice point in this situation, you might choose to go out and walk briskly for thirty minutes. Exercise not only releases neuropeptides called *endorphins* that are known to produce a positive mood and a sense of well-being, but it also helps improve your cardiovascular health and elevate your metabolism, which aids in maintaining a healthy weight. It even helps prevent Alzheimer's!

The pitfall is that watching television seems easier than thirty minutes of brisk walking. What's *easier* is infinitely more appealing than what's *harder*, particularly when you're depressed. And this is compounded by the belief that what changes your mood *right away* is preferable to what'll change it over the *long term*. The paradox, and the problem, is this: Some short-term strategies help you feel better *right now*, but in the long run, they create more depression. Watching the movie only *artificially* changes your mood; exercise literally does it.

Once you gain new skills for shifting your perspective, you can choose positive coping behaviors, experience their benefits, and begin to build a new behavior pattern. You do this by learning to select long-term solutions over short-term strategies when you're at a choice point.

JUDY'S STORY

Judy is a thirty-three-year-old mother of two children, ages nine and eleven. She has been married for twelve years. Her husband, a construction worker, usually drinks a few beers after work with his buddies before coming home. He often has a couple more beers at home. Judy began to feel depressed several years ago, after she discovered that her husband had an affair with a woman he met at the local watering hole. She chose to forgive her husband even though she felt terribly rejected by his infidelity and by his frequent comments about her physical appearance. Judy had gained weight after her second pregnancy and she believed that this triggered her husband's interest in other women.

Judy believes that he drinks to avoid interacting with her, but she hasn't said anything to him about it. She's afraid that confronting him might cause him to leave her or start another affair. Because of her limited job skills, she doesn't think she'd be able to make it on her own if he left her. She feels lonely but doesn't see her friends because she doesn't want them to know that her marriage is in trouble. Her day is basically organized around her household and childcare duties, reading magazines, watching TV, and napping. She enjoys being with her children, and she takes pride in her cooking and cleaning, but she had hoped for much more in life.

Let's take a look at what Judy came up with when she took an inventory of her depressed behaviors and their short-term and long-term results. It'll help you prepare for when you do the same, later in this section.

Judy's Inventory of Short-Term versus Long-Term Results

What I've Done to Control My Depression	Short-Term Results	Long-Term Results
I take a lot of naps during the day.	My mood gets a little better after I sleep. I don't have to think about my husband coming home.	Later I feel guilty about not doing more with my day. It increases my feeling that life is passing me by.
I avoid large social gatherings because they sap my energy.	I feel relieved that I don't have to put on a happy face in front of others. My husband goes without me now and criticizes me for not liking to party. That makes me feel like I'm letting him down.	I haven't seen one of my close friends for months and feel like I'm letting her down; her mother died a while back and I know this is a hard time for her. I feel more and more guilty about this.
I try to talk to my husband about how depressed I feel.	He doesn't seem to listen and just starts lecturing me. I feel like he's criticizing me for being depressed. When he drinks, this gets so bad that I leave and go to my room.	I feel more and more isolated over time because my husband isn't helping me through this. These interactions are making my depression worse. I probably need to look for another person to talk to.
I take lots of walks with the dog.	This does give me peace of mind and helps my mood for a little while. I feel better after walking and don't see my problems in such a dark way.	The exercise has helped me feel more physically fit, so that's at least one problem I've actually been addressing.
I don't argue with my kids because it makes my depression worse.	I feel relieved that I don't have to battle with them and deal with their tantrums. I wait for my husband to get home so he can deal with them.	My kids are having more behavior problems at school, and I feel like I'm not helping them. This makes me feel like I'm failing as a mother.
I smoke cigarettes to calm down and de-stress.	I guess it helps me distract myself from things for a while. When I get stressed out, I can always step outside and relax with a smoke.	I feel like I'm getting more addicted to cigarettes and that they will hurt my health in the long run.

In Judy's answers, you can see the usual mixed bag of short- and long-term strategies that people use to try to control feelings when depressed. Notice that the strategies she assesses as least useful are basically avoidance behaviors (napping, smoking, and avoiding social situations and confrontations with her husband and children).

In reflecting on this exercise, Judy realized that she needed to stop using avoidance strategies that were not helpful. She puzzled over why she had used them for as long as she had. Judy reasoned that the avoidance strategies were easier and more familiar to execute than her more-active approach strategies. She heard a voice saying, "Just lie down and take a nap; you'll feel better when you wake up... Just have a cigarette and focus on something else... Let your husband deal with the kids—he's their father." And those strategies made sense when Judy's goal had been to control her mood. But her real goal—and yours—is to solve problems and live a vital life.

INVENTORY OF SHORT-TERM VERSUS LONG-TERM RESULTS

In this exercise, think back over the time since you first began to struggle with depression. In the left-hand column, describe the main strategies you've used to control your depression. Then consider the short-term and long-term results of each strategy, and describe those in the next two columns. If you need more space, print a copy from this book's website (http://www.newharbinger.com/38457).

What I've Done to Control My Depression	Short-Term Results	Long-Term Results

Further Exploration. What did you discover in this exercise? Were you able to identify some short-term coping strategies? When you step back and look at them objectively, how did these strategies end up working in the long term? Did you determine whether any of your strategies have helped in the long run? If so, you'll want to use these strategies more often.

Depending upon your situation, you might have piled up a lot of short-term strategies that produce miserable long-term results. When your attempts to manage your depression don't work in the long run, you know it because you don't feel like you are living the life you want to live. Is your life working better than it did a month ago? A year ago? Is your life satisfaction improving or deteriorating? Are you living your life the way you want to live it? It's important that you honestly look at whether a particular coping behavior is working or whether it's hurting. If it doesn't work, try something different. And ask yourself, "Does the new behavior work better?"

As mentioned, depression is fueled by avoidance of emotionally challenging situations. Avoidance strategies normally are short-term-relief oriented; their goal is to reduce or eliminate your emotional distress right now. But you do have a choice in which strategies you eventually select! In the exercise that follows, you'll have a chance to play with the choices you have, both the short- and long-term ones.

APPROACH VERSUS AVOIDANCE INVENTORY

To begin, either select an item you endorsed in the Depression Risk Inventory in chapter 2, or pick a different depression trigger in your life. Then, on the lines below, describe how you could avoid dealing with the situation, followed by how you could approach the situation. Try to describe these options in terms of behaviors.

Please don't use this exercise as an opportunity to beat up on yourself; cultivate the kindness for yourself that you would give to someone else in your position. You've been doing the best you can, and this program will give you the new perspective and skills you need to make changes in your life. Just stick with us; we are your partners in change.

Relationships in my life: _____

Strategies I could use to avoid dealing with the problem: _____

_____

Strategies I could use to directly deal with the problem: _____

_____

Work/study behavior: _____

Strategies I could use to avoid dealing with the problem: _____

_____

Strategies I could use to directly deal with the problem: _____

_____

Leisure/play behavior: _____

Strategies I could use to avoid dealing with the problem: _____

_____

Strategies I could use to directly deal with the problem: _____

_____

Health behavior: _____

Strategies I could use to avoid dealing with the problem: _____

_____

Strategies I could use to directly deal with the problem: _____

_____

Further Exploration. This is another way of looking at depression triggers. In this exercise, did you detect problems you didn't identify in the Depression Risk Inventory? If so, great. Do take these into account as you move toward experimenting with new strategies in dealing with problems in your life. If you didn't note any new problems, then consider this exercise as confirming and perhaps further clarifying what you learned from your Depression Risk Inventory. Was it difficult for you to describe what you would do if you chose to deal directly with the problem? If you did, you are certainly not alone! The good news is that you can retrain your brain to pursue those long-term coping strategies more often.

Judy's Results

When Judy did this exercise, she had some interesting observations on what was going on in her life and how her penchant for avoiding rather than dealing with life challenges was fueling the fire of her depression.

Relationships in my life: *My marriage is going downhill fast.*

Strategies I could use to avoid dealing with the problem: *Neither one of us ever brings up the fact that we don't get along. Instead we just nitpick each other and criticize what the other person does. I try to stay out of his way when he seems to be in a bad mood. I don't let myself think about how unhappy I am; the prospect of having to deal with the marriage is just scary. I may end up being a single mother.*

Strategies I could use to directly deal with the problem: *I would have to sit down with him and have a heart-to-heart talk about what is going on in our marriage. We might need to get marital counseling. At least I could let him know that the relationship matters to me and that I want to try to save it.*

Work/study behavior: *I have not developed my job skills or created a career even though I intended to after my kids were old enough to stay at home by themselves.*

Strategies I could use to avoid dealing with the problem: *I have a lot of worry about going back to work. I know my skill sets are out of date, so I talk myself out of looking at job ads or talking to friends about my interest in a career.*

Strategies I could use to directly deal with the problem: *I could go to unemployment and get help with developing a résumé and a job search strategy. I could talk with my friends and get information on how they coped with going back to work after having kids. I can also ask them to keep an eye out for me—for just part-time work.*

Leisure/play behavior: *I have very few activities or hobbies that give me joy.*

Strategies I could use to avoid dealing with the problem: *I just don't think about it. I do my housework, cook, take care of the kids, and call it a day. I tell myself that that's all I need and that I don't have the energy for anything else anyway. When friends call to invite me to go out, I make up an excuse for why I can't go.*

Strategies I could use to directly deal with the problem: *I could look for hobbies that I can do at home, like sewing or reading. I could join a book club or just say yes to invitations. It would be easy for me to volunteer at my children's school; they are always asking for parent helpers.*

Health behavior: *I've gained more than thirty pounds in the last three years, and I smoke too much.*

Strategies I could use to avoid dealing with the problem: *I'm afraid to quit smoking or change my diet because smoking and snacking are how I stay calm. I worry that I would feel more down and maybe even gain more weight if I quit smoking.*

Strategies I could use to directly deal with the problem: *I could get a fitness evaluation at the YMCA and maybe an exercise coach to help start a program. I could set a modest weight-loss goal so I would feel successful. I could call the quit-smoking line; I have it on the card my doctor gave me.*

As her answers clearly show, Judy struggles with her tendency to avoid addressing her major life issues. In completing the exercises, Judy realized that she was spending too much time and energy on managing her feelings by avoiding things, and she also realized that she has good ideas about how she could deal with the big problems in her life.

Judy's Journey Toward a Vital Life

Judy had the realization that her life was steadily going downhill and that she would have to be the one to do something to turn it around. She realized that the mess she was in was caused in large part by her reluctance to deal directly with her husband's affair and his lack of accountability about it. So one night when their children were staying at a friend's house, Judy brought up the affair and asked her husband to take responsibility for his behavior and apologize to her. She also informed him that his drinking wasn't going to work for her and that he needed to get help. He got up and left the table without saying a word, got into his truck, and drove off.

Even as Judy wept, she felt released from her prison of silence, numbness, and isolation. At that moment, she accepted that she might not be able to save her marriage, but in her heart she knew she could and would create a better life for herself and her children. Her husband returned after a couple of hours and agreed to seek treatment for his alcoholism. He apologized for being unfaithful and insisted that it didn't have anything to do with the way Judy looked but was more about his own insecurity and impulsivity. He asked her to forgive him, and this time he meant it. Judy was optimistic about going to counseling with her husband, but her first priority was continuing to focus on creating a vital life for herself, whether she shared it with him or not.

USE WORKABILITY AS A LIFE MANTRA

A unique feature of the workability approach to daily living is that it owes no allegiance to any doctrine about how to live life. A life worth living comes in about as many flavors as there are people. And how you get there isn't about style points—it's about getting out of life what you want out of life. As we said before: It isn't about what *should* work, it's about what *does* work. When you're zeroed in on using workability as your guide, you'll find yourself asking these kinds of questions:

Is drinking to relax working for me?

How has it been working for me to avoid dating?

Is skimping on sleep working for me?

Is not talking to my partner about our sexual problems working for me?

Is not looking for a more satisfying job and career path working for me?

What am I doing in my life right now that is working for me?

What am I doing in my life right now that's not working?

Is working two jobs working for me in terms of my family life?

How did my choices today work for me?

Is waiting to be motivated to take a walk working for me?

Is eating ice cream every night working for me?

Is not going to church working for me?

It takes courage to ask workability questions. Very often, the mere fact that you're asking means that you've begun to recognize a difference between what your mind is promising you and what you're getting in terms of results.

So before we end this chapter, let's size up the questions you might be carrying around about the workability of certain aspects of your life in the four life domains. Remind yourself that it is okay to ask workability questions without necessarily assuming that the answer is going to be negative. It is like checking the air pressure in your tires. You don't know if there is a problem until you put the air pressure gauge to work!

MY WORKABILITY QUESTIONS

In the space provided, write down your workability questions in the four key life domains: relationships, work/study, leisure/play, and health. They might resonate with ones we've just listed, or they might be totally different. You don't need to answer these questions now—not yet. Just jot them down.

Relationships: _____

_____

_____

_____

Work/study: _____

_____

_____

_____

Leisure/play: _____

_____

_____

_____

Health: _____

_____

_____

_____

Further Exploration. Were you able to come up with some questions about workability in all of the life domains? If you did, welcome to the human race! There are few people in this world who have everything figured out in even one life domain, much less all of them. Because life is dynamic, unfolding, and challenging by nature, you can expect workability questions to surface, subside, and resurface over time. In some life arenas, you probably have an inkling of what's not working for you right now. We will go into that in greater depth in future chapters.

One thing we want to make abundantly clear is that we aren't blaming you for at times engaging in unworkable behaviors. We all do it. We understand how difficult it is to remain focused on living in accordance with your values. It's why so many people experience symptoms of depression at some point in their lives. At the same time, there is a connection between your actions (or lack thereof) and the results you're getting in life. We view this as a positive rather than a negative truth. You do have control over your behavior, even if your mind tries to bully you into following unworkable rules.

If you identify the strategies that aren't working in your life right now, you can try something new. And trying something new introduces the opportunity for learning something new—and then trying something else. It's all about variability in our behavior—experimenting, noticing, and noting the direction in which we want to head, of course! We think this classic Zen saying offers inspiration: *The journey of a thousand miles begins with the first step.* You are taking that step right now, and the journey is under way!

IDEAS TO CULTIVATE

- Workability is a powerful tool designed to help expose rule following and test whether the rules you are following are actually working.

- To know what works, you must learn to notice your behavior and analyze the consequences of your behavior.

- Short-term strategies for coping with depression tend to be focused on controlling emotional pain.

- Long-term coping strategies don't offer the quick fix you might want, but they provide stable, workable results that promote your sense of vitality.

- Ultimately, it's better to solve problems than avoid them, and better to face difficult emotions than run from them.

- Taking inventory of how your lifestyle is working right now, scanning the horizon for depression risk situations, and forming a problem-solving plan oriented toward approach rather than avoidance can help you create a better life.

CHAPTER 4

Understanding the Mind and Mindfulness

Hold to the now, the here, through which all future plunges to the past.

—James Joyce

If living life on autopilot sets the stage for you to veer toward a depression-producing lifestyle, then the antidote is to create a lifestyle intentionally: one in which you choose to live in ways that expand you as a person. If rule following and the emotional and behavioral avoidance it produces lead you away from your inner vitality, then learning to approach and embrace all emotions, even those you don't like, is a more positive path for relating to your inner space.

In the previous chapter, we gave you a chance to imagine what living an approach-based life would look like. But if it were that easy to turn your life around, you no doubt would have already done that—and you probably wouldn't be holding this book in your hands. It might surprise you that one of the things making the change so hard for you is *your mind*.

Your mind is not necessarily going to cooperate in helping you achieve your goals. As we discussed in chapter 2, your mind is full of rules for you to follow, and it will incessantly tell you to follow them. Your mind has been programmed to tell you that controlling your depression—and all other sources of personal pain—is job one in life. Your mind wants you to assume that nothing else important can happen until you get rid of your depression. When it comes to this issue of emotional control, you and everyone else do indeed have a one-track mind.

We can guarantee you this: Your mind is not going to stop chattering at you about the virtues of control, suppression, and avoidance. And it is hard to ignore your mind, because it is always with you, and it *is* helpful to you in many ways. What is needed is a different way of relating to your mind so that you can listen to it when it pays to do so and follow your own intuitions when that is the better path.

In this chapter, we want to better help you understand how the mind functions and how cultivating your mindfulness skills can help you relate to your mind in a more productive way. To accomplish this important objective, we will delve deeper into the architecture of the mind using the perspective of *relational frame theory*. You will quickly see why you might want to take your mind's advice with a grain of salt.

Along the way, we will discuss two major modes of mind that you have access to in daily living. One is based in the linear, rule-based system of language and social control and is likely to push you in the direction of emotional avoidance; the other originates in your values, intuitions, and passions and will lead you into a state of awareness of, openness to, and curiosity about your internal experiences—all while being engaged in the life pursuits that matter to you. One mode of mind is the source of suffering; the other is the source of inner calm, compassion, and vitality. In ACT, the goal is to help you use this second mode of mind to make you *psychologically flexible.* This involves you being able to stay in the present moment, stay open to and accepting of your inner experiences, and simultaneously engage in life pursuits that matter to you.

The mindfulness skills we teach you in this book contribute directly to psychological flexibility; they will help you to be present and open—receptive to your inner experiences—while increasing your ability to initiate and sustain a lifestyle that creates positive emotions and that is consistent with your values. In this chapter, you'll have a chance to make direct contact with—really experience—what they feel like in practice.

We will end by giving you a chance to assess your mindfulness skills as they stand at present and then help you develop a plan for strengthening them. Remember: Neuroscience studies suggest that even a brief daily practice of mindfulness skills can result in quite rapid, permanent, and positive changes in brain functioning (Deshmukh 2006; Hankey 2006; Lutz et al. 2009; Davidson and Begley 2012).

WELCOME TO YOUR MIND!

In this book, we use the word "mind" to refer to the ongoing process of *fusing with* and *reacting to* thoughts, feelings, memories, and sensations. The mind is not a thing in the literal sense. Instead, it is a dynamic, unfolding process in your awareness. When you're fused with your mind, you're likely to obey its instructions, just as a child minds a parent. Only you can relate to your mind, because no one else has access to the word machine inside your head. It's just you and your mind going at it. Your relationship with your mind is unique and determined by your learning history. In this way, no two minds are alike, even though we are trained from birth to comply with similar social rules, norms, and expectations. For a moment, we want to examine how the mind originates within the operating system of language and thought.

RFT holds that human language and thought originate from a surprisingly small number of symbolic relations called *relational frames*. Examples of these core relations include now/then, if/then, and here/there, to name a few. RFT researchers are very interested in how these frames develop, expand in number, and multiply to create the vast capabilities of human language.

The most basic relational frame in language is the *deictic frame*. The deictic frame establishes that I am different from you, and this is the very beginning of the ability to adopt a point of view wherein my point of view is different from your point of view. Very young children can't engage in this type of relation, so they're unable to distinguish the emotions of others from their own emotions. If a parent starts crying in front of a year-old infant, the infant will also start to cry.

Acquiring the ability to frame deictically is the beginning of conscious self-awareness. Indeed, in Buddhist philosophy, it is this emerging sense of self as separate from others that is the first cause of human suffering. Once you know that you are separate from others, you can begin to evaluate how you are different from others. This leads to a whole host of potential sources of suffering.

Deictic frames also allow us to distinguish things from the perspective of the observer: here and there, now and then, and so on. In language, this allows us to make such statements as "The photograph is there, in front of me" and "I was five in this picture; now I'm fifty." In thought, it allows you to clearly distinguish between "me" and "my mind," such as being able to say, "I'm having the thought that I'm sad about where my career is headed." Turning the deictic frame inward can be very difficult, as it might not feel intuitive or even true at first. But once you've established the relation "me and my mind," you're able to say, "I'm having the thought that I'm lonely" or "I'm having the feeling of being sad." And this is a major step toward improving your ability to stay in the moment, open to your experiences—and transcend depression.

At first, this distinction may seem surprising, maybe even mind-boggling, but just as you aren't the same person as someone sitting across from you, *you aren't the same as your mind*. It's more accurate to say that you are able to observe your mind's activities, but, as the observer, you are separate from your mind. Learning to step back from unworkable rules produced by the mind, therefore, comes down to strengthening your ability to deictically frame in an inward direction, be it through the practice of meditation, prayer, mindfulness exercises, or a combination of these. Now there's a paradox—using the word "mindfulness" to describe a way of separating yourself from your mind! Luckily, that one's just semantic.

REVEALING THE BRITTLE SHELL

The activities of mind are so subtle and hard to apprehend by nature that we tend to take them for granted. On the surface, it seems essential and correct to use the mind as the go-to for daily functioning. It helps us organize, plan, predict, and engage with the world. The reality, however, is that the mind is just an operating system. The mind displays output at a constant rate on the screen of your mind's eye on a 24/7 basis. But don't mistake the operating system for the computer that houses it! Like any operating system, the mind is not as capable as you might think it is. This guided audio exercise will help you understand this counterintuitive idea.

Get an egg out of your refrigerator, hold it in your open palm, and concentrate on it for a minute. What do you see? What do you feel? You see a white or brown shell, with a smooth, slightly sandy texture. Now notice how perfectly made the shell is in terms of its function. The entire structure is necessary for the shell to do its job. It is built exactly right and has been that way since the moment it came into existence as a tiny, tiny shell. Can you see the location where the shell started to become a shell? Is there an obvious starting point? What was the last part of the shell to grow? And finally, what is the living part of this egg? The shell—or what is inside the shell? When you are ready, return to the book to complete the remainder of this exercise.

Now that you've had a chance to really study the shell, you may be thinking how perfectly designed it is for the job it has to do. Now, let's change the context a little and see what happens to the shell. What if we asked you to let the egg drop onto a floor? Would you resist? Perhaps you would, as you know that would result in the end of the egg in its current form—and a mess on the floor!

The shell, as perfect as it is for providing a lightweight protective covering for the potential life mass inside, is not designed to protect the life mass from every possible physical insult. If you dropped the egg on your bed, it would probably make it, but not if you dropped it on the floor. Something that's a perfectly protective cover in one context can turn out to be exactly the wrong form of protection in a different context—just like your mind!

CRACKING THE SHELL OF LANGUAGE

If the mind is like an egg, the shell is the operating system of language and thought. The main products of this system are thinking, feeling, remembering, and the awareness of physical sensations within the body. It turns out that this shell grows and matures just like an eggshell, and it's also very brittle. How brittle is it? The following guided audio exercise has been used for decades (and in Hayes, Strosahl, and Wilson 1999, 154–6) to demonstrate the transparent nature of language and thought.

First, think of the word "orange." Let all the sensations, memories, and images associated with that word come into your mind. Do you sense the tangy odor or the texture of the peel? Can you imagine the slightly bittersweet taste? Do you see color? Can you see the sections of the orange in your hand? Can you sense the gush of juice as you bite down on a section? Give yourself a minute or so to get a full picture of an orange in your mind's eye.

Now find a clock with a second hand on it. For the next forty-five seconds, we want you to say the word "orange" over and over again as fast as you can. Just keep saying the word as fast as you can until the forty-five seconds are up. If you have trouble pronouncing it or lose your concentration on the task, just get back to it and keep repeating the word as best you can. Time to start. Go!

When you are ready, return to the book to complete the remainder of this exercise.

What happened to your relationship with the word "orange" as you did this exercise? Did you notice that the more you repeated the word, the more it started to sound like gibberish? Did you have more trouble pronouncing the word over time? What happened to the images and associations you had in the first part of the exercise? Did they disappear?

Let's consider the implications of the orange exercise for a moment longer. Initially, when we asked you to use the word "orange" as it's supposed to be used in your language system, the system functioned beautifully. It gave you not just the word "orange" but a variety of images and associations from your past history with oranges. Then, when we asked you to use the word in a way that violates the rules of the system, it turned into an odd collection of sounds, mostly devoid of images and associations. You were simply uttering a sound that had no functional connection to your shell. You could try this again with almost any word and the result would be the same.

Activities like this essentially crack the shell of language and reveal its limitations, which often has a freeing effect on people. Once you realize how context dependent your reactive mind is, it is easier to react to it with skepticism, particularly when it involves dealing with your inner space. There is some formidable and essential wisdom in this part of your awareness, just as the essence of the egg is not the shell but what's inside the shell. The reason the egg is there isn't because of the shell. If there wasn't any life mass inside, there would be no need for the shell in the first place.

Learning to recognize that your shell is different from your essence is fundamental to living a vital life. You are the life mass, and although the shell protects you in some contexts, it's ineffective—or worse—in other situations. We'll help you learn when you can use your shell and when you need to shed it so you can access other important aspects of your mind. Don't worry about cracking the shell of language! It's very robust and will pull itself back together quickly.

THE TWO MODES OF MIND

Functionally speaking, the mind is organized into two main modes: *reactive mind* and *wise mind*. One mode (reactive mind) involves the linear, analytical, judgmental problem-solving operations of the mind. These activities are largely based in the semantic processing and reasoning areas of the brain. The second mode (wise mind) involves nonverbal forms of intelligence such as intuition, prophecy, inspiration, creativity, compassion, transcendent experiences of self, morality, and so forth. The mental abilities of both modes reside in distinctly different regions of the brain. Thus, the brain seems organized to give us two different ways to approach, understand, and respond to events inside and outside our skin.

The problem in depression is that the verbal, analytical mode of mind dominates awareness, squeezing out the nonverbal forms of knowing. In the sections that follow, we examine this dichotomy a little more closely, because it points directly to the question of why mindfulness practice will be such a powerful ally in retraining your brain to help you transcend your depression.

Reactive Mind

The reactive mind is a direct creation of your language system. It is linear, judgmental, and directive in nature. It chatters at you, wants to discourse with you, and serves up an unending stream of "woulds," "shoulds," "musts," and "oughts," regardless of whether its advice is wanted or needed. Your reactive mind is full of judgments, categories, comparisons, and predictions. It strings together concepts that describe who you are in the here and now and how you got to be the way you are. It will tell you that you don't have enough of something, like love in your life, and too much of something else, like body hair or fatty tissue around your waist. It tells you what will happen if you engage in some behavior ("If you leave your job, you'll never find another one") and what will happen if you don't ("If you don't quit, your boss will keep insulting you and you'll have no self-esteem"). This type of comparative, evaluative, and predictive activity is a breeding ground for depression, because overidentifying with the products of your reactive mind can get you caught in the trap of rule following and make you unable to adapt. In Buddhism, the reactive mind is viewed as a small and limited form of self that must be held lightly in order for you to cultivate healthier forms of self-experience.

Let's be clear: We aren't trying to bash reactive mind across the board. In many life circumstances, such as when you're planning a work task, balancing a bank account, or crossing a busy intersection, reactive mind is very useful. As we noted earlier, reactive mind is able to plan, evaluate, and predict with considerable success in the external world. We would be lost without its organizational and problem-solving functions.

The problem is that the functions of reactive mind creep into areas where they are not useful. This includes making unhelpful evaluations, comparisons, or predictions about your thoughts, emotions, memories, self-worth, and how others perceive you, to name just a few. In these inner-world situations, reactive mind backfires miserably, causing your behavior to be governed by unworkable rules that foster emotional and behavioral avoidance. Further, and as we discussed in chapter 2, the rule following that originates in reactive mind directs your attention away from the actual real-world results of your behavior, thus making it difficult for you to identify strategies that don't work.

Remember Bob from chapter 2? After his family left, this is exactly what he had to confront. His reactive mind was telling him to avoid being with his friends or setting up visitation with his children because he would just be a burden to them. His reactive mind was advising him to engage in a strategy designed to control his depression, but the strategy actually made his depression worse. His reactive mind advised him to work even more than he had prior to losing his family and to stop feeling sorry for himself.

The more Bob followed this advice, the more he struggled with anger and sadness, and the more often he resorted to drinking alcohol to relax and to sleep. Drinking, of course, did not stop the mental chatter of his reactive mind. It kept telling him, "Other people are able to take care of their patients and make time for their families. Why can't you?" Bob's mental advisor simply couldn't admit that its strategies were never going to work, because it didn't have another plan of action to offer. Until Bob learned to listen to his direct experience, he was powerless to resist the constant chatter of his reactive mind.

Wise Mind

It was Buddha who coined the term "wise mind." Wise mind is deeply rooted in basic awareness and the nonverbal forms of knowing that surface when we can separate ourselves from the incessant chatter of reactive mind. The Dalai Lama likened wise mind to the clear blue sky that remains after the clouds created by reactive mind have been removed (Dalai Lama, Lhundrub, and Cabezon 2011). He suggests that the wise mind is the final source of the you that you know as you. It is the repository of consciousness itself, and this is something you have been in touch with since you first became an aware human being.

There is something comforting, safe, and secure about simply being in contact with self-awareness. This experience doesn't change, even when things are changing all around you in the external world. In this way, the wise mind can become a sanctuary when you are in troubled waters. It is in the sanctuary of wise mind where you really grab hold of the sense that you are here, now, and alive. Your senses come alive such that you become much more tuned in to what is going on inside your body (for example, your rate of breathing, heart rate, sensations in your limbs) and on the outside as well (for example, seeing colors and hues differently, noticing new smells, seeing your partner's face differently).

When you make sustained contact with wise mind, you may also have a sense of being interconnected with all things and experience a deep sense of compassion for the suffering of others and yourself. Self-compassion, as we explain later in this book, relieves you of the burden of having to be perfect in order to be worthy of your own kindness and affection. When you sense that you are interconnected with everyone, you quickly realize that everyone has flaws and shortcomings. Welcome to the human race!

Remember the egg we had you experiment with before? Wise mind is the essence inside the shell; it is what persists underneath the brittle surface of language and conceptualized versions of self. It is not defined by thoughts, feelings, memories, and sensations. Wise mind can see the shell of language and thought for what it really is, not what it says it is. The shell has a specific purpose that is important and useful in the right situations. But its use is ultimately limited—as is reactive mind, which depends on language and thought, and the limited context of verbal rules, to function. By contrast, because it is not in the world of evaluation, labeling, comparison, or prediction, wise mind is naturally curious, empathic, and focused on the here and now. It is fearless in standing in the presence of immediate experience and is keenly interested in the you that is doing the experiencing.

Much of the work we ask you to do in this book and on your own is to continually and patiently shift from the mode of reactive mind to the mode of wise mind. With patience and practice, you will get better and better at making this very important shift! In fact, an easy way to start is to give your reactive mind a nickname. Go ahead, try it—the sillier the better. Maybe a name like "Blow Hard" or "Know It All" or "Inner Critic" will get you thinking. As soon as you name it, you've made an important distinction between you and your reactive mind—and this is an important step toward being able to access your wise mind when you need it.

WISE MIND AND PSYCHOLOGICAL FLEXIBILITY

Spending more time in the mode of wise mind will lead you to have greater and greater levels of psychological flexibility. Wise mind inherently involves being in the here and now, open to and curious about even painful inner experiences, and in touch with your overarching life principles. This is not only good for your health and well-being, but it also helps to quickly turn the tide on your depression. Wise mind mode frees you from rule following and having to use avoidance strategies, because when you are in the sanctuary of wise mind, there is no need to run from your own experience of being human. You can roll with your inner experiences instead of resisting them, focus on being present and in the moment, and base your actions in your beliefs about what matters to you in life. This is when the fun begins!

Note that even psychologically flexible people can fuse with unworkable rules and behave in values-inconsistent ways at times. However, they possess the mindfulness skills necessary to keep them moving in the direction of their values, and they can "get back in the game," even after going through a challenging period in their life. Prior to moving on to a discussion of the mindfulness skills that produce psychological flexibility, it will be useful to examine each of these three core attributes of psychological flexibility—awareness, openness, and engagement—in more detail.

Being Aware

Being aware is the ability to be present, in the moment, and to pay attention to what is in front of you in a flexible, effective way. It is no accident that almost every meditative tradition emphasizes some type of breathing or attention-focusing task. It is a widely accepted spiritual truth that being present is the portal to peace of mind and transcendent experiences.

On a more mundane level, being aware of what you are doing as you do it is the solution for many of the problematic results of automatic living, including depression. Being aware is the skill that keeps you tuned into what is actually happening around you. This allows you to notice mistakes and learn from them, rather than slipping back into following unworkable rules that your mind is giving you. When you are paying attention, you don't tend to pick mindless, automatic behaviors; you can see their unhelpful consequences and instead choose a behavior that is beneficial to you.

Sadly, the ability to be "here and now" is seldom valued or taught in Western culture. It is often labeled as a New Age idea that is practiced only by weirdos and monks. We are taught instead that automatic living is the preferred way to go: Complete your daily routines, follow the social conventions you've been taught, and turn your life over to the system, and your depression will surely give way to happiness. Unfortunately, you may not choose daily routines that actually support your health, and the pace of daily living may not allow you to smell the roses, so to speak. What a shame, because intentionality in choosing daily routines is critical—and the roses do smell good!

The ability to be present on purpose also supports your ability to treat yourself and others with compassion and kindness. For example, you may find that you're less likely to judge a friend who has done something that hurts you. You may even become aware of things you did unintentionally that contributed to the problem. When you suffer a setback or make a mistake, being able to get present and pay attention to your reactive mind's harsh judgments of you will allow you to treat yourself with kindness and self-acceptance.

Being Open

Being open is the ability to take an accepting, curious, detached stance toward all of you inner experiences. All humans have an unending cascade of thoughts, emotions, memories, images, and physical sensations, all of which are experienced privately. However, people vary widely in how they respond to these experiences. A basic difference has to do with whether they *approach* or *avoid* the distressing, unwanted internal experience. While avoidance works sometimes, such as when you jerk your hand away from a hot burner, habitual avoidance of painful emotions and thoughts exacts a heavy toll on a person's quality of life. On the other hand, taking an open, curious, receptive stance reduces the need to control, avoid, or numb uncomfortable feelings, and it allows you to move forward in chosen directions.

Let's say you want a new job and you find a possibility. You send in your information, and you're called in for an interview. With each step, you may naturally experience some anxiety and apprehension.

You may have some tightness in your chest when you think about the upcoming interview, and you may notice thoughts such as, "What if I get so uptight that I screw up the interview?" If your response style is one of *avoidance* (being closed), you can easily get caught up in trying to control these unpleasant thoughts, which saps your energy, diverts your attention, and may actually prevent you from succeeding in the interview. If your response style is one of *approaching* (being open), you can simply notice the feelings and thoughts that come up around your vulnerability and continue to invest your energy in moving forward with your plan.

Being Engaged

Being engaged is the ability to approach situations, events, or interactions with the intent of acting according to your values, even if doing so involves experiencing painful emotions, distressing thoughts, disturbing memories, or uncomfortable physical symptoms. When you engage life, you take the bull by the horns. You can focus on solving difficult personal problems. You accept the reality that distressing, unwanted experiences often are part of living a valued life. For example, an engaged person might seek out a friend who had said something hurtful and try to move through the problem, even though the conversation might be tense. Although there's no guarantee that addressing this conflict will restore the relationship, an engaged, approach-oriented person would do it anyway.

In contrast, when you're disengaged you tend to withdraw from situations that are emotionally upsetting and challenging. You might believe in letting the situation take care of itself, rather than messing with it and possibly making it worse. Alternatively, you might overfocus on getting out of the situation and take an impulsive or aggressive action that conveys a lack of attention to the needs of others. For example, you might decide not to talk with a friend who hurt your feelings, based on the belief that another bad interaction might end the friendship altogether, or you might decide to tell your friend off, thinking that that is what your friend deserves. In reality, your friend may not even be aware that you feel hurt.

Being disengaged can feed the cycle of depression because many challenging life situations will only get worse if you sit back and wait for them to get better on their own, or if you lash out and offend others. This style of withdrawal or impulse actions may also increase your sense of being out of control and trigger a variety of additional negative emotions, such as frustration, anger, rejection, or shame.

FIVE FACETS OF MINDFULNESS

Defining the core features of mindfulness has spurred a hot debate in psychology and in the religious community. The term "mindfulness" is actually somewhat of a misnomer, because most of the core skills involve learning how to get *out of* your mind, not get fully *into* your mind. But it would be a hard sell to call this "mindlessness training"!

Pioneering research by Ruth Baer and colleagues (Baer et al. 2006; Baer et al. 2008) was done to shed more light on the core features of mindfulness. If it is not a single trait ability, then what it is? Baer and her research group compiled all of the known existing self-report scales of mindfulness and then administered all of their items to several large samples of subjects, ranging from college students to people seeking psychotherapy for mental health issues. Her findings suggest that there are five distinct skills, or facets, of mindfulness. As the term "facet" suggests, each skill complements the other skills, much like each facet of a diamond contributes to the overall luster of the diamond. The more facets of mindfulness you learn to cultivate, the greater the level of your psychological flexibility will be across the board. We have organized section 2 of this book to help you understand, practice, and strengthen each facet so that your diamond shines bright.

Using Baer's five-facet approach, we define mindfulness as a set of unique mental skills that, taken together, help you get present and pay attention to your thoughts, emotions, sensations, and memories in a curious, receptive, nonjudgmental way (see also Kabat-Zinn 2005). Mindfulness involves cultivating a sense of being interconnected with all people and all things, and extending compassion toward the suffering of self and others. Most important to our way of thinking, mindfulness involves being aware and intentional in your daily actions. This allows you to experience life on purpose and to link your daily actions to the things that you value in life.

SELF-ASSESSMENT: FIVE-FACET MINDFULNESS INVENTORY

We want you to learn more about what each facet of mindfulness is and what it looks like in daily practice. To that end, we'd like you to complete a survey known as the Five-Facet Mindfulness Questionnaire—Short Form (Baer et al. 2008). In the sections that follow, we briefly describe each of the five facets and then provide a format for you to complete a short self-assessment of your skills in that area. While this may sound a bit technical, the results provide crucial information for you to use in transcending depression and creating a vital, purposeful life! In fact, we suggest that you periodically repeat this survey so you can see how your mindfulness skills are improving with the brain training practices we will introduce you to in section 2.

Facet 1: Observe

Observing skills consist of being able to "just notice" things that are happening both inside of you (physical sensations, thoughts, feelings, memories) and outside of you (sounds, sights, colors, smells, activities of others). In observing mode, you hold still mentally and focus attention in a singular way—as if you are using the zoom function of a camera lens.

The following items of the FFMQ represent the Observe facet. Using the 1–5 rating scale below, please indicate in the box to the right of each statement how frequently or infrequently you have had each experience in the last month. Please answer according to what really reflects your experience rather than what you think your experience should be. When done, add your answers to get your total Observe score.

Never or very rarely true	Not often true	Sometimes true, sometimes not true	Often true	Very often or always true
1	2	3	4	5

		Your Answer
1.	When I'm walking, I deliberately notice the sensation of my body moving.	
2.	When I take a shower or a bath, I stay alert to the sensations of water on my body.	
3.	I notice how foods and drinks affect my thoughts, bodily sensations, and emotions.	
4.	I pay attention to sensations, such as the wind in my hair or sun on my face.	
5.	I pay attention to sounds, such as clocks ticking, birds chirping, or cars passing.	

6. I notice the smells and aromas of things.	
7. I notice visual elements in art or nature, such as colors, shapes, textures, or patterns of light and shadow.	
8. I pay attention to how my emotions affect my thoughts and behaviors.	
Observe score	

Further Exploration. Take a moment to review your individual answers to these questions. Did your ratings tend to vary a bit? Most of us differ in our ability to observe different aspects of the internal or external world. For example, you may find it easy to tune in to bodily sensations but find it difficult to notice thoughts, feelings, or memories that are showing up. Your abilities may also change depending on the situation you are in (for example, while riding a bus to work versus lying in your bed at night). Some people may be able to pay attention to sounds and colors in their environment, while others can more easily attend to internal sensations like breathing. The good news is that you may be able to use your strengths in one area of observing to grow in your abilities in other areas.

Facet 2: Describe

Describing refers to your ability to use words to organize and convey what you are aware of either inside or outside of you at any moment in time. Some people use the phrase *being a witness*. The job of the witness is to just tell the truth, the whole truth, and nothing but the truth.

There are several core features of being a witness. First, witnessing needs to be anchored in the present moment, as it unfolds in front of you. For example, witnessing involves being able to label strong emotions at the moment you make contact with them, such as feeling both sad and ashamed after you get into a heated argument with your partner and say some mean things.

Second, descriptions of direct experience must be as objective as possible. This involves a focus on the immediate qualities present using *descriptive words*. For example, in describing sadness a witness might say, "My eyes are tired and want to close... My body feels heavy... I'm having the thought that I don't want to be in this relationship." The witness does not use the mind's interpretations or judgments of events—these would come out as *evaluative words* ("I shouldn't be feeling sad... I'm wrong to want to leave this relationship") The witness simply describes events to the fullest extent possible, without inserting judgments about them.

The following items of the FFMQ represent the Describe facet. Using the 1–5 rating scale, please indicate in the box to the right of each statement how frequently or infrequently you have had each experience in the last month. When done, add your answers to get your total Describe score.

Note that for questions 3, 4, and 5, you will need to subtract the number associated with your answer from 6 to obtain the adjusted score for the item. For example, if your answer to statement 3 is 4 (often true), you will subtract 4 from 6 to get an adjusted score of 2.

		Your Answer
1.	I'm good at finding words to describe my feelings.	
2.	I can easily put my beliefs, opinions, and expectations into words.	
3.	It's hard for me to find the words to describe what I'm thinking.	6-
4.	I have trouble thinking of the right words to express how I feel about things.	6-
5.	When I have a sensation in my body, it's hard for me to describe it because I can't find the right words.	6-
6.	Even when I'm feeling terribly upset, I can find a way to put it into words.	
7.	My natural tendency is to put my experiences into words.	
8.	I can usually describe how I feel at the moment in considerable detail.	
	Describe score	

Further Exploration. Take a few moments to look at your answers to the individual items. Did you notice differences in some of the ratings? For example, is it harder for you to describe what you are experiencing when you are upset but much easier for you when you are just feeling normal? Think about your ability to use descriptive words that are closely tied to the direct qualities of an experience, while avoiding evaluative words that give positive or negative meaning to an experience. Whereas we want you to *attach* to descriptive words and develop your vocabulary in that area, we want you to *detach* from labels that create a positive or negative evaluative tone. Try to look at the pattern of your responses and see if there is an area of describing skills that you would like to shore up with practice.

Facet 3: Detach

To detach means that you dispassionately allow any thoughts, feelings, memories, and sensations to simply be present without becoming absorbed in mental evaluations of them. Detachment is sometimes described as *letting go*. When you can detach from a thought, feeling, or sensation, you are able to notice that private experience without getting lost in trying to analyze it. In a sense, you are willing to just let experiences be there and let it play out in your awareness. This is difficult to do, particularly when the thoughts are compelling, the feelings are painful, and the memories create the impression that we are reliving the past. We want to avoid pain and suffering, and so we have our own unique escape strategies. Detachment skills help us develop the ability to notice the appearance of an escape move and stay present with whatever it is that we want to go away.

The following items of the FFMQ represent the Detach facet. Using the 1–5 rating scale, please indicate in the box to the right of each statement how frequently or infrequently you have had each experience in the last month. When done, add your answers to get your total Detach score.

	Your Answer
1. I perceive my feelings and emotions without having to react to them.	
2. I watch my feelings without getting lost in them.	
3. In difficult situations, I can pause without immediately reacting.	
4. Usually when I have distressing thoughts or images, I am able just to notice them without reacting.	
5. Usually when I have distressing thoughts or images, I feel calm soon after.	
6. Usually when I have distressing thoughts or images, I "sit back" and am aware of the thought or image without being taken over by it.	
7. Usually when I have distressing thoughts or images, I just notice them and let them go.	
Detach score*	

Further Exploration. Take a moment to think about your strengths in this area. Do you find it easier to detach in some contexts more so than in others? For example, is it easier to detach when a coworker makes a snide remark than it is when your spouse criticizes your appearance? Do you tend to overreact to and fuse with certain types of feelings but not others? Do you have some ideas about particular methods or strategies that you can use to activate your detachment skills? Sometimes saying something as simple as "Breathe in and let go" can serve as a reminder that it is time to step back and give yourself some inner breathing room.

Facet 4: Self-Compassion

The ability to practice acceptance and kindness to yourself is a powerful tool for creating a state of wise mind. This is sometimes referred to as practicing *self-compassion*. It is an important concept in Buddhist writings about human suffering and how to relieve it. The potential benefits of treating yourself with care and kindness are garnering more and more attention in the depression-treatment literature. People caught up in depression behaviors tend to overuse self-criticism and may, at some level, believe they are unlovable and unworthy. Practicing self-compassion involves adopting exactly the opposite stance—totally accepting yourself, flaws and all.

The following items of the FFMQ represent the Love Yourself facet. Using the 1–5 rating scale, please indicate in the box to the right of each statement how frequently or infrequently you have had each experience in the last month. When done, add your answers to get your total Self-Compassion score.

Note that you will subtract the number associated with your answer from 6 to obtain the adjusted score for all items. For example, if your answer to statement 1 is 2 (not often true), your adjusted score for item 1 will be 4.

		Your Answer
1.	I criticize myself for having irrational or inappropriate emotions.	6-
2.	I tell myself that I shouldn't be feeling the way I'm feeling.	6-
3.	I believe that some of my thoughts are abnormal or bad, and I shouldn't think that way.	6-
4.	I make judgments about whether my thoughts are good or bad.	6-
5.	I tell myself I shouldn't be thinking the way I'm thinking.	6-
6.	I think some of my emotions are bad or inappropriate, and I shouldn't feel them.	6-
7.	I disapprove of myself when I have irrational ideas.	6-
8.	Usually when I have distressing thoughts or images, I judge myself as good or bad, depending on what the thought or image is about.	6-
	Total Self-Compassion score	

Further Exploration. Take a few minutes to go back and review your answers to these questions. Completing this facet is usually an eye-opener for depressed people, because they tend to be their own worst critics. Did you notice that it is hard for you to accept difficult inner experiences without criticizing yourself? When you get lost in your reactive mind's judgments about how you are doing, it is very difficult to cut yourself some slack. Remember that self-compassion is unconditional; it is an attitude of deep respect that does not depend on your performance or accomplishments, and it does not rely on approval from others. People who cultivate self-compassion show concern for their well-being; can experience failures, setbacks, or disappointments without getting lost in self-criticism or self-rejection; and are willing to walk into their pain—and they do all of this with a sense of warmth and gentleness.

Facet 5: Act Mindfully

Acting mindfully means being aware of what you are doing as you are doing it. This is sometimes called *acting with intention*. Acting with intention means being squarely located in the present moment and behaving in a way that reflects your beliefs and principles. The experience of intentional action is qualitatively different than the automatic-living mode that is characteristic of depression. Rather than going through each day in a haze, acting mindfully brings you to your senses so that you can choose each activity based upon your values.

The following items of the FFMQ represent the Act Mindfully facet. Using the 1–5 rating scale, please indicate in the box to the right of each statement how frequently or infrequently you have had each experience in the last month. When done, add your answers to get your total Act Mindfully score.

Note that you will subtract the number associated with your answer from 6 to obtain the adjusted score for all items. For example, if your answer to statement 1 is 2 (not often true), your adjusted score for item 1 will be 4.

		Your Answer
1.	I find it difficult to stay focused on what's happening in the present.	6-
2.	It seems I am "running on automatic" without much awareness of what I'm doing.	6-
3.	I rush through activities without being really attentive to them.	6-
4.	I do jobs or tasks automatically, without being aware of what I'm doing.	6-
5.	I find myself doing things without paying attention.	6-
6.	When I do things, my mind wanders off and I'm easily distracted.	6-
7.	I don't pay attention to what I'm doing because I'm daydreaming, worrying, or otherwise distracted.	6-
8.	I am easily distracted.	6-
	Total Act Mindfully score	

Further Exploration. Take a few minutes to carefully review your answers to each item of this facet. Do you tend to go on autopilot for some activities but not others? Which activities are most likely to lull you into an automatic mode of living? Are there situations in which you are much more aware and intentional? Of all the facets of mindfulness, being intentional is where the rubber meets the road and, because of that, it is the most demanding of the five mindfulness skills. Think about ways that you could deliberately increase your daily level of intentional action.

Putting It All Together: How Mindful Are You?

Now it's time to summarize your assessment results to create a profile of your five-facet mindfulness skills. Record your scores for each facet in the table that follows. Notice that we include a column for your scores three months from now, because we would like you to complete this survey again to help gauge the impact of additional exercises we introduce later in this book.

Five-Facet Mindfulness Questionnaire Summary Sheet

Facet/Skill Area	My Scores Today	My Scores in 3 Months
1. Observe		
2. Describe		
3. Detach		
4. Self-Compassion		
5. Act Mindfully		

TARGETS FOR MINDFULNESS PRACTICE

Reflect on your scores for each of the five facets now and develop a mental image of what it would be like if your skills were even stronger than they are today. For example, you might have a decent score on the Observe facet; imagine what it would be like to have a superhigh score, meaning you were able to practice observing even in the highest depression-risk situations. What would life be like if you got really good at loving yourself and practicing self-compassion in a moment of suffering? What if you beefed up your detachment skills such that you could pull yourself out of a spiral of rumination and worry, even in a high-conflict situation? Would life be better if you could do even one of these things a little better? We think so!

A FORMULA FOR RADICAL CHANGE

The way to transcend depression is for you to be open, receptive, and curious about your inner landscape; to be more mindful and intentional in your daily living; and to focus positive energy on the things that matter to you in life. The mindfulness skills that promote psychological flexibility don't operate in a vacuum; instead, they tend to be interrelated and to support each other. For example, the more open you are to distressing, unwanted internal experiences, the easier it is for you to be present, and to be intentional in your actions. The more mindfully you approach your daily life, the more likely you are to treat yourself and others with compassion. The more you approach and try to solve problems in spite of being in emotional pain, the more you learn that being free from emotional pain is not necessary to feel alive and full of purpose.

This leads us to the three principles of living that will let you transcend depression and radically change your life:

1. **Spend as much time as you can each day trying to be present.** Practice waking up your senses so that you are exquisitely tuned in to what is going inside you and all around you. This is where the joy of living is!

2. **Be open, curious, and nonjudgmental about your inner experiences, even the hard ones.** They can't harm you unless you get into a struggle with them. You can learn from all of your inner experiences, not just the ones that you like.

3. **Set up your daily routines to reflect your values.** This will give you an active sense that you are living intentionally and behaving with purpose. Even tough life situations can produce growth in you when you respond according to what you believe in.

When you live out these principles on a daily basis, you will begin to notice that your life outlook has improved, that you have more positive emotional experiences, and that you have a distinct sense that it is just easier to be you. In part 2, we are going to teach you nine specific ways you can practice and apply mindfulness skills to create the type of life you have always dreamed of living. If you are intrigued with this prospect—and we would be surprised if you aren't—then read on!

IDEAS TO CULTIVATE

- The mind is a product of the operating system of language and thought. It is not a thing but rather a dynamic, unfolding process that you can observe without getting caught up in it (with training and practice).

- Reactive mind is a built-in rule follower. It can be helpful in some situations, but not in all. Developing a new relationship to your reactive mind is an important step in overcoming depression.

- Wise mind is the ultimate sanctuary from reactive mind. It is a source of peace, tranquility, and compassion for yourself and others.

- Psychological flexibility involves being open, receptive, and observant of distressing emotions (and the thoughts, memories, or sensations that trigger them); being present in the here and now; and engaging in intentional, valued action at the same time. Your goal is to develop greater psychological flexibility in painful moments rather than chase after the holy grail of "happiness."

- Five unique and interrelated skills contribute to mindfulness, at any given moment. You can strengthen all of these skills with practice.

9 Mindful Steps to Transcend Depression

The journey of a thousand miles begins with the first step.

—Chinese proverb

In this part of the book, we'll teach you nine powerful steps you can use right now to transcend your depression and claim the life you would like to live. If avoidance, fusion, and living on autopilot are the pathways into depression, the way out must be to get present and approach and solve emotionally challenging situations in a way that reflects your basic values. Mindfulness and all of its elegant functions will serve you well on the quest to transcend depression. We will teach you how to connect with your values and create an overarching sense of life vision and purpose, how to live in the present moment, how to remain detached in the presence of reactive mind's chatter and destructive self-stories, how to be self-compassionate, how to be intentional in daily life, and how to make and keep promises to live by your values. Once you learn to apply these powerful mindfulness strategies in daily life, your depression doesn't stand a chance!

Here's a worksheet to help you keep track of your sense of confidence in being able to use each of the nine powerful strategies outlined in this section of the book. After reading each chapter in part 2, come back and rate your grasp of the material presented in that chapter. As before, use a scale of 1 to 10, whereby 1 indicates that you need more help and 10 indicates that you've totally got it.

You may already have practical experience with some of the strategies we offer. If so, don't be shy about devoting a lot of energy to using those, especially at first. It's best to work your way through the chapters sequentially, as some of the later chapters build on concepts and exercises in earlier chapters. However, it's fine to focus on the strategies that feel most natural to you. Other strategies may seem new and unusual; they might even fly in the face of what you thought was true. If this happens, try to maintain an open mind. You're likely to have an aha moment later on as all of this starts to come together.

PART 2 CONFIDENCE WORKSHEET

Need More Help		Somewhat Confident		Confident		Got It!	
1	2	3	4	5	6	7	8	9	10

Chapter		Confidence Level
5	Step 1: Find Your True North	
6	Step 2: Use the Present Moment as Your Anchor	
7	Step 3: Practice Nonjudgmental Acceptance	
8	Step 4: Detach and Let Go	
9	Step 5: Don't Believe Your Reasons	
10	Step 6: Hold Your Stories Lightly	
11.	Step 7: The Leap: Practice Self-Compassion	
12	Step 8: Live with Vision and Intention	
13	Step 9: Make and Keep Promises to Yourself	

Further Exploration. If your confidence level is 5 or less after reading any chapter, this may be a signal that you would benefit from rereading those parts of the chapter that were confusing for you. If you still have a low confidence rating after doing a second reading, consider asking a friend or other companion to read it and discuss it with you. This type of interactive dialogue and support can help keep you motivated.

CHAPTER 5

Step 1: Find Your True North

If you don't figure out where you are going, you are bound to end up where you are headed.

—Chinese proverb

Living without a sense of life purpose or meaning is often the emotional calling card of depression. The antidote is to define your values for living and then take inventory of your current life direction to see if you are on track. While you might not always like the results of the inventory, connecting with your values stimulates positive emotion and strengthens approach motivation pathways in the brain. This will give you a powerful sense of life direction, even during difficult moments.

In part 1, we explained that mindfulness is the conduit to wise mind. In wise mind mode, you can be aware of the ongoing chatter of reactive mind without getting drawn into it. In this section, we take you through a nine-step program designed to strengthen all of the mindfulness muscles in your brain. As your mindfulness skills get stronger with practice, you can use them to listen—not to the misguided advice of your reactive mind but to the soft, reassuring, empowering intuitions and visions of wise mind. Anchoring yourself in wise mind mode will let you clearly determine what is working—and what isn't—in your life right now. You can then get on to the tasks of downsizing unworkable life strategies that fuel your depression and of adopting new strategies that will help you live a vital, purposeful life. Now it is time to get down to business and delve into each mindfulness skill in much more detail!

In this chapter, we'll introduce you to the first step in your campaign to transcend depression and reclaim your life: *getting in contact with your values*. Stephen Covey's (1989) first habit of highly effective people makes the point better than we can: *Begin with the end in mind*. If you could choose the life that you would like to live, what would that life be like? That life is what we are going to help you create, and we need to start by helping you identify what you are shooting for. When you plot a new course in life that's based on your values, you'll immediately notice that your sense of health and well-being improves. Your motivation grows and you gain confidence in your ability to address problems in a different, healthier way. Your values, like a compass, will point you toward rich, meaningful life experiences. In this chapter, we help you both investigate and clarify your values. Think of living a valued life as following *true north*, the compass heading that imbues you with a sense of vitality, meaning, and purpose.

WHAT ARE VALUES?

When we talk about values in this book, we are referring to your most deeply held principles of living. Your values are yours and yours alone. They are your personal beliefs about the way you want to live your life and what you want to stand for in your life. Here are some examples of values statements given to us by clients:

- I want to be well educated and pass on my knowledge to other people.

- I want to be a loving, kind, responsible parent for my children.

- I want to be a spiritual being, and I will honor all forms of spirituality in others.

- I want to be a loving, compassionate, and supportive life partner.

- I want to continually challenge and improve myself as a person.

- I want to promote a safe and healthy life for animals.

- I want to contribute to my community by performing acts of charity and volunteerism.

- I want to improve the lives of people who are economically challenged.

- I want to promote my physical and mental health over my life span.

- I want to protect the Earth and promote a clean, sustainable planet.

- I want to be there for anyone I care about in his or her time of need.

We emphasize values because living according to them will justify any pain or suffering you have on your journey through life. In the chapters that follow, we ask you to exchange *emotional avoidance* for *emotional acceptance* and *values-based living*. We ask you to enter into potentially painful life situations rather than avoid them. We encourage you to stand in the presence of emotional distress and act according to your values.

It would be unfair to ask this of you unless there is a higher calling involved. That calling is your desire and intention to live life according to your own principles, not according to the principles of fear and avoidance. When you get in touch with your values, they can provide motivation for action even in the midst of depression experiences. They are a mental fuel that can propel you on the path toward a life full of meaning. In almost any life situation, there is no position to take that is more empowering than standing for your values.

NeuroNote: Values Produce Intrinsically Positive Motivation

As you may recall, relational frame theory (RFT) is a field of scientific study that aids in identifying new strategies for helping human beings live more purposeful lives. In RFT, a value does two things: it creates the motivation needed to initiate action, and it organizes behavior in pursuit of a desired outcome. Connecting with a value may also trigger a positive emotion, and this, of course, boosts the likelihood that we will act in accordance with the value.

From a neuroscience perspective, there are three distinct neural pathways involved in our experience of values and our engagement in values-consistent actions. One pathway is responsible for creating the moral intuition that a value represents. This involves *forming the will*, or the desire, to behave in a particular way in certain life contexts. The development of will has been associated with increased activation within the default mode network (see chapter 1; Fox et al. 2005).

A second broadly distributed neural pathway creates an emotional response to an imagined action and related outcomes. There are at least six distinctive patterns of brain activation involved in emotional experience. One of those patterns is seen when memory and self-referential reasoning are involved in mental rehearsal of future action. This type of emotional experience is heavily supported by the insula and anterior cingulate nucleus, and by processing in the medial prefrontal cortex (Phan et al. 2002). These are the regions of the brain implicated in self-control, moral reasoning, and self-related processing.

The third neural network is responsible for producing different motivational states. It's composed of two neural systems—one located in the right hemisphere and one located in the left. *Approach motivation*, also known as *reward anticipating motivation*, is associated with greater activation in the left prefrontal cortex, particularly activity in the ventral, tegmental area (Fields et al. 2007). *Avoidance motivation*, also known as *punishment anticipating motivation*, is associated with greater activation in the right prefrontal cortex (Phan et al. 2002).

What does all this neuroscience have to do with how values relate to depression? Principally, it means that focusing on and engaging in valued actions activates regions of the brain that downregulate the depression pathways in your brain. When you are depressed, most of the ideas you have about the future are negative; this in turn causes a negative emotional tone, which activates the avoidance motivation system in your brain.

In contrast, values allow you to mentally rehearse a future in which you do something positive, something that is important to you. This creates a positive emotional tone in your brain, and, subsequently, the approach motivation system is activated. Over time, you will experience more and more positive emotion and an ever-growing motivation to approach situations in which you can enact your values. Downsizing depression means fueling a life worth living!

RUNNING ON EMPTY

If values are the fuel that will propel you into a vital life, living without them is akin to running on empty. Without them, you fall into patterns of daily living that don't reflect what matters to you, and you find yourself without energy and enthusiasm. For example, let's say that one of your dearest values is to be in a caring, cooperative, and mutually supportive relationship. If you go through a period in which your primary relationship devolves into a cold war, you'll probably begin to feel a reduced sense of vitality because you're in a situation where you aren't living your values. All kinds of negative factors can push you in this direction and keep you there: You may feel overwhelmed. You may be afraid of the consequences of expressing your needs or standing up for your values. Your reactive mind will pump you full of messages that encourage you to reduce the amount of conflict in your life.

As Amy's story demonstrates, when the avoidance rule kicks into high gear, it is extremely difficult to follow a valued course of action, or even to remember that you have a valued course of action.

AMY'S STORY

Amy, a forty-six-year-old divorced woman, lives with her cat, Emma. She struggled with depression during her twenty-one-year marriage to a charismatic man who had more than one affair. Amy had loved him, and the affairs hurt her deeply. More than once she had threatened to leave him, and his response had further destroyed her confidence. He'd say things like "Good riddance! You'll never find anyone desperate enough to want to be with you, and you'll end up alone. Go ahead if you think you're so hot—because you're not." Amy began to wonder if he might be right. For many years, she made deals with him that she would stay if he promised to be faithful. And she made a deal with herself that she would stay until their sons left home. The final straw came after the boys had left, when she caught him sleeping with one of her friends.

Now, four years after the divorce, Amy goes to work, tends to Emma, and sees her sons when they find time to visit. She continues to work as an office manager at the same company she's been with for eighteen years. Years ago, she loved her work. It was challenging, and she felt creative and valued. But over the years a series of management changes had put a real dent in her job satisfaction. Now, she works just to earn her paycheck and keep her health care and retirement benefits.

Amy doesn't have any close friends at work or in the community. Her husband remarried, and he and his new wife are involved with the group of friends that Amy had when she was married. She feels like her depression makes it hard for her to be social, and so she hasn't made any new friends. She works long hours and doesn't feel she has the energy to do anything else. She's heard that exercise is supposed to help with depression and has started walking programs several times, but she doesn't follow through on them. Even though she imagines meeting someone and forming a relationship, she recently told her mother that she didn't think she could go through that again.

From a valued-living perspective, Amy is running pretty close to empty in some areas. She does value being reliable and acting as a team player, and her work at her job is a tribute to these values. One of Amy's complaints about her life is that it is boring, that she doesn't have a passion for what she's doing. She values creativity and intimacy, but activities consistent with these values have been pushed aside during this rough patch in her life.

HOW VALUES GET LOST IN THE SHUFFLE OF LIVING

In fairness to Amy, it's hard to live a life that reflects all of your values on an ongoing basis. We're trained from birth to be responsive to the demands of our society—to work hard, to get good jobs, to stay faithful to our partners—even though the interests of society don't always coincide with those of the individual. The first step toward a more meaningful life is often that of identifying your values and connecting with them so that you can begin integrating them into your style of living. Amy's deeply held principals have always been there, but her actions have taken her farther and farther away from her values. To live a life full of meaning and purpose, her allegiance to being a "good mother" and a "hard worker" needs to be replaced with a determination to live by her true north instead.

While living by your true north doesn't guarantee happiness or pleasure on a day-in, day-out basis, we can guarantee you this: Breaking away from rules about how to live your life, and embracing your personal values, will provide you with the opportunity to experience greater well-being and satisfaction with your life. A life worth living can't be measured by the number of chances you *didn't* take, the distressing moments you avoided, or your allegiance to rules about feeling only positive feelings. It's measured by the vitality that comes from living in accordance with your values and being willing to face both pleasurable and distressing experiences directly in the service of those values.

Values and Depression

You might still be wondering, "What do values possibly have to do with depression? Isn't the point of psychological interventions to help people gain control of emotional problems so they can be happier?" This thinking is very common. In fact, we hear it all of the time in our practice. Most people believe that getting rid of depression means targeting the emotion itself—overwhelming sadness—and fixing it. Then, and only then, can we get on with the job of living a good life. But that's a big misconception. In fact, there is an important connection between how you *live* your life and how you *feel* about your life. When you feel as though your life isn't going very well, it's usually because your day-to-day life isn't giving you enough meaning. So the reality is that your day-to-day actions can produce very powerful positive, or negative, emotional results.

When you begin to examine your values and how they are (or aren't) embodied in your daily activities, you may feel uncomfortable. This is because you're beginning to take note of what matters to you. Noticing a difference between what you do and what matters to you should and will cause concern. For example, if you value being a good friend but notice that you're frequently turning down invitations to be with your friends, you might feel bad about not living up to your values. This is actually a useful type of discomfort, as it can motivate you to have more awareness and intention, and to make choices that are more true to your values.

Be patient, go slow, and let the discomfort be your reminder of what's important. Your values can be your guide. In the following set of exercises, we help you begin an ongoing process of revealing where true north lies in your life.

STRANDED

This exercise will help get you in the mood to do some serious work on clarifying your values. We recommend downloading the audio version of this exercise at http://www.newharbinger.com/38457; the guided audible component will make this exercise an enjoyable and powerful experience for you. Afterward you will jot down answers to some questions. Allow yourself about ten minutes of uninterrupted time to complete this exercise. Just relax, go along with the prompts, and be open to where it takes you. The more you put into it, the more you'll get out of it. Close your eyes to help you better imagine the scenario.

Imagine that you're on a trip to the South Pacific, and during a sightseeing trip in a small boat you rented, you experience engine trouble. As your boat starts to drift toward the breakers, you realize that you'll have to swim to a nearby island to avoid a catastrophe. You swim for your life, and you end up on the shore of a tiny, deserted island. You sleep in the sun, and when you are rested, you awaken and take stock of your surroundings. You look around and find some interesting things to eat and a protected place where you can rest. You realize that you have no way to communicate where you are, as everything was left in the rental boat. You hope that eventually you'll be found, but you don't know when that might happen.

Then your thoughts turn to your family and friends—the people back home. They will hear that you've disappeared without a trace and are presumed dead at sea. There will be tears. They will come together and speak of you and your life. They don't know that you're okay and that you'll be back with them soon. Eventually, they decide to remember you in a memorial service. They agree to write eulogies and come together to share them with each other to remember you. Eulogies usually speak to the more lasting qualities a person is remembered for and the impact they had on the lives of those they left behind.

Imagine now that you can be there unobserved, like an invisible bird flying above them, and you listen to these heartfelt speeches of acknowledgment. What does your life partner say about you as a person? How does your life partner describe you as a lover, a companion, and a playmate? If you have a child or children, what words do they use to describe your life and your advice about living life? How do they sum up your efforts to prepare them to go forward without you? What would your friends, your coworkers, and your neighbors say? What would people say about your spiritual life? What would you hear about your participation in the community in which you live? How do the mourners remember you in terms of your ability to have fun, relax, or engage in leisure activities? When you are ready, return to the book and complete the remainder of this exercise.

After you have completed this imagery exercise, take all the time you need to seriously consider and answer each question on the worksheet below.

STRANDED WORKSHEET

Based on how I'm living my life *right now*, what did I hear in the eulogy…

From my partner? _____

_____

From my children? _____

_____

From my closest friends? _____

_____

From my coworkers? _____

_____

From members of my community? _____

_____

From people in my spiritual community? _____

_____

If I could have lived my life any way I wanted to, what would I like to have heard…

From my partner? _____

_____

From my children? _____

_____

From my closest friends? _____

_____

From my coworkers? _____

_____

From members of my community? _____

_____

From people in my spiritual community? _____

_____

Further Exploration. Is there a difference between what you think you'd hear if the memorial service were held today and what you'd ideally like to hear? Any differences give you important information. First, look at what you wrote down for what you would most likely hear based on how you're living *right now*. You probably listed some things that warmed your heart, since you certainly do things that reflect your values that are noticed by loved ones. At the same time, you may have written down things you're not very proud of. This is something to pay attention to, because it might be an invitation for you to do some corrective work in that area. By the way, we *all* have those areas, so don't get down on yourself about it!

Second, comparing what you would currently hear with what you'd ideally like to hear at your memorial service highlights values that you may have placed on the back burner. These may be important values that are being undermined by your avoidance of emotionally charged life problems or that just have not been prioritized recently.

BULL'S-EYE

You're probably familiar with a bull's-eye target, whereby the goal is to hit the bull's-eye in the center. The closer you are to the bull's-eye, the more points you get; sometimes you might miss the target altogether, in which case you don't get any points. Keep the bull's-eye notion in mind as you read through the rest of this chapter, because you'll be using it to complete the following set of exercises, based on the work of psychologist Tobias Lundgren (Lundgren et al. 2012). This exercise will help you better clarify and target (pun intended) your values, building on the work you did in the Stranded exercise.

Do you recall the four major life domains discussed in chapter 3? They are relationships, work/study, leisure/play, and health. You'll now work on identifying your core values in these areas, and then you'll assess the extent to which your daily activities have been consistent with your values. Let's start with a brief overview of each life area.

Relationship Values

In regard to values about relationships, most people are much more alike than different. Most of us value honesty, trust, dependability, the ability to laugh and to forgive, the pursuit of win-win solutions, sensitivity, strength, and so on. Relationships are played out in many areas of life. For many people, the most important relationship is with a spouse or life partner. Other important relationships are with friends and family members, including family of origin, extended family, and children. Some values, like being compassionate or respectful of others, are usually relevant to all relationships, whereas other values, such as being a role model, may be more pertinent to a particular kind of relationship, such as being a parent versus being a friend.

As you consider different kinds of relationships you have or wish to cultivate in your life, think about how you want to apply your values in each situation. In the worksheet below, describe where you'd like to be headed in your relationships. Describe the qualities that are most important to you in each type of relationship.

Relationship Values

Spouse or life partner: _____

_____

Family: _____

_____

Parenting: _____

_____

Friendships: _____

_____

Other: _____

_____

Further Exploration. After writing down your values about relationships, reflect on how you acted in relationships during the last couple of weeks. To what extent were your day-to-day choices consistent with your values about relationships? To what extent did your actions support the quality of relating that expresses your values? Did your interpersonal behaviors reflect a commitment to preserving and furthering relationships with those you love as well as those you're less close to? Consider these and other behaviors, and then decide how consistent your choices were with your values about relationships.

Don't worry if you find that some of your choices haven't been consistent with your values. When you're depressed, it's hard to stay in touch with values because the effort required to make it through each day is so great. It's as if you're in a fog. Making an effort to name your values will help clear this fog so that you have a better day-to-day focus and more opportunities to lessen the gap between what you care about and what you do.

On the target below, make an X to indicate how close or off the mark your activities were in relation to your bull's-eye values about relationships.

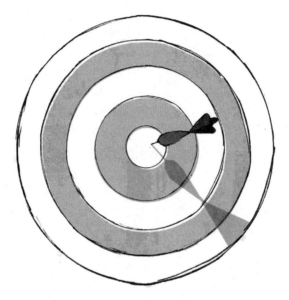

To help you focus on opportunities for positive change in the area of relationships, write down a few examples of behavioral choices that show consistency with your values and a few that show inconsistency with your values.

Examples of actions that were more consistent with my values: _____

_____

_____

_____

_____

Examples of actions that were less consistent with my values: _____

_____

_____

_____

_____

Work/Study Values

Now it's time to describe your values about work or educational pursuits. By work, we mean any regular activity that makes you feel of use on a regular basis, whether it's a meaningful job, going to school, being a homemaker or caregiver, or donating your time to community or other volunteer activities. Many types of work don't involve getting paid; the activity is done because of other values you might have. And just because you get paid to do a job doesn't mean that you are living according to your values while you work. For example, after doing this exercise you might discover that you are acting much more according to your values when you volunteer at a food bank than when you work for pay as a server at a restaurant.

Examples of important work values might include being reliable, maintaining focus, being persistent, cooperating with others, taking a team approach, being creative, helping others, always doing your best, being on time, and promoting more lightheartedness. In the worksheet below, describe where you'd like to be headed in terms of work.

Work/Study Values

Work (includes homemaking, caregiving, volunteerism, and attending a trade school or college):

_____

_____

_____

Further Exploration. After writing down your values in regard to work, reflect on your actions during the past couple of weeks. To what extent were your day-to-day choices consistent with your values about work? If you value being cooperative or creative, to what extent did your daily activities reflect this desire?

On the target below, make an X to indicate how close or off the mark your activities were in relation to your bull's-eye values about work.

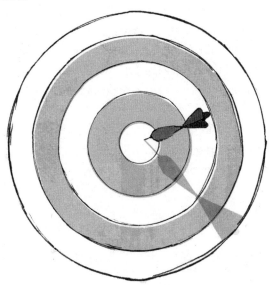

To help you focus on opportunities for positive change in the area of work, write down a few examples of behavioral choices that show consistency with your values and a few that show inconsistency with your values.

Examples of actions that were more consistent with my values about work or school: _____

_____

_____

_____

_____

Examples of actions that were less consistent with my values about work or school: _____

_____

_____

_____

_____

Leisure/Play Values

Now we want you to describe your values about play activities—any recreational or leisure pursuits that you enjoy and that allow you to relax and smell the roses in life, so to speak. The ability to "recharge your batteries" through play is essential in today's stressed-out world. As we noted, when you engage in pleasurable activities, you strengthen the reward and approach motivation circuitry in your brain. We know the task of being playful might be a struggle for you—a depressed mood doesn't leave a lot of emotional space to engage in fun, spontaneous, or relaxing hobbies or activities. That is why you're reading this book! But bear with us; exploring and strengthening your values related to play activities almost always pay dividends.

If you can't think of anything enjoyable that you have done recently, think back to a time when you were less depressed. What did you do for fun then? It's likely that the values you had then are still with you and are still as meaningful. Alternatively, imagine what your values would be if you were happy in your life and didn't have your current life challenges.

For this exercise, it might be helpful to picture yourself in the activity (imagine what you would be doing, and where, what you'd see and hear, and so on). In the worksheet that follows, describe where you'd like to be headed in terms of play, and make note of any relevant imagery as well.

Leisure/Play Values

Having fun: _____

_____

_____

Relaxing: _____

_____

_____

Recreational pursuits: _____

_____

_____

Creative activities: _____

_____

_____

Further Exploration. After writing out your values in regard to play, reflect on your actions during the past couple of weeks. To what extent are your day-to-day choices consistent with your values about play? If you did engage in playful activities, to what extent were your values about play demonstrated during those activities? Did you discover that you had lots of activities in one area (relaxing) but few or none in another area (creative activities)?

On the target below, make an X to indicate how close or off the mark your activities were in relation to your values about play.

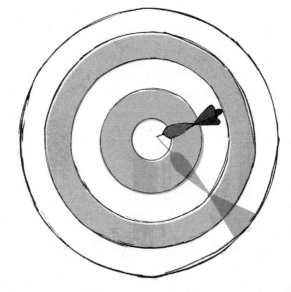

To help you focus on opportunities for positive change in the area of play, write down a few examples of behavioral choices that show consistency with your values and a few that show inconsistency with your values.

Examples of actions that were more consistent with my values about play: _____

_____

_____

_____

_____

Examples of actions that were less consistent with my values about play: _____

_____

_____

_____

_____

Health Values

Only by protecting your physical, emotional, and social health can you be in a position to perform valued actions in the realms of family, work, play, and community. Conversely, even if you have a physical impairment like chronic pain or a chronic condition like diabetes, this doesn't mean you're unhealthy. In fact, you can amplify your mental and social health while coping skillfully with a chronic disease—and greater participation in valued activities in life is critical to this outcome. Here is just a sampling of values that can contribute to success in this life area: balance, calmness, kindness, courage, harmony, fitness, faith, self-reliance, cleanliness, and compassion.

Promoting health also means you have the self-care skills to address life stresses in a way that preserves your ability to move forward in a positive direction. Core self-care skills involve engaging in healthy behaviors in terms of diet, exercise, sleep habits, spiritual practice, self-growth, and hobbies. Avoiding or minimizing negative lifestyle habits (such as using tobacco or street drugs, or overreliance on caffeine and/or alcohol) is also health protective. In the worksheet opposite, describe where you'd like to be headed in terms of promoting your health.

Health Values

Diet: _____

_____

_____

Exercise: _____

_____

_____

Sleep habits: _____

_____

_____

Lifestyle habits (including ways to reduce stress): _____

_____

_____

Spirituality practices (including prayer, affiliating with a spiritual community, yoga, meditation, etc.): _____

_____

_____

Further Exploration. After writing out your health-related values, reflect on your actions during the past couple of weeks. To what extent were your day-to-day choices consistent with your values about health? Did your eating behaviors reflect a commitment to preserving and furthering your health? To what extent did you purposefully engage in exercise and relaxation activities? How much and how well did you sleep? Did you use tobacco, alcohol, or drugs this week? If so, is this consistent with your values about promoting your health? Consider these and other behaviors, and then decide how consistent your choices were with your values about health.

On the target below, make an X to indicate how close or off the mark your activities were in relation to your values about health.

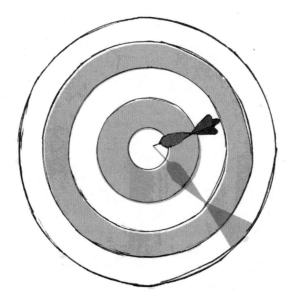

To help you focus on opportunities for positive change in the area of personal health, write down a few examples of choices that show consistency with your values and a few that show inconsistency with your values.

Examples of actions that were more consistent with my values: _____

_____

_____

_____

_____

Examples of actions that were less consistent with my values: _____

_____

_____

_____

_____

Further Exploration. In each of these life areas—health, relationships, work/study, and leisure/play—maybe you're mostly on target, maybe you're not. Whatever the results, view this exercise as an opportunity to clarify what your values are and where you're at in terms of pursuing them, at this point in time. Most of us don't hit the bull's-eye on a frequent basis, but being clear on a value provides you with a focus. With a focus and with practice in choosing activities strategically, your aim will improve!

AMY'S RESULTS

Amy was shaken when she completed the values exercises in this chapter. She placed her X in the outer ring of the health target; her biggest problems were a poor diet and a sedentary lifestyle. Seeing this helped her realize that she didn't feel physically or emotionally healthy much of the time. Amy's mark at the greatest distance from her bull's eye was in the area of relationships. Her value was to have an intimate relationship based on trust, intimacy, and equality. Yet, she wasn't dating and, recently, had turned down an invitation from a man to have coffee together. In regard to work, Amy wrote that her greatest work value was to be involved in a career that would use her natural strengths as a leader and to do her job with reliability and good team spirit; she placed her X in the middle range and noted that she wanted to find ways to exercise more creativity at work. In regard to play, Amy placed her X in an outer ring of the target. She played with her cat every day, but she had no regular way to be playful with people and no creative hobbies. She had enjoyed crochet and had lots of yarn stored away, but her needles remained idle.

Amy's Journey Toward a Vital Life

Looking carefully at her values gave Amy some ideas. She began to put them into action. First, Amy decided to enroll in night school so she could get an advanced degree in human resources. When word got out to her supervisor that she was going to night school, he called her into his office and asked what she was working toward. She told him that she was studying human resources because she would eventually like more innovation opportunities in her work. Much to Amy's amazement, her supervisor offered to provide some financial support for her course of study and said he would look for a way to move her to the HR department as soon as she was ready. Amy also developed a plan for eating better, which included bringing her lunch to work. And to further promote her health she started walking with a coworker at lunchtime. Amy made a call to a friend to see if a community crochet group focused on making baby blankets for the neonatal unit at the local hospital was still meeting. She'd read about this in a newsletter months ago and thought it would be a good way to spend time regularly with others.

And Amy finally consented to have coffee with a male friend. She was petrified because she believed that the only way she could deal with her fear of rejection was to stay away from any situation that might open the door to romantic feelings. Nevertheless, she made the choice to go into the situation with an open mind—*and* to allow her fear to come along. The man became a close friend over time, and there was never romance involved. This challenged Amy's fear that men were overly interested in sex and didn't value friendship. She realized that she could make herself available should the right man come along, and that she could just roll with her fears and anxieties. By living according to her values rather than her fears, she could begin to inject more meaning into her life and transcend her depression in the process. Amy was beginning a more mindful pursuit of a chosen life!

BRAIN TRAINING TO POINT YOU TOWARD TRUE NORTH

Like all of the mindfulness skills we introduce you to, the more you practice living according to your values on a daily basis, the more you will stimulate and strengthen the positive emotion and approach motivation pathways in your brain. It will help you get your feet on the ground and meet each day with a greater focus and sense of purpose. The following brain training exercises are relatively brief and can easily be practiced at home on a daily basis.

A DAILY PROMISE

Before jumping out of bed in the morning, reflect on the value statements you came up with in the Bull's-Eye exercise and pick one value as your focus for the day. Think for a few moments about how you might embody this value in your behavior today. It doesn't have to be a heroic act; it can be a small one. Then, make this promise out loud: "Today, I promise to myself that I will act upon my value of _____ in a conscious, purposeful way." If you find it hard to keep your promise, don't give up. Simply try again the next morning.

VALUE THERMOMETER

Measuring your day in terms of how consistent your actions were with your values is a great way to keep your eyes on the prize. The value thermometer works like this: Each day, choose one of the four core life domains of the Bull's-Eye exercise to focus on: relationships, work/study, leisure/play, or health. Circle the domain you will focus on at the top of the column. At the end of the day, rate how consistent your behavior was with your values in that area on a scale of 1 to 10, with 1 meaning you didn't do anything that was consistent with your values and a 10 meaning you were totally consistent all day long. The goal is to chart this every day, so print extra copies from http://www.newharbinger.com/38457.

Temperature	Relationships	Work	Play	Health
10				
9				
8				
7				
6				
5				
4				
3				
2				
1				

Further Exploration. As you do this over days, weeks, and months, look for day-to-day differences in your value thermometer ratings. Note circumstances that seem to support more values-consistent actions. Is there a person who seems to bring out the best in you? Are you more consistent in some areas (like work) than others (like home)?

THE FLIP SIDE OF PAIN

Are there situations in your current life that challenge your sense of personal integrity? It might be an unresolved issue that both you and your intimate partner avoid discussing, even though it is hurting your relationship. It might be not getting a job promotion that you thought you deserved, but you've never discussed being passed over with your supervisor. It might be a friend who has been gossiping about you behind your back.

Often, when we first come into contact with emotional pain produced when a value is violated or neglected, we fixate on the pain, not realizing that the flip side of this coin is the value we hold close. Thus, emotional pain may be a reflection of what matters to you. You can take any emotionally painful life situation and work backward from it to discover your values. If it didn't matter to you, you wouldn't have any feelings at all about it. Right? In this exercise, we want you to think about a hurtful life situation. In the space provided below, describe the situation, how it makes you feel, and then work backward to identify the value that seeks your attention. You can do this *any* time you run into emotional pain in daily living.

Describe the hurtful situation. _____

_____

Describe what emotions are present. _____

_____

What value(s) are at stake? _____

_____

Further Exploration. What did you discover about the connection between your painful inner experiences and your values? For most people, seeing the link provides a bit of emotional relief with the knowledge that they are not suffering senselessly—and that their pain in fact honors their values. What values were present for you in this situation? Could you backtrack and see how coming up short in terms of what matters to you directly produces the painful inner experiences you recorded? Any time you run into a painful or challenging life moment, you can use this simple exercise to remind yourself that your pain is legitimate, not a sign of weakness or being abnormal.

REMINDER: BE GENTLE WITH YOURSELF

In ACT, we like to say that you "vote with your feet in life." This means you walk the walk every day and in every way. All of the exercises in this chapter are meant to be a start toward this, toward a valued way of living. And if you did well with your values today, you still have to get up tomorrow and do it again. This exemplifies another of our favorite sayings: *Practice doesn't make perfect; practice makes permanent.* No one lives life in a perfectly consistent way, and you won't either. What you are consciously striving for is to put your values into play as much as you can in your daily life. And if you stick with it, you will get better and better at doing it. If you've been struggling with depression, you may be tempted to beat yourself up because you aren't living out your values as perfectly as your reactive mind thinks you should. If this thought shows up, just thank your reactive mind (remember your silly name for it) for giving it to you and move on!

IDEAS TO CULTIVATE

- Your values can get lost in the fog of depression. An important step forward in your quest to transcend depression is to reconnect with them and act in ways that move your life in that direction.

- Your actions in life are what you'll be remembered for, not what is going on between your ears.

- While you may not always be consistent with your values, describing them, thinking about them, and talking about them will strengthen your connection to them.

- A better connection to your values means greater harmony in core life domains: relationships, work, play, and health.

- Finding new ways to practice living according to your values will both stimulate and strengthen the reward and motivation centers in your brain.

- It takes courage to go out and do something new. Be willing to experiment, look at the results, and use what works. Let your feeling of vitality, purpose, and meaning be your measure of success!

CHAPTER 6

Step 2: Use the Present Moment as Your Anchor

The present moment is filled with joy and happiness. If you are attentive, you will see it.

—Thich Nhat Hahn

When you practice being in the present moment, you strengthen neural pathways responsible for mental efficiency, self-awareness, empathy, compassion, and creative problem solving. The ability to focus your attention solely on the here and now allows you to take a stance of just noticing, rather than getting hooked by, painful emotions, negative thoughts, or distressing memories. Practicing being here—right now—activates your parasympathetic nervous system, puts you into wise mind mode, and allows you to experience a sense of well-being as you act in the service of your values.

In chapter 4, we described one facet of mindfulness as the ability to get into the present moment and simply observe, or be aware of, what is going on inside and outside your skin. We have already explained how mind wandering, rumination, worry, and similar lapses of attention are linked to depression. Our clinical experience has shown us that when depressed clients learn to stay present and control their attention in the moment, they are better able to process their distressing emotions and to solve the real-life problems that are producing them. If you think of depression as the result of unresolved personal pain combined with the avoidance of life situations that trigger pain, you can see why learning to get present, and stay there, is powerful medicine.

In this chapter, we will teach you to use the present moment as an anchor in the service of acting according to your values in each domain of your life, and creating a more meaning-filled life overall. The ability to focus and maintain attention is a fundamental skill in behavior change because being in the present moment allows you to make values-based choices about your behavior. It is also the place where you can connect powerfully to your values and use them to propel you to behave in new ways.

THE IMPORTANCE OF PAYING ATTENTION

The ability to focus and sustain your attention on what you want to pay attention to (not what your reactive mind is telling you to pay attention to) allows you to access the space of wise mind. In that space, you are less influenced by the chatter of reactive mind, better able to gain perspective on your life situation, and better prepared to create action based on your values rather than your fears. To punctuate the importance of being here, *now*, consider the following words of wisdom from Agnes Baker Pilgrim, chair of the International Council of Thirteen Indigenous Grandmothers and spiritual elder of the Confederate Tribe of Siletz:

Yesterday is history,

Tomorrow is a mystery,

Today is our gift, and we better use it wisely. (Schaefer 2006, 16)

Take a minute to think about your personal experiences with just being in the present moment, an increasingly rare event in this day and age of fast-paced, autopilot living. You may have had brief present-moment experiences that occurred spontaneously, perhaps in a particular setting. Maybe you had an awareness of the present moment while in a garden or forest, or sitting on a bench at the park. Perhaps you experienced the present moment while studying the actions or speech of a child or grandchild while in a state of genuine love and acceptance. Children tend to spend more time in the present, and we can pick up on this. When we do, we may feel a sense of peace and well-being, and a freedom from the need to act. Maybe you have practiced meditation or prayer and had the experience of suddenly being free of something that troubled you, such as a negative evaluation of an event, situation, or interaction. Think back on such moments and remember the qualities of the experience. These may have included simply noticing your surroundings or how your five senses—touch, sight, taste, hearing, and smell—were engaged. Or, as you were playing with a child, you suddenly realized you are completely engaged in the act. Or maybe you've had feelings of expanded awareness, almost as if you were tuned in to a cosmic radio channel, as you felt a profound sense of clarity and well-being. Either way, the exercises in this chapter are designed to help you become more aware of the present moment more often. You'll soon discover that the more space you give to intentional mindfulness, the less room there is for your depression.

NEURONOTES: THE CONTINUUM OF ATTENTION

Neuroscientists regard the act of paying attention as one of the most broadly distributed, complex functions of the brain. At every level of our evolved brain there are neural pathways to help us pay attention. Further, all levels of the brain interact when we pay attention, ranging from the primitive midbrain all the way up to the highly evolved neocortex.

There are two key principles to remember when thinking about attention. First, it exists on a continuum from simple to more complex forms and functions. Simple forms of attention evolved to support survival and procreation. Complex forms of attention are closely tied to higher-order symbolic abilities such as self-awareness, perspective taking, and social judgment. Second, you must realize that attention is a finite brain resource. We don't have an endless supply of it and, under certain conditions, the ability to pay attention can be depleted very rapidly.

Depression tends to be associated with a very narrowly focused, basic form of awareness called *bottom-up attention*. Bottom-up attention originates in the primitive structures of the limbic system. It evolved to help us scan for immediate threats to our survival. In bottom-up mode you tend to focus attention on negative information and either ignore or disregard positive information. This is the type of attention that you might have to deal with when you are depressed—unless you consciously shift out of it. This is why people with symptoms of depression complain about being indecisive and less able to mentally process complex information. In essence, the problem is one of using a narrow, or lower-order, form of attention to perform tasks that require a higher form of attention. This mismatch contributes to the likelihood of making errors of judgment or reacting impulsively in stressful situations.

The good news is that there is another type of attention that allows you to remain flexible and effective, even if symptoms of depression are present. This mode is called *top-down attention*, and it originates in the higher-order brain structures of the insula and regions of the dorsolateral prefrontal cortex. Top-down attention is much more flexible and dynamic in nature. It is sometimes referred to as the *executive control system* of the brain. Executive control is a process of deciding how much attention resources will be allocated to any particular task, thus helping you balance any competing demands for your attention. This allows you to quickly shift your attention inward or outward, depending upon what is needed in the moment. Your senses become more acute, so you might be aware of sounds or sights that you hadn't noticed before. If you shift attention inward, you can observe how your body is responding to what is in the moment (for example, heart rate, respiration rate, muscle tension). Paying attention to these internal cues is thought to be a crucial step in the process of regulating negative emotions. You first have to be aware of how you are feeling before you can do something about how you are feeling.

The other benefit of top-down awareness is that it helps decrease activity in the default mode network by activating the task positive network, which activates the reward-anticipating motivational system. This means you will likely approach problematic life situations using values as your fuel, rather than avoiding them using fear as your fuel. Activating your top-down attention system has the effect of bringing you out of the fog of default mode network dominance and back into contact with values-based actions. Importantly, mindfulness practice has been associated with increased activation of the neural circuitry responsible for producing top-down attention.

THE THREE PERSPECTIVES OF EXPERIENCE

As human beings, we are capable of adopting three different perspectives on our experience: *participant*, *participant-observer*, and *observer*. We spend almost all of our awake time shifting between these three modes. No single mode is arbitrarily better than the other; however, some perspectives work better than others in different contexts. To help you get a better feel for how different these perspectives are, let's apply them to the experience of taking a roller-coaster ride at an amusement park. What is the rider's experience?

The first perspective we can take is that of a *participant*. In this mode of observing, you climb into the front car of the roller coaster and take the ride with the sole intent of thrill seeking. You directly experience the thrills and terror of the ride; you are really not interested in anyone else who is riding the coaster with you; it is all about your immediate experience. The more you "get into" the ride in this mode of being, the better! In some life contexts, being a simple participant in your experience is highly desirable, for example, when playing with a child or engaging in sexual relations with a partner.

A second way to experience a roller coaster is in the role of *participant-observer*. In this approach, you once again hop on the roller coaster, but this time you are both riding the coaster and paying attention to the reactions of your fellow riders. Your attention is divided between the thrills of being on the coaster and at the same time noticing all of the different verbal and nonverbal reactions of your fellow riders. What you see your fellow riders doing might even influence your reactions, for example, throwing your arms in the air and screaming as you plunge downward. Again, this form of experiencing is highly useful, for example, in groups where the effort is to cocreate and build on the responses of others in an effort to come up with the best option for the entire group.

The third way to experience a roller coaster is in the role of *observer*. As an observer, you don't actually ride the roller coaster but position yourself so that you can see all aspects of the roller coaster in a larger context (the platform and rails, the operator and ticket taker, the number of people in the cars, the sounds of the riders). As an observer, you want to see the whole picture without being drawn into any particular part of it. This perspective allows you to see where the riders have come from and where they are going, and to perhaps assess their emotion level by the volume of their collective voice. The observer perspective is useful when adopting a broader point of view is needed, such as when you get into an argument with a friend or partner. Adopting an observer perspective will let you notice your emotional responses while not reacting to them or being controlled by them. This nonreactive point of view might make it easier for you to better understand the perspective of your friend or partner.

As you can see, all three types of experiencing play an important role in helping you live a meaningful life. In depression, there is a bias toward adopting a participant perspective. On a roller coaster, that translates into getting lost in the thrills of the ride; with depression, it means getting you absorbed in rumination, worry, or self-criticism. The task is to learn which perspective is going to work the best for you on a situation-by-situation basis, and then learn how to shift flexibly among them.

Be an Observer

Now that we've discussed the three perspectives you have access to, and you've learned the importance of paying attention, which perspective do you think is the focus of this chapter? You are right if you guessed being an observer. The observer perspective is a key component to being mindful and in the present moment. Now let's discuss how to become a better observer.

There are three fundamental skills an observer must learn:

- **Centering:** the act of letting go of whatever is demanding your attention and marshaling all of your attention on the present moment. Centering can involve an act as simple as slowing your breath, connecting with the sensation of your feet on the ground, and softening the focus of your eyes in an effort to shift your perspective so that it is larger and more spacious. The more often we practice centering, the more it tends to happen without much effort. Centering acts as an anchor to the present moment.

- **Focusing:** a skill that kicks in after centering has happened. It involves selecting one thing as the focus of your attention. That thing can be an internal sensation, such as the temperature of the air as it enters and exits your nose, or it can be an external object, such as the flicker of a candle. When your attention wanders (and it will), you bring it back to the chosen focus. Focused attention is sharp and concentrated, and it allows you to zero in on the most important parts of your experience. For example, if you are feeling sad about something and are starting to experience an urge to distract yourself from sadness, you can focus your attention on where you feel sadness in your body. Maybe there is a sensation of a lump in your throat, as if you are about to cry. Focusing in, while remaining in the observer role, allows you to more fully contact and understand what is going on inside.

- **Flexibility:** the ability to shift your attention from one aspect of your immediate experience to another without losing control of your attention or falling out of the observer role. It is like you are bird-watching, using a pair of binoculars to look at a number of different, rare birds. First, you look at one bird, and, without dropping the binoculars, you shift your view so that you see a second bird you are interested in; then you might shift to the first bird again. All the while you are in observer mode. The binoculars have never come away from your eyes.

Going back to the example of being an observer of your sadness, being flexible with your attention might include first noticing the lump in your throat and the urge to cry. Then you might become aware of a memory of another time like this in your life when you felt the same way. Then you might notice a picture on your desk that seems to have triggered sadness, followed by noticing the warmth of a tear running down your check. All the while, your attention to sadness is *mostly* centered and focused.

The reality for most people is that lapses of attention are common, because we don't typically practice attention-strengthening skills. So an equally important observer skill is to learn to notice when you are no longer paying attention. You might have been sucked into a participant perspective without knowing it, and the type of attention required to be a participant is typically more bottom up than top down in quality. When you notice that this shift has occurred, you can consciously and gently reengage your top-down attention pathways to allow you to once again center, focus, and flexibly shift attention.

As an observer, you can center, focus, and shift your attention around or choose to stop paying attention at all. Just for fun, try it. Find something in your immediate environment that interests you, and keep your attention focused on it. Notice what happens. Do you have the urge to look at something else? Does your reactive mind distract you into thinking about something else? If you notice this shift of attention happening, can you redirect your attention back to what you were first looking at? This is a very simple attention strengthening exercise you can practice anytime—at work, school, or home.

TIMELINE

To help you learn how to get into the present moment and stay there as much as possible, let's do an exercise to find out what time zone—past, present, or future—you are inhabiting at the moment. Think of time as a continuum ranging from your most remote memories of early childhood to future projections that go all the way to the moment of your death—and possibly beyond. There is nothing good or bad about where your mind goes, so try not to think in those terms. The goal is simply to get to know your reactive mind and better understand its preferences.

Timeline				
Distant Past	Recent Past	Present Moment	Near Future	Distant Future

In the time continuum graphic, the present moment is the middle of the line. Go ahead and place your index finger there, and then read on or listen to the guided audio instructions.

The first step of this exercise is to close your eyes, take some deep cleansing breaths, and put the cares and concerns of the day to one side, as best you can. Just try to clear your mind so that you can stay in the present moment for a few minutes. If you notice your mind wandering, simply notice that it is wandering and begin to move you finger. Slide it to the left if your mind is drifting into the past. For a distant childhood memory, your finger would go all the way to the left. More recent memories would bring you finger closer to the present-moment notch on the timeline. If your mind heads way into the future—say imagining your life at a very old age—your finger would go all the way to the right; a more immediate thought of the future, like what present to buy for a friend's birthday next month, would move your finger toward just right of the center of the timeline.

Just let your mind drift in whatever direction it wants to drift, without forcing it to change course. See if you can just notice where your mind is on the timeline at any moment in time. If you suddenly realize you got pulled out of this exercise, just recall the time orientation of the last thought or memory you had. Gently put your attention back onto just noticing where your mind is traveling when you give it free reign. When you are ready to come back to your normal waking state, take some time to complete the written timeline that goes along with this experience.

How often did you find yourself in the present moment (for example, noticing the sensation of your finger on the paper, or your breathing)?

_____

Where on the timeline did your mind tend to take you when you left the present moment?

_____

Did particular thoughts, feelings, memories, or sensations lure you out of the present moment more than once or on an ongoing basis? If so, describe them:

_____

_____

_____

_____

_____

Further Exploration. Did you find it hard to stay in the present moment during this exercise? For most people, this 2- or 3-minute exercise seems like ten! In modern society, we hardly ever take the time to just sit and explore the present moment. Did you have the experience of suddenly realizing you weren't in the present moment at all, almost like you woke up and found yourself somewhere else? We all do. The process of fusing with our thoughts, emotions, and memories happens automatically and often. This is why practice and intention are fundamental to shifting attention back to the present moment.

Remember what we know about the reactive mind? It isn't designed to be in the here and now. Its job is to look backward, try to make sense of what has occurred, and then look forward and make predictions. It likes to evaluate, analyze, and solve problems. In moment-to-moment terms, you will notice that your reactive mind darts back and forth along the time continuum. Some minds like to hang out in the future, and the most common symptom of that future orientation is problems with worrying. Other minds like to hang out in the past, and the result is falling into a pattern of rumination. Some minds are really hyperactive and like to move back and forth between the past and the future. The result is a double whammy of both rumination and worry, a common feature of depression.

Most people find it very difficult to stay present because there's really not much for their reactive mind to do there. As you learn more and more about how to use the present moment as your anchor, you can change where your mind tends to hang out on the timeline of your life. This is when mindfulness practices that allow you to access wise mind come in. Over time, you can learn to access your wise mind when there's no problem to solve and you simply want to be. So what do we mean by just being?

SIMPLE AWARENESS

Almost every meditative and mystical religious tradition uses some type of mindfulness practice to create a "doorway" to more expansive forms of conscious awareness. The main mechanism here is the ability to pay attention, on purpose, and to avoid becoming entangled in the ongoing chatter of reactive mind. As the Dalai Lama notes (Dalai Lama, Lhundrub, and Cabezon 2011), the reactive mind functions like the clouds in the sky, always creating new weather systems for us to be preoccupied with. All the clouds that appear will eventually move out of view, and new clouds will be formed to take their place. Whatever happens with the clouds, the clear blue sky that contains them is consciousness itself. You are the conscious being that is there looking at the clouds of the conceptual mind. The act of being aware of your awareness is sometimes called *simple awareness*.

Along with helping you bring your attention into the present moment, simple awareness frees you of the need to form judgments or construct attachments. This is a place where you can experience whatever arises in your reactive mind and just notice that it is you who is doing the noticing. This is the *you* that you have known since you became aware that you existed. This part of you has never changed since you first became aware. It is not influenced by the trials and tribulations of life. It is the lens through which you experience what you experience. It is your clear blue sky. When you practice exercises that help you cultivate your ability to experience simple awareness, you will begin to see that this mental space is a place of safety and sanctuary for you.

As you learn to touch your simple awareness, you increase the ease with which you can shift between reactive mind and wise mind. This allows you to access the mode of mind best suited to demands of the moment. At the start, you will notice that reactive mind continues to have the upper hand, as it will quite effectively interfere with your practice of just observing what is present and staying inside simple awareness. As you develop a daily practice routine and your wise mind grows stronger, the predominance—or at least the speed—of your reactive mind will change, making it easier to access the spaciousness and slower pace of wise mind. These skills pave the way for more creative and meaningful experiences in key areas of life.

Once you learn how to step back from your reactive mind and access the sanctuary of simple awareness and wise mind, you can pursue wellness and vitality in relationships, work, leisure, and health without fear that you will somehow be consumed by emotional pain if things don't work out the way you had planned. Just as there are no edges to the blue sky, there are no edges to your consciousness. Just as the clouds form in the sky, unexpected life events, setbacks, and personal losses may temporarily cloud your existence. These events are both inevitable and transient. The one thing that doesn't change is that you are the one who is there to be conscious of each and every life moment as it unfolds.

In a state of wise mind and using the present moment as your anchor, you can initiate new life activities or engage in familiar activities in new ways. As we mentioned in the last section, contact with wise mind instantly puts you in contact with what matters most to you in life. Wise mind has a direct link to your heart. This link will help you steer toward your true north, rather than rule following and emotional avoidance. Wise mind also provides you with a new perspective on knowing and understanding the world around you. It will help you balance logic, reason, and verbal forms of knowing with intuition, imagination, inspiration, and compassion. We often tell clients that, although the quest to transcend depression often begins in the head, it almost always ends up in the heart.

MOONRISE MOUNTAIN MEDITATION

This exercise is designed to test your ability to remain in a state of simple awareness, even in the midst of something that might seem more like fantasy than reality. But is it? When your consciousness is simply "on the loose," lots of interesting things can and do happen! According to Native American thought, the sun is a symbol for male energy and the power to make an effort. Similarly, the moon represents female energy and the ability to relax, perceive, imagine, and allow. Balance in living comes from having both sun and moon energies present in our lives. There is a great deal of conflict in the world today, and a great deal that modern society expects of us, which brings with it a tendency for us to push ourselves to action. When life presents contradictions to us, it's important to create a space that is large enough to hold them and, from that space, take action.

In preparation for this meditation, take a moment to reflect on contradictions in your life. What is it that you feel the urge to fight or get away from? Is it an injustice at work? Is it some type of social inequity? Do you want to fight or just get a break from worrying about problems with your health or the health of the planet? Is there a relationship problem that brings you a lot of pain but also love? Accessing wise mind through simple awareness can help you with this, as it has the ability to find a still place where a new perspective can emerge. Before starting this exercise, go back to the end of chapter 3 and review the workability questions you generated related to any of the four life domains. You can take all of these questions with you on this journey, all the way down to just one or two that really have you concerned.

To complete this fantastic journey, please download the fully guided version at http://www.newharbinger .com/38457. Alternatively, you might make your own recording by reading the following passage and then playing it back when you're ready to meditate.

Take a moment to focus on your breath. Allow it to slow and deepen naturally and easily. Follow it and feel the rhythm and the ease of its motion, in and out, up and down. Your breath is a constant, a foundation, and place from which you can travel. Now focus on using your attention to create a dream, a dream that can help you better understand yourself. With better understanding, you will have more compassion for yourself. With the ability to care for yourself and trust your wise mind, you can perceive new possibilities in your life and say yes to them. This is the spirit of this, the Moonrise Mountain Meditation. In and out, your breathing continues effortlessly as you begin to imagine a warm summer day.

Yes, days are long now and you've been walking with friends. They go on ahead to pursue another trail, and you choose to stay by a creek. You like the way you feel as you stand beside the creek and breathe. You are tired from a long day's walking and you sit down. You take off your shoes and walk into the creek. The cool water is refreshing, and you reach down and cup your hands to draw the cool water to your face and neck. Then you lie down on a flat, warm rock beside the creek and listen to the movement of the water, the rustling of the leaves in the trees, and the birds. They sing for you, and you listen and breathe.

You are aware of the transitory nature of your experience, and this makes it all the more precious for you. The birds, the trees, and you—all have a beginning and an end. Only the rock you lie upon will live forever. You consider the warm rock and the strength it offers as it holds you lightly, confidently, and endlessly. Perhaps you doze off for a few moments, knowing that you don't have to hold yourself now; the rock will support you.

Rested, you are drawn to walk back into the forest you came from. You're filled with new energy and your senses are heightened. You smell the forest—the rich earth and the green trees. You come to a fork in the trail, and you decide not to take the path that will lead you back to your car. You are drawn to take a new path, a path to Moonrise Mountain. You quicken your pace in anticipation of being there for sunset. Your legs move easily and effortlessly, and your breathing is slow and deep. Then, you pause for a moment in your walk because something catches your eye. You understand that the forest is offering you something to help you remember this moment and the trust you feel in your future. Look closely. What is it? Go ahead and pick it up; it's yours and you can take it with you. It will help you remember this moment and your ability to be fully present and connected—connected with your silent mind, the rock, the water, and now the forest.

Now you arrive at the foot of the mountain at sunset. You see a steep path that will take you up to a good viewpoint, and you take it. Again, it is amazingly easy to walk this path, and you breathe in and out, slowly and deeply, as you climb up and up and up. You arrive at a large red rock with a smooth, warm surface, and you sit down. You watch the sunset and reflect on your life—what you have done, and what you wanted to do. You understand the things that have impeded your actions. You accept your fears, your sadness. The sunset is long and beautiful, and the clouds make it all the more interesting and unpredictable. There's really nothing to control or avoid, no problems to solve as you consider your life and this precious sunset. It just is.

Now darkness is falling upon you and the mountain, and you decide to look around for a place to stay the night. You walk a little farther along the trail, and you notice a cave in the side of the mountain. You go there and find a bed of pine needles. It is soft and warm. Someone has stayed here recently, and it is an inviting place to rest. You feel protected and ready to rest. Before you lie down, you step outside and look toward the sky. There it is—the rising moon. It is full, and it is huge. You look at the moon, and the moon looks at you. You look for the edge between your looking and seeing, between the moon and you, and this edge blurs. You are the moon, and the moon is you. You feel a pulsing, and with this pulsing a sense of rising or falling. Your silent self has something for you, something to help you with the conflicts and contradictions that concern you at this time in your life. What is it? Pay attention. It might be an image, a thought, a verse. Listen and learn. If you experience strong emotions at this time, allow them. Remember your gift from the forest and continue to pay attention.

When you are ready, go back into your body in the cave and rest. Your understanding of what your silent self offers you may deepen as you descend into sleep. Caves are special places for dreaming, and your dreams here may be particularly helpful for you.

And soon, the morning light wakes you slowly. Although you have not slept long, you are rested and ready to see the sunrise. You walk to the entrance of your cave, and you see the moon setting and the sun rising. A butterfly rests on a nearby tree that grows from a small indentation between the rocks. The butterfly spreads its wings so that you can enjoy its colors. You are ready to return, and you walk down the mountain path and through the forest. You remember the secrets that silent self revealed to you, and your gift from the forest. You know you can return here whenever you want, and you thank your mind for allowing this. Now allow yourself a few minutes to savor this moment in your life journey. And when you are ready, return to the book for further exploration of your experience on Moonrise Mountain.

Further Exploration. Take a few moments to make notes on your experience during this meditation. Did you experience some type of new intuition or insight about any workability question you took with you? Did the question seem as "serious" and life changing during your journey as it seems to feel in your daily life? Very often, the perspective of wise mind to tends to soften the hard emotional edges we create around more important workability questions. There is a great deal of variability in what people experience with this meditation, and if you repeat this exercise, your results are likely to be quite different from what they are today. You might consider creating a Moonrise Mountain journal, wherein you write down insights or intuitions that occur to you during this meditation. If you found this meditation emotionally helpful, you might want to repeat it periodically to help keep you focused on what matters to you in life.

LESLIE'S STORY

Leslie, a hardworking and proud single mother, had raised her son, Sam, without support from his father, and Sam was the center of her life. He was accepted into a good college with some financial aid, but attending would still involve considerable expense. Leslie took a night job to support Sam in getting the best education possible, and he moved to a distant town to attend college. Leslie missed Sam and tried to call him daily during the break between her jobs. If she didn't reach him, she had trouble sleeping.

Sam was ambivalent about his mother's frequent calls; he missed her and only felt more down after they talked. Although he maintained average grades, he started hanging out with a group of students who drank excessively on weekends. Halfway through Sam's second semester, Leslie received a call from the emergency room. Sam was being treated for an alcohol overdose. In an effort to calm herself and find direction in this difficult situation, Leslie used the Moonrise Mountain Meditation, asking, "How can I help my son and support him now that he no longer lives with me?"

In the forest, Leslie discovered a rare blue butterfly; she'd read about this type of butterfly but had never seen one. At moonrise, Leslie had an image of a beautiful horse racing around a track. The horse was wet with sweat and gasping for breath. She saw herself mounting the horse and slowing his pace to a canter, a trot, and then a walk. Finally, he relaxed and then stopped altogether. She dismounted and began to groom him, and he allowed this. In fact, he accepted her attention lovingly, as it was offered freely and without reservation, and Leslie began to cry.

After the meditation, Leslie felt as if a burden had been lifted. Although she wasn't sure what she would do differently, she knew she was better prepared to perceive her own needs, as well as her son's. She understood that being in the present moment was as elusive as a rare butterfly, and that if she relaxed her grip on Sam, he would settle in and find his way in life. She saw that she couldn't control him and didn't need to. If she simply expressed the fact that she loved him, and would be there for him, that would be enough.

BRAIN TRAINING TO STRENGTHEN YOUR INNER OBSERVER

Strengthening your ability to adopt an observing, self-aware stance will be an important ally in your quest to transcend depression and pursue a more vital life. Any number of daily practices can help you develop the ability to be here and now, and we encourage you to experiment with and find those that work the best for you, even if you come up with them on your own. For example, one of us (PR) likes to develop her observer skills through daily yoga and meditation practice. The other (KS) enjoys a daily practice of morning yoga and a viewing of the sunset while accepting private events, ranging from familiar disparaging stories about himself to random moments of unexpected laughter.

The following brain training exercises are designed to help you learn to pay attention in a focused, flexible way and to make contact with the more expansive qualities of simple awareness. If you practice any or all of these exercises on a regular basis, you will notice that your ability to organize, focus, and shift your attention is getting better and better, as you are literally creating new neural pathways as well as strengthening existing ones in your brain. As we have discussed, neuroscience studies have shown that practicing such strategies regularly for as little as a month can have a positive impact on your ability to be here, now.

All of the following exercises are supported by very specific, detailed audio instructions. The audio component will make it easier for you to follow along and practice the skills that we want you to learn. We recommend you take the time to download them now from http://www.newharbinger.com/38457, so that you can use the one(s) you like the most as part of your daily brain training routine.

THE BREATH OF LIFE

In order to foster present-moment experience and expand awareness, you must learn to control and deepen your breathing. The breath is the center of your being. It controls not only your respiration but also your heart rate, brain waves, skin temperature, and a host of other basic biological functions. Coincidentally, deep regular breathing of the type we have you practice has been shown to help downregulate the hypothalamic–pituitary–adrenal axis, which controls the brain's fight-or-flight system, and is a source of negative energy for the reactive mind. So what we call *belly breathing* actually optimizes the neural pathways responsible for calming the nervous system and producing a state of wise mind.

Indeed, the Buddhist term for this type of deep breathing practice is *pranayama*, which literally means "the breath of life." How powerful is pranayama? Research shows that people who can be aware of each breath report improved ability to pay attention in real life, report less daydreaming and mind wandering, and experience more positive mood with lessened depression (Levenson et al. 2014). The benefits of this breathing practice were observed to occur within two weeks of starting!

Find a comfortable place to sit and make sure the clothes you're wearing aren't tight so that you can breathe very deeply. Get your body in a comfortable position and close your eyes for a few minutes. Begin by focusing your attention on your breath. Just notice your breathing for a while without trying to change it in any way. Take your time to get present with your breathing. This is the present moment in your life, and there is no reason to rush through it. Just allow yourself to breathe in and out however your body wants to do it.

Now imagine there's a balloon in your belly that you want to fill with the air you inhale. As you breathe in very slowly and deeply, you're filling the balloon in your belly. When you are filling the balloon, you will notice that your belly is pushing out and down. When the balloon is full, pause for a second and then gradually let the air flow out of the balloon. When you empty the balloon, you will notice that your belly pulls in and up slightly. As you inhale and exhale, your chest and shoulders should remain almost still. If you notice that your chest and shoulders are rising and falling, try to send your breath into your belly and allow your chest and shoulders to remain still and relaxed.

Now, as you inhale, purse your lips and breathe in through your nose. Notice the sensation of the air coming up through your nose and down into the balloon in your belly. Imagine this flow of air as an upside-down umbrella handle. You start at the crooked end of the umbrella handle, then bring your breath up into your nose and back down the handle into the balloon. As you exhale, open your lips and reverse the umbrella handle. Your breath leaves the balloon, comes up the long, straight handle, then travels over the arch and out of your mouth. Now, as you continue to focus only on your breathing, notice any sensations you experience as the breath goes in through your nose and back down to your belly. Do you notice the temperature of the air as you bring it in? What does it feel like as it goes through your nose? And as you exhale, does the air seem warm or moist as it passes your lips? If you notice your attention shifting away from breathing, just gently redirect it to what you have come here to do. Continue to fill and empty the balloon for 5 minutes.

Further Exploration. What experiences did you have when you practiced this basic breathing exercise? Were you able to consciously fill the balloon in your belly? Did you notice your mind wandering while you were breathing? Were you able to bring your attention and focus back to the task at hand? Don't get frustrated if this exercise is difficult at first. The simplest things, like breathing, can seem like a big mental task when your reactive mind tries to get in the way. We strongly recommend that you practice this or another breathing exercise that you like at least once a day—even better, several times a day, morning, noon, and night. The more you practice pranayama, the more accustomed you will become to using the present moment as an anchor on your life journey

TONE-GUIDED PRANAYAMA

In this breathing practice, you will hear two distinctly different chords. The first chord is the signal for you to breathe in, and you'll continue to do so as long as you hear the chord. Wait until you hear the second chord before beginning to slowly breathe out, and continue breathing out as long as you hear the chord. The silence in between chords is a signal to do nothing with your breath and simply notice the quiet space of non-breathing The pattern will continue for 5 minutes, until you hear a bell ring. That will be the signal for you to slowly bring yourself back to your normal state of awareness.

INSIDE AND OUTSIDE

Using pranayama as a platform, this exercise will let you practice the three main observing skills (centering, focusing, and attention flexibility) using your body as a primary focus. When you practice this exercise, you develop the ability to direct your attention and awareness from the inside to the outside and back again.

Begin by downloading the guided audio version of this exercise from http://www.newharbinger.com /38457. (Alternatively, you may record the following passage in your own voice to play back later.)

For this moment, simply breathe in and out, filling your lungs and emptying them slowly. Notice the sensation of air flowing through your nose and throat and into your lungs, slowly and effortlessly. Feel your chest and abdomen rising and falling with each slow inhalation and exhalation, creating the feeling of a wave endlessly ebbing and flowing over your body. In and out goes the wave, and upward and onward goes the energy outside the skin of your chest and abdomen as it moves to accommodate the rhythmic flow of your body in response to the flow of air in and out of your body.

Notice your heart. Can you feel a pumping sensation? Can you feel a pulse? If you like, place your fingers lightly on one of the carotid arteries in your neck or on the inside of your wrist. That's your pulse—the rhythm of your heart's moving the oxygen in the air you breathe to all parts of your body, your blood's flowing like a river with many tributaries, all so perfectly designed, all of this happening with your awareness and acceptance.

Now shift your consciousness to the edge between your body and what it is touching. Feel your clothes on your skin, your shoes on your feet. If you are lying down, notice the places of contact between your body and the floor, bed, or couch. If you are sitting, notice the places of contact among your body, the chair, and the floor that supports your feet and the chair. Describe these points of contact to yourself.

Now focus your awareness on the space you are in, the room that holds you and the things that surround you at this moment. Listen for small sounds in this space—a fan, a bird just outside the window. Hold these in your awareness and then move beyond them to the larger physical space around you, the entire house or building that holds the room that holds the chair or bed that holds your clothes and all your things—and you. What is this building like? What are its sounds and smells? Are there cars passing by? If so, notice them and hold them in your awareness—their noise, their smell, the people they carry. You can be aware of this, and so much more, as you pay attention to the points of contact between you and the objects and events occurring in your awareness.

Now, if you are willing, shift your attention to the city, town, or geographic area that holds the building where you are. See it from an eagle's-eye view. There it is below you, the building you're in; the other buildings; and the parks, dogs, cats, and people—young and old. They are there, and you are watching, allowing all of this as you continue your approach to a larger and larger experience of the context of your experience. Now you are seeing the entire world and looking deep into space, where many stars look back at you. Stay here as long as you like and see the edge of your consciousness.

When you become aware of something smaller, like a thought or sensation in your physical body, say hello to whatever it is and let it go. Allow yourself to expand back to the edge of your consciousness, where your experience is inclusive and accepting. And when it is time for you to return, allow yourself time to retrace your path of expanding awareness. Go from the galaxy slowly and take in the beautiful colors of Earth as you approach your first hemisphere… your city or town… and then your building… and your room.

When your attention is back to your body, connect again with your pulse and feel the rhythms of your body. Feel the movement of your body as it takes in the air needed to sustain it. When you are ready, you can return to the book.

Further Exploration. What happened when you required your attention to shift back and forth? Was it easier to pay attention to some things than others? Did you lose control of your attention during the practice? Did something hook you? What? The better you get at moving your attention around in a flexible way, the more keenly observant you will become of what is happening in and around you. This sense of being in intimate contact with everything you are aware of produces a unique kind of serenity that is associated with expanded awareness.

DANCING WITH THE QUIET

This exercise will give you a chance to be more tuned in to inner experiences that tend to draw you out of the observer role. There are two basic forms of inner experience that you will be concerned with: events inside of you—thoughts, memories, emotions, or certain kinds of physical sensations—and events outside of you—sounds, smells, and activities of other people, pets, and so on.

To begin, practice pranayama or the Breath of Life exercise for several minutes. Afterward catalog on the worksheet below any experiences you encountered that drew you out of observer mode.

Dancing with the Quiet Worksheet

Events Inside the Skin	Events Outside the Skin

Now take a moment to review all of these distractions. Then practice pranayama again. This time you will be vigilant for each distraction: pay soft attention to the distraction, then release your attention and put it back to simply observing your breath. The goal is not to eliminate these events but rather to learn to keep your attention under control in their presence.

MINDFUL EATING

One of the most ancient meditative practices is to approach a common everyday activity with mindfulness. An old Buddhist koan makes this point: *Before enlightenment, chop wood, carry water. After enlightenment, chop wood, carry water.* This means that you can practice being present with many daily activities, including preparing and eating food. Most of us are conditioned to take a "gobble, gulp, and go" stance toward eating, to get done with it and simply satisfy our hunger. Like breathing, eating is an everyday necessity for nourishing the body and mind, and part of this nourishment comes from the mental well-being that healthful eating creates.

For this exercise, get an orange, find a quiet place to sit at a table, then close your eyes for a moment and clear your mind of any concerns or attachments. Then, follow the guided audio version or, alternatively, read through or record the script below for yourself.

Sit with your hands in your lap and study the orange you have in your hand. Note its color and size. Can you smell it? Notice when your thoughts wander and you think about something you plan to do later or something you wanted to do earlier. Let those thoughts come and go, and return your attention to the orange. You will probably need to keep returning your attention to the orange; your reactive mind is likely to offer numerous instructions and concerns as you move toward the present moment with the orange on the table.

When you're ready, place your hands on the orange. Touch it lightly and feels its texture. What words describe it best? Is it cool? Bumpy? Now hold the orange more firmly. Does it feel solid? Soft? As you are ready, place a fingernail into the skin to pierce it. Do you feel the oil of the orange skin? What does it feel like? Smell your finger and consider the smell. Notice the thoughts and feelings that come with smelling the orange oil. Look at these thoughts and feelings and let them go.

Now remove the peel little by little. Notice any urge to finish quickly or "do it right," and simply continue to slowly peel the orange. Once the skin is removed, hold the orange again and study the lines that reveal its sections. Look at their particular pattern; every orange is slightly different from all other oranges. When you are ready, open the orange at a section line. Look inside, to the center of the orange. Study how the sections are connected to one another inside the orange.

Notice any evaluative thoughts you may be having. Let them be there and let them go. Continue to study the sections. And when you are ready, choose one to separate from the others. Bring it to your nose and smell it. If you like, place it in your mouth. Hold it there for a moment and consider its history—what brought it to this moment. And then, when you are ready, chew the section until you are ready to swallow. When you swallow, feel the movement of the piece of orange from your mouth to your throat, then your esophagus, and then your stomach. You may continue to choose one section at a time to smell, taste, chew, swallow, and follow in its path to your stomach. Finally, take the peels in your hands and hold them for a while as you simply sit and observe. When you have completed your mindful eating, you can return to the book.

Further Exploration. What happened as you went through this exercise? Did you have moments when you were perfectly present with "orangeness"? Did you notice your reactive mind attempting to pull you out of this exercise? Did you notice a sense of wanting to hurry up and just eat the orange? Did your reactive mind tell you that this whole mindful eating thing is a big joke? That it won't work for you because you have bigger issues to deal with? When your reactive mind showed up and tried to spoil the party, were you able to gently redirect your attention back to the experience of eating an orange?

If you like this type of observer training, you can repeat this exercise with almost any object—a raisin or a cup of tea, for instance. You can also try this exercise with a crystal, a flower arrangement, or anything else that would expand your contact with your senses within the present moment.

CHOOSE EACH STEP

This exercise, which involves walking mindfully, can be done inside or outside. Before beginning, decide where you want to take your walk and how long you will spend. We recommend 10 to 15 minutes, but as little as 5 minutes will help you contact the present moment and move into the observer mode. When possible, it's nice to do this exercise barefoot, as this allows you to better sense the contact between your feet and the ground. There are four points on each foot that need to be in contact with the ground to give you maximum stability. The picture below shows these four points.

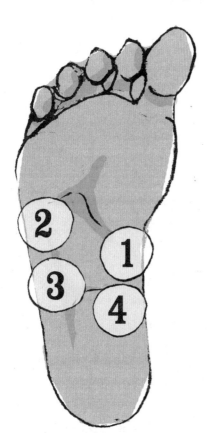

Stand with all eight points in firm contact with the ground. Your task is to choose each step you take and then take that step consciously. Your reactive mind will want to race through this and, in its frustration, might even give you the urge to take a lot of steps quickly. Your reactive mind is not accustomed to having you, the human, observe, accept, and choose rather than allowing it to evaluate, struggle, and avoid!

In addition to choosing each step, you can also choose not to take a step; in so doing, you are choosing to stand in place. If that's what you choose to do, notice how the process of simply standing feels. It takes conscious choosing on a second-by-second basis to hold still—the same type of second-by-second choosing it takes to walk mindfully.

As you stand or move, choose how many of the four points on each foot are in contact with the ground. Notice what it's like to stand with intention and to make a decision to move or not to move. Notice what it's like to have maximum contact between your feet and the earth or less contact. Maybe you'll choose to lift two points off the ground on your left foot. What happens? Does it have an effect on your right foot? Are you going to take a step now? Toward what? Away from what?

Notice any thoughts about this exercise and its value or lack of value to you. Notice how the reactive mind runs on with suggestions and stories. It can be very hard for the reactive mind to accept standing still or moving slowly, feeling the earth, and choosing every step. Notice this sense of tension if it's there and simply make room for it. Notice if there are unpleasant or pleasant sensations in your body. Where are they? What are they? What do they feel like? Are they hot, cold, flowing, pinching, itchy, or something else? Make room for those sensations and continue to choose to stand or step.

Notice how many points on each foot are on the ground at any moment. Can you feel each point as it leaves the ground and touches the ground when you take a step? As you're focusing on and continuing your steps, do you notice a thought about needing to get someplace? If you do, that's okay; just notice it and choose your next action in the moment. See if you can bring all of your attention in the moment so that it is completely focused on each step. Stop when you hear the bell and return to the book.

Further Exploration. How did you do with this exercise? The interfering effects of your reactive mind can make it extraordinarily difficult to make even simple choices, such as where to put your foot down. We're used to walking toward something and doing it on autopilot. This is a reflection of the tremendous impact that turning your behavior over to the environment has on your sense of internal pace and purpose. Like so many aspects of developing a mindfulness-based lifestyle, it all comes down to consciously going off autopilot, showing up in the present moment, savoring what is there without the pressure of time, and taking back control over your behavior. That is a surefire formula for living in the depression-free zone!

IDEAS TO CULTIVATE

- A core mindfulness skill is to be an observer of your inner experience, and to participate in that experience when it pays dividends to do so.

- Your wise mind is the source of true knowledge, intuition, and compassion.

- When you learn to find the present moment as an anchor for your experience of life, your awareness expands and your ability to accept also grows.

- Simple awareness is a special place from which you can look at all things with greater understanding and compassion.

- Present-moment awareness can be practiced in seemingly mundane daily activities, like eating, walking, or breathing.

- You can use daily brain training exercises to strengthen neural pathways in your brain that produce robust and flexible forms of attention.

- Accessing wise mind through the portal of present-moment awareness will enrich your life on this planet in each moment as it unfolds and teach you about the bigger role you play in the universe.

CHAPTER 7

Step 3: Practice Nonjudgmental Acceptance

We cannot control the wind; we can only adjust the sails.

—Kahlil Gibran

In depression, you tend to become attached to and judgmental of your thoughts, feelings, memories, and physical sensations. When you practice emotional acceptance, you simply allow these mental experiences to exist in awareness, without struggle or evaluation. Practicing this stance strengthens the neural circuitry responsible for regulating emotions and your action tendencies. Learning to let things be without struggle or judgment will become a go-to skill on your life path.

One reason it can be so hard to be in the present moment is because, when we get there, we usually come into direct contact with feared and avoided mental experiences like painful emotions, self-critical thoughts, distressing memories, or unpleasant bodily sensations. We often tell clients that, for better or for worse, their inner experiences are waiting for them just beyond the doorway of present-moment awareness. Taking an open, accepting stance with respect to these experiences is much easier said than done because our primitive brain is hardwired to do the opposite: evaluate the experience in terms of its positive or negative emotional tone; assess the danger level when the emotional tone is appraised as negative, dangerous, or threatening; and engage in self-protective behavior if danger is present. This demonstrates how destructive fusing with and following the emotional avoidance rule can be in situations involving emotional distress.

The rules we have been socially trained to follow define painful private experiences as threats. Thus, your brain is primed to react with impulses to escape and avoid. This is why your knee-jerk response is to evaluate painful experiences as something you would rather avoid than approach. Adopting a stance of openness to and acceptance of distressing emotions in the present moment requires that you learn to view them in a different way—not as threats, as your reactive mind tells you, but rather as just clouds in the clear blue sky of your wise mind's simple awareness. Instead of pulling away in horror from your pain, we want you to lean into it with a stance of openness and curiosity.

Of course, your reactive mind has other plans for you. It is not just going to roll over and let you enter the space of wise mind. Instead, it will do everything to get you to view your emotional experience as the enemy within. Reactive mind tells you to continue avoiding both the painful experience and the values-based action that you're capable of. It's important to learn to recognize the tricks and antics of reactive mind without getting caught up in them. We will examine several of the challenges to being open and accepting, and what to do about them, in coming chapters, so read on!

In this chapter, we introduce the general idea of *acceptance* as an alternative to avoidance. We define what acceptance is and isn't, as well as the types of events and experiences that require acceptance versus those that we can attempt to change or modify in some way. Like many mindfulness concepts, acceptance is not a single mental skill but rather is the end result of practicing two highly interrelated mindfulness skills:

- **Emotional resilience:** the ability to use mental and behavioral strategies that minimize the impact of negative emotions in response to some life event or challenge (Smith and Ascough 2016). In ACT, we want you to adopt a stance of leaning into difficult, emotionally challenging experiences in a way that promotes health and well-being. Emotionally resilient people utilize painful moments in life to increase self-knowledge and improve their coping abilities. Emotional resilience involves the ability to observe private experiences and then use words to distinguish among different types of them. It involves both understanding and countering biases and action tendencies that make negative emotions more challenging. Equally important is the ability to simply describe emotions as well as other private experiences, without buying into the reactive mind's evaluations of them. It is only by remaining in this judgment-free zone that you become resilient to the urge to struggle with, avoid, or change what is there.

- **Willingness:** a stance of voluntarily approaching events, situations, or interactions that are likely to trigger distressing and unwanted emotions, memories, thoughts, or physical reactions. We often tell clients that willingness is the behavioral equal of acceptance. In order to practice acceptance, you have to be willing to approach situations that might be emotionally difficult for you. Without a stance of willingness, you are likely to steer clear of those situations, leaving no opportunity to practice acceptance.

ACCEPTANCE: THE ALTERNATIVE TO EMOTIONAL AVOIDANCE

It's likely that you're already familiar with the concept of acceptance in the form of the Serenity Prayer so widely used in Alcoholics Anonymous and other similar programs: "God grant me the serenity to accept the things I cannot change, courage to change the things I can, and the wisdom to know the difference." The reason this simple prayer is so widespread, and so effective, is because it describes an important fork in the road we face over and over again in the process of pursuing a vital life.

From an ACT perspective, learning to discriminate between things that can and can't be changed is one of the keys to personal health. Whereas things that can be changed require one type of response, things that are beyond your control require an entirely different approach. In this section, we teach you how to make this very important distinction. When you learn what you have control over, you can direct your efforts toward exercising control when it's possible to effect change. And once you can identify what you can't control, you won't get sucked into the trap of expending your energy on strategies that lead to a dead end. Instead, you'll be able to practice an alternative strategy: acceptance.

Acceptance involves consciously choosing to practice an open, curious, and nonreactive stance toward distressing, unwanted internal experiences. Rather than attempting to suppress or avoid a troublesome emotion, thought, memory, or sensation, you simply allow it to be there. In ACT we sometimes describe this stance as "making room" for something that's distressing you. By practicing acceptance when it's called for, you can free up, or make room for, incredible amounts of time and energy that can be redirected to aspects of your life that you *can* control.

In a way, acceptance is letting go of any urge to resist or avoid what shows up in your mental space. Your immediate life dilemma won't suddenly disappear because you accept it, but acceptance does put you in a position to do something other than practice unworkable avoidance strategies. It gives you a chance to check your values compass and make a new move toward your true north. Practicing acceptance is extremely difficult when you're confronting personal pain, but the alternative is to struggle with something that can't be controlled. This struggle not only exhausts you emotionally, it also worsens your personal pain and harms your overall health.

There are many mistaken notions in the community about acceptance that we want to dispel:

- *Acceptance does not mean you are resigning yourself to defeat and endless suffering in life.* You aren't giving up hope for yourself. To the contrary, we would argue that people suffer because they won't or can't accept something that is an unchangeable, fixed feature in their life, such as the death of spouse or child, a divorce, or losing a job. In this sense, acceptance is a new, powerful strategy that gives you the freedom to try something different, and possibly better.

- *Acceptance doesn't mean you choose to tolerate something up to a certain point of intensity, and then you won't accept it anymore.* Acceptance is a choice to make room in yourself for whatever comes your way. This can be a daunting challenge if you're already depressed, because the decision to escape from a situation is often done to protect you from further emotional pain. It is natural for us to want to move away from pain—that is usually the first impulse we have. Acceptance means that you will remain present when something hurts, even while your reactive mind is telling you to run. Rather than get into an argument with your reactive mind about whether you will or won't escape a difficult situation, you make an advance commitment to hold still in a difficult situation and let the pain wash over you. Sometimes, when you let pain wash over you, you can almost feel like you are getting "clean," psychologically speaking.

NeuroNotes: Emotion Recognition Is a Key Mindfulness Skill

Neuroscience is shining new light on how human beings experience and process stress-related emotions at the level of brain circuitry—and recent discoveries make even clearer the benefit emotional acceptance can have. The practice of emotional acceptance is correlated with activation of the anterior cingulate cortex (ACC). This is the area of the brain responsible for comparing an idealized outcome with a realized outcome. For example, if you expected to have an exciting evening with your partner, but instead you got into a really bad argument and decided to break up, the resulting discrepancy in outcomes would be communicated by the ACC to the dorsolateral prefrontal cortex (DLPFC). This is the area of the brain responsible for executive control, including the management of conflicting emotional states and their associated action tendencies. The DLPFC also has neural projections into the amygdala, the brain's emotion center. So the DLPFC will both stimulate an emotional state and then help regulate the intensity of the emotion and urges to act (Tang and Posner 2009; Shackman et al. 2011).

A number of studies have shown that mindfulness practices are associated with unique patterns of coactivation in the ACC and DLPFC. This pattern is particularly strong under conditions of emotional distress. Individuals practicing mindfulness for even brief periods of time seem much more attuned to their emotions and perform well in spite of them (Tang and Posner 2009), and they are also very adept at practicing emotional acceptance (Goldin and Gross 2010; Niemiec et al. 2010). One recent study showed that emotional acceptance seems to be the key mechanism in fostering positive executive control and improved performance conflict monitoring (Teper and Inzlicht 2012). The long and short of it is that, along with the ability to stay in the present moment, a second defining feature of mindfulness is the ability to quickly and accurately identify emotions when they appear without becoming consumed by them (Williams 2010).

Another recent study documented changes in the brains of people with back pain who participated in acceptance training using the ACT approach. These people were also dependent on opioid medications. The changes included the same alterations to the DMN that are often seen with meditation practice, as well as changes in the resting state connectivity in pain-related areas of the brain. People in the control group who received health education did not experience brain changes (Smallwood, Potter, and Robin 2016). In essence, practicing acceptance of pain sensations resulted in a significantly reduced rate and intensity of pain signals sent to the brain for processing.

The results of the chronic pain study raise another important point about the role of acceptance in processing distressing, unwanted private experiences. We typically tell clients that there is no guarantee what will happen if they practice acceptance. Their pain might go up, go down, or stay the same. The temptation could be to see acceptance as a really powerful emotional avoidance strategy. You might think, "If I accept my pain hard enough, maybe it will go away!" The reality is that the original pain *doesn't* go away, but the pain that is generated by struggling with the pain *does*!

As we have shown, when you struggle to control or suppress emotional pain, it rebounds in a very invasive way that can be quite distressing in its own right. So practicing acceptance really is kind of an emotional-control strategy after all: when you practice acceptance, you reduce the unnecessary pain that is added when you use avoidance and suppression strategies.

BILL'S STORY

Bill is a fifty-one-year-old man with chronic back pain and depression. He injured his back while lifting a pallet on the job fifteen years ago. He returned to work after two months of leave but found that his back pain was too intense for him to continue his work. He quit his job and filed for permanent work disability, but his claim was denied after an independent medical examiner determined that there was inadequate evidence of a permanent back injury. Nevertheless, Bill continued to experience pain on a daily basis. He was offered a vocational retraining option by the state but declined because he didn't feel he could work at all with his pain.

Bill consulted with several surgeons and underwent a spinal disk fusion that initially helped his pain but eventually left him with even worse pain. He was prescribed narcotic pain medication ten years ago. Now he's dependent upon the medicine but still experiences a lot of pain. His current doctor has refused to increase his dosage and even recommended that he reduce his dose. Bill is furious that his doctor isn't helping with the pain. He feels that none of his doctors have taken very good care of him.

Bill describes his pain as a burning, stinging sensation, like someone is putting a needle in his back. Pain sensations radiate down his right leg, where he experiences numbness and tingling. Bill's daily routine is to spend a lot of time at home lying on the sofa, as this gives him some relief. He doesn't go out much because upright activity tends to cause pain. He used to go to church with his wife a couple of times a week, but he stopped going after he had to leave a church luncheon because of a pain flare-up. There's a lot of tension in the household. Bill's wife complains that he doesn't help around the house and that he's short with her and their kids. They don't have much intimacy anymore, as intercourse is painful for him.

Bill believes his depression is caused by his chronic pain. The more he struggles to control his pain, the more angry and irritable he tends to get. He often thinks about the day he hurt his back and whether he could have done something to prevent his injury. He doesn't see much hope that his life will turn around unless the pain is somehow eliminated. He's disappointed in himself for not being a good breadwinner, and he feels bad when he yells at his kids for no good reason. More than once, he's thought of killing himself because he feels his family would be better off without him.

Almost anyone hearing Bill's story would feel sorry for him. He experienced an injury, was weaseled out of his disability payments, and ended up basically homebound without much in the way of a fulfilling life. He wakes up every morning with a knot of anger in his stomach, disappointed and embittered at a world that seems to have given him a raw deal. Bill is a good person who loves his wife and children, and he was a good provider until he was injured. Then *poof!* His life was vaporized by an act of fate, and depression became his daily companion.

IDENTIFYING WHAT CAN'T BE CHANGED

Let's examine Bill's situation from the perspective of the Serenity Prayer. Does Bill know what he can and cannot control in his current situation? Is he practicing acceptance of the aspects that can't be controlled? Is he exerting control over the things that he can control? Take a few minutes to study the aspects of his situation listed below. For items that Bill can't change, circle A for acceptance. For aspects he has control over, circle C.

Events or Situations in Bill's Life

1. Bill suffered an on-the-job injury.	A	C
2. Bill experiences back pain on a daily basis.	A	C
3. Bill was denied a disability pension.	A	C
4. Bill has thoughts that he has too much pain to work at any job.	A	C
5. Bill refuses to go through vocational retraining.	A	C
6. Bill underwent an unsuccessful back surgery that left him with more pain.	A	C
7. Bill spends a lot of time on his sofa to control the pain.	A	C
8. Bill doesn't go to church.	A	C
9. Bill doesn't exercise regularly because of the pain.	A	C
10. Bill takes larger and larger doses of narcotics to control his pain.	A	C
11. Bill experiences burning and stinging sensations in his back.	A	C
12. Bill experiences sensations of tingling and numbness in his leg.	A	C
13. Bill feels angry and irritable when in pain.	A	C
14. Bill remembers the injury.	A	C
15. Bill thinks about how he could have prevented the injury.	A	C
16. Bill yells at his children.	A	C
17. Bill is short with his wife.	A	C
18. Bill doesn't have sexual relations with his wife because his back hurts.	A	C
19. Bill has thoughts that life has given him a raw deal.	A	C
20. Bill has thoughts that he would be better off dead.	A	C

Key: *Acceptance:* 1, 2, 3, 4, 6, 11, 12, 13, 14, 15, 19, 20; *Control:* 5, 7, 8, 9, 10, 16, 17, 18

Further Exploration. Now compare your answers to those in the key. Did they differ? As we assess his situation, it becomes clear that Bill has some control over quite a few things. He can influence the amount of time he spends on the sofa, his attendance at church, his participation in daily exercises, his use of narcotics, his behavior toward his wife and children, and his sexual relationship with his wife. And he could choose to challenge his assumptions about his pain and try vocational retraining. Do these answers surprise you?

Take a close look at the events and experiences that Bill has no immediate control over: not just physical sensations but also his spontaneous thoughts, feelings, and memories related to his pain and his personal history. Being in pain causes predictable private experiences, including negative emotions and thoughts. Unpleasant feelings, thoughts, and images show up in the moment for all of us in response to pain—and they show up more when we try to suppress or avoid them. What we have to do instead is to observe them, then decide what to do in response, according to our values.

What Can Be Changed

Like many people with chronic pain, Bill is focusing on controlling uncontrollable aspects of his life, such as the physical sensations of pain, thoughts about pain, emotional distress related to pain, and memories of the injury experience. Meanwhile, he's spending less energy addressing controllable aspects of his life, such as engaging in meaningful activities or participating in activities that would promote and preserve his health. Bill seems to have unintentionally stopped trying to exert control over aspects of his life that he could influence in significant ways, perhaps because the burden of depression makes it difficult for him to get started. Change could indeed be difficult in some of these areas; Bill may need to acquire some new skills and obtain support from others. However, it is entirely possible for him to have both chronic back pain *and* a meaningful life.

When we first suggested this possibility to Bill, he was frustrated. His first response was, "How could anyone expect me to do more when I'm in such horrible pain?" We asked Bill to slow down, pause momentarily, and then ask himself whether his pain literally made it impossible for him to show more kindness to his wife and children, to participate in a daily exercise program, to attend his church, or to enjoy sexual pleasure with his life partner.

In essence, Bill had fallen into a trap of struggling so hard with his pain that he ended up heading more toward true south than true north! When Bill thought this through, he realized that his pain didn't actually preclude him moving in the direction of his values compass. When he considered the merits of continuing with his present approach versus bringing values-based behaviors into his life, he decided to go for it, even though making some of these changes would challenge him. He decided to go see his doctor and ask to be referred to a pain management class at the medical school.

What Must Be Accepted

Bill's life situation demonstrates another common feature of complex life situations: There is often a grab bag of things that we can or can't control and an intermixture of things that can and can't be changed running in parallel, and our job is to sort this out. Bill can't control the fact that he suffered a back injury that left him disabled. He can't control what the disability insurance system decides to do with his claim. He can't rewind his back surgery so that the outcome is better than it was. Bill also can't control that his back injury will prevent him from engaging in daily routines enjoyed by people who don't have back injuries.

Many difficult life situations, like Bill's back injury, make the process of sorting out what we can and cannot change a real challenge. As the famous AA mantra says: *Stuff happens!* And, when it does, your best positive response is to take an accepting stance, connect with your humility, and believe that you can find ways to live a thoughtful and purposeful life.

If instead you respond with indignation, blaming, avoidance, and withdrawal (in an effort to protect yourself from pain), you end up losing more of your connection to the things that matter. You also risk losing behavior you can control. By trying to wash your hands of responsibility for any aspect of the situation, you're likely to lose insight into which aspects of the situation are actually in your lane. Bill got off track by spending inordinate amounts of energy trying to control aspects of his life situation that cannot be changed:

- Spontaneous feelings
- Spontaneous thoughts
- Spontaneous memories
- Spontaneous physical sensations
- A single life event, act of fate, or ongoing life stress
- Other people's behavior
- Past events and personal history

These experiences occur within us in a very personal and immediate way. What could be closer than your own thoughts, feelings, memories, or sensations? What could be more in your face than rejection or criticism from someone you love deeply or the fading health of someone you care about? When the inevitable and transient challenges of life show up, the best course of action is to become an observer of your experience, connect with the bigger life perspective that simple awareness and wise mind provide you, and move forward in a way that is consistent with your values.

Here's a key concept that will go a long way in helping you learn to accept difficult thoughts, emotions, and memories: Painful private events aren't toxic. They feel like they're toxic and you may *think* they're unbearable, but they aren't. As a human being, you're perfectly built to experience whatever you experience in response to the situation you're in. These private events are normal, natural, and healthy—and, more important, they can't be prevented. They don't require alteration, and they don't need to be packaged to look or feel good. While they don't feel good, you can feel them well! See them as the newest set of clouds in the vast blue sky of your simple awareness.

Remember this truism: Everything changes on its own. Nothing is permanent. All you have to do is watch as life unfolds in front of you. Respond according to your values, when doing so will make a difference. Hold still, and relax, when life's twists and turns are outside of your control. There is an ancient Buddhist saying that makes this point better than we can: *What can you do, when you can do nothing?* Basically, you can just be.

This is what acceptance looks like on the ground: having distressing, unwanted experiences without judgment and without struggle. If you just let your reactions be, they will function the way evolution has designed them to function. Have no doubt: Your own reactions aren't toxic to you, but avoiding your reactions through suppression or avoidance can be very toxic indeed.

FOSTERING EMOTIONAL RESILIENCE

Emotional resilience starts with being open to and accepting of unwanted, painful inner experiences. There are three main qualities of emotional resilience that will allow you to use your emotions to help you instead of hurt you:

- the ability to use words to accurately describe experience

- the ability to remain nonjudgmental about what you are experiencing

- the ability to regulate your action tendencies

Describe What You See

Words help us both organize and make sense of what we are experiencing. By linking words with the various aspects of your inner experience events, you can slow down the pace of your experience and better understand what you are feeling or thinking. This allows you to peel away the layers of your experience, like the layers of an onion. This lets you contact each layer, without having to deal with the whole experience at once, which can feel overwhelming.

An important step in building your emotional resilience is to increase your ability to use a wide spectrum of words to describe different types of experiences (emotions, thoughts, memories, sensations) and their emotional tones (negative to neutral to positive) along a continuum of intensity (mild to intense). The more words you have at your disposal to describe your state of mind, the more you can get located inside of your experience.

Here's a simple way to test this out for yourself: Imagine that you know only ten emotion words and you must use them to label one hundred different emotional states. How would you do that? You would be forced to use the same few words repeatedly to describe completely different emotional experiences. Because your words organize your inner experience, you might end up treating very different emotions—sadness, guilt, or loneliness, for example—as if they were one and the same. You basically lose the information contained in each emotion by having to lump them into one category. Your coping strategies will be less diverse and your perspective more narrow.

Now imagine that you have fifty words to describe one hundred different emotional states. Would it be easier? You'd be able to match different emotion words to different emotional experiences far more accurately. To do so, you would need to pause, slow down, and choose thoughtfully. So, the take-home message is that the more words you have at your disposal to describe your state of mind, the more you can observe and describe your experience.

Consider the following words that apply to the emotional experience of depression: dejected, dispirited, discouraged, demoralized, blue, down in the dumps, sad, lonely, lost, left behind, inconsolable. Think of each of these words as occupying a specific space on the continuum of depressive emotions. However, there is a big difference between feeling lonely and feeling inconsolable. It is the ability to distinguish these nuances of your emotional world that gives you a huge advantage in processing emotional experience in a healthy way. You will be much less likely to overreact to an emotion-producing event if you can name your feelings precisely. You will get a chance to test your word skills in the exercise Buff Up Your Emotional Vocabulary near the end of this chapter.

Be a Witness

Another important component of emotional resilience is to remain objective and nonjudgmental. What is so tricky about the reactive mind is that it will silently intermix *descriptions* and *judgments* of events or situations. When you are depressed, your reactive mind is full of judgments. It judges you, it judges people around you, it judges how life is treating you, and it judges your private events. When we talk about learning to use words that describe emotional experience, we are deliberately steering clear of words that judge emotional experience. Attaching to judgments is toxic because doing so can quickly trigger avoidance and escape behaviors. Plus, when you attach to negative judgments, you experience secondary emotional shock waves. Judgments trigger emotional reactions that might compound an already difficult situation for you. Therefore, it is important for you to learn to recognize the difference between simply describing an event in objective terms versus being judgmental about that event.

If you look at a vase full of flowers, you can describe what the vase looks like (its shape, texture, color, height, and so forth) and what the flowers look like (size, shape, color, whether the stems are smooth or thorny, and so on). If we ask ten people to write a description of that vase full of flowers, we would probably see a lot of consistency in the primary attributes. The aspects of situations, objects, or events that are perceptible to the senses are primary properties. They are an integral part of the event, object, or situation being described.

If we then ask the same ten people to write their impressions of this vase full of flowers, their responses would vary much more widely. Some might report that they don't like hybrid flowers, or view cut flowers as frivolous or destructive to the environment. When we unleash the judgment engine in reactive mind on even a simple object like a vase of flowers, the result will be all over the map. Descriptions of situations, events, or interactions anchor us to the ground and allow us to perceive things accurately, whereas judgments of situations, events, or interactions will send us flying off in all directions.

Here's the rub: It's impossible not to have judgments of situations, events, interactions, and so forth; that's what the reactive mind does for a living. The problem is that sometimes we can't tell the difference between a judgment and a description. This is particularly the case when what we are confronting is emotionally challenging for us. When this happens, it's extremely difficult to discriminate between what actually happened and what your reactive mind thinks happened. As Bill's case demonstrates, once this distinction is lost, depression can quickly spiral out of control. Bill got so absorbed in his judgments about the events and people in his life that he went completely off course. He became reactive rather than nonreactive, and it's very, very difficult to practice acceptance when you are in a reactive state of mind.

A term we use to describe this detached, objective stance is *witnessing*. The witness simply reports on what is seen, without elaborating on it or inserting interpretations or evaluations into testimony. The witness's job is to report only what he or she knows firsthand through direct experience—and not offer interpretations of an event. Any deviation from being completely objective makes a witness's testimony less useful in court.

So, in order to be a good witness, you must not only be a good observer but be good at using language nonjudgmentally. Your goal when you try to describe an unpleasant private experience is to stay with facts ("I'm feeling sad right now") without inserting any judgments that might negatively color the meaning of your experience ("I shouldn't be feeling sad when I have so many things to feel happy about"). This is the slippery part of learning to use words to help you understand and deal with emotionally challenging moments in life. Depending upon the words you use, you can either calm your feelings or escalate them!

OBSERVE YOUR JUDGMENTS

This exercise will help you practice making the distinction between describing things and judging things.

In this exercise you'll study an object in your environment, a person you know, and an event in your past. For each, we ask that you observe your reactive mind's tendency to be more interested in judgments than facts. When you notice this happening—for example, if you end up judging the chair you're sitting on for being too stiff to be comfortable—just say to yourself, "Thank you, mind, for giving me the evaluation that…" "Thank you, mind, for giving me the evaluation that this chair is too stiff to be comfortable." This exercise also gives you an opportunity to see similarities and differences between your reactive mind's responses to objects, people, and events.

Select an object that you want to focus your concentration on for few minutes: a teacup, a piece of furniture, a picture, a flower arrangement, anything specific. Concentrate on this object for a few minutes, focusing only on describing—not judging—the object. Write out your description of the object in the space provided in the workbook, or on any piece of paper you have to hand.

_____

_____

_____

Next, write down any judgments that may have crept in.

_____

_____

_____

Finally, thank your reactive mind for handing you each of these judgments.

Now do the same for a person—describe this person, using only descriptions; no judgments.

_____

_____

_____

What judgments are creeping in? Remember that with people, judgments may involve the person's state of mind, what you think the person thinks of you, or what you think is good or bad about that person. Write the judgments down.

_____

_____

_____

Finally, thank your reactive mind for handing you each of these judgments.

Now, bring to mind a difficult event in your life. It could be from your childhood, teenage, or adult years. Choose something that's been a problem for you in terms of the emotional reactions it triggers. Focus your mind's eye on this event until you're sure you have the image in full detail; then write your description of the actual event.

_____

_____

_____

Note any judgments that creep in as you write. These may include how the event affects you now, how it has changed your life, or evaluations of right and wrong or good and bad, such as "What I did was disgusting" or "What she said was thoughtless." Write the judgments down.

_____

_____

_____

Once again, thank your reactive mind for handing you these judgments and return to the book to complete the remainder of this exercise.

Further Exploration. What did you notice as you proceeded through this exercise? Often, reactive mind tends to insert more evaluations as the emotional stakes become higher. Setting aside your judgments about a cup is very different than setting aside your judgments about a painful personal memory. You might have noticed that you remembered your painful life event primarily in terms of judgments about it. For some people, judgments are so built in that it's actually hard to get back to the original event and describe it in factual, objective terms.

Regulate Instant Appraisals and Action Tendencies

Once you've supplied words to your experience and have freed yourself from unhelpful judgments, the next skill of emotional resilience is the ability to step back from your immediate emotional experience, pause, and describe the feeling tone of the emotion you are having. Is the emotion *pleasant, unpleasant,* or *neutral* to you when you first make contact with it? For most of us, this split-second appraisal can move us down the path of avoidance. An unpleasant feeling is likely to activate further emotional arousal in the amygdala and will trigger activation of the fight-or-flight system, whereas a positive or neutral feeling activates the calming and reward circuitry in the hippocampal and DLPFC regions of the brain. Thus, at the moment of first contact with a distressing emotional experience, we want you to first pause and be aware of any movement in the direction of pulling away from or avoiding what you've come into contact with. At that moment, pause, take a deep breath, and access the sanctuary of wise mind, where there is no need to make impulsive choices. The more deliberate you can be in just noticing your feelings, the more likely you will be able to reduce the intensity or sticking power of any urges to escape or avoid.

Emotions spur us to action, and we want you to use your emotions to help you be flexible and effective in your coping responses. An *action tendency* is an urge to act in a certain way once a certain type of emotional tone appraisal is made. Is there an emotion—sadness, helplessness, fear, anger—that you try to get the heck away from, the moment it arises? Generally, if you are unwilling to approach an unpleasant emotional experience, that avoidance will just add to the intensity and negativity of that experience. This is true for everyone, but it is a particularly important issue if you are struggling with depression. Approaching a pleasant experience is fairly easy, but even there, not pausing to regulate your action tendencies can add fuel to the fire. For example, you might go for seconds on a rich dish or a heavy dessert and later experience the results on your stressed-out digestive system! Better to savor the positive emotional experience and let it go when it ends.

WILLINGNESS: THE ALTERNATIVE TO BEHAVIORAL AVOIDANCE

In ACT, the concepts of *willingness* and *acceptance* are considered to be bedfellows. Think of willingness as choosing to enter a difficult situation instead of avoiding it. Willingness means you voluntarily face the problem intentionally and with purpose. Willingness allows you to expose yourself to what you are afraid of. Practicing acceptance is what you do when you get there.

Willingness not only involves approaching big life events, situations, or interactions that might bring you into contact with personal pain, but it also applies to how you live your daily life. There are lots of opportunities in daily living to either check out or check in. As we discussed in part 1, a big contributing factor to depression is living life on autopilot, or simply not being present and aware of what you are doing as you do it. Some of this lack of awareness comes about because we might be unwilling to feel what will show up when we slow down a bit. An opportunity could be something as simple as taking a shower in the morning or commuting to work. Because willingness and intentionality go hand in hand, it is important to identify little opportunities to show up (willingness) and take an accepting stance to whatever surfaces in awareness.

From a neuroscience perspective, the more you practice checking in, the better your brain gets at staying checked in. Alternatively, the more time you spend checked out, the better your brain gets at keeping you in an emotionally numb state. You might say that we want willingness to become a lifestyle marker. We want you to walk around—whether in the privacy of your home, at work or school, or at a public event—with an attitude of openness and curiosity toward all aspects of your experience. This intentional act will bear directly upon not only your daily levels of depression but also your sense of feeling alive inside.

WILLINGNESS, DEPRESSION, AND VITALITY DIARY

When you begin studying your willingness level in daily life, you will notice that it vacillates minute by minute. However, the realities of contemporary living make it very difficult to stay focused on such intricacies in the moment, even though doing so is an important element of vital living. Because of this, you'll need to practice some type of observation of your willingness levels on a daily basis. The daily diary form here can help you in this regard. You may wish to make copies of this blank form (or download it from http://www.newharbinger .com/38457) so you can continue to keep the diary over time.

Complete the form later in the day, perhaps after dinner, when you can reflect on the entire day to come up with your responses. You'll assess your *willingness* in the column labeled "W," your *depression* in the column labeled "D," and your *vitality* in the column labeled "V." Assess each using a 1 to 10 scale, whereby 1 means none and 10 means extremely high.

First, rate your willingness to experience unwanted and possibly distressing experiences over the course of the entire day. In the notes column, describe any factors that may have contributed to higher or lower levels of willingness. Next, rate your depression level and, again, describe any factors that pushed your depression level up or down. The third rating is the most important. Assign whatever number best reflects the extent to which you felt your activities were purposeful and meaningful during the day and, in the notes column, describe anything that contributed to a higher or lower sense of vitality. Make particular note of any spontaneous, natural moments when your willingness or vitality levels were high. At those times, what were you doing that elevated your willingness or vitality?

My Willingness, Depression, and Vitality Diary

Day	W	Notes	D	Notes	V	Notes
1						
2						
3						
4						
5						
6						
7						

W = Willingness (1–10), D = Depression (1–10), V = Vitality (1–10)

Further Exploration. Did you see one or more relationships between your daily willingness level, depression level, and sense of vitality? Did your willingness and vitality ratings fluctuate day to day? That's typical when you first start experimenting with willingness. Being willing takes daily practice, focus, and persistence to master. What occurrences seemed to spark higher levels of willingness and vitality? What factors decreased your willingness level? When you notice factors that drive your willingness down, you might consider putting together a new willingness and acceptance plan to use when those factors are at play.

To give you a sense of how this daily practice played out for someone else, let's take a look at Bill's responses. This will show you how much information can be gleaned from doing this exercise in earnest for just one week.

Bill's Willingness, Depression, and Vitality Diary

Day	W	Notes	D	Notes	V	Notes
1	1	Many doubts, pain was real bad, was down on myself	10	On the couch most of day	3	Reviewed my values, read from a book of poems and the Bible
2	3	Thought about what I could do even with pain	7	Outside for a while in a.m. and p.m., helped to be in sunshine	4	Read more poems, wrote one, offered to garden with wife
3	4	Wrote more on values	7	Decided I would go to pain class	4	Told wife and kids about class
4	5	Shared values about family with kids and wife	6	Class supportive of me, told me they'd be there	5	Told wife about class and asked her to help me keep moving
5	4	More pain, angry at life and doctors for screwing me up	8	Mostly watched TV all day, bored and feeling life is going nowhere	3	Trying not to think about pain, trying to be positive
6	8	Decided to plan day with walking, activity, and getting out	2	Outside a.m. and p.m., called a friend	7	I can choose where I want to go in life; I'm not a prisoner
7	9	Called someone from class for coffee, invited wife to a movie	2	Outside a.m. and p.m., less pain meds needed, felt I belonged	8	Long embrace with wife, had the thought that I can do this

As you can see from Bill's diary, his ratings of willingness, depression, and life vitality tend to dance together in certain patterns. As his willingness goes up, his depression tends to go down and his sense of vitality tends to goes up. Although the overall trend is for the better, Bill's diary does show a day when his willingness level goes down and his depression goes up. This is common, and occasional setbacks are inevitable. To Bill's credit, he doesn't stop trying, and he uses his experience to figure out effective strategies to restore his willingness.

Bill's Journey Toward a Vital Life

After he had practiced emotional acceptance and willingness for a few weeks, Bill noticed that he enjoyed social connections with his classmates and that his pain levels seemed to decrease when he was focused on others in the pain class. He was surprised to find that he could go to a movie and sit through the whole thing without a pain episode of huge proportions afterward, as had always happened to him in the early years of his chronic pain problem. He realized that he had previously gone to the movies alone; he wondered if the difference this time was his willingness to go with his wife and experience pain in order to do something positive for their relationship. Bill began to plan daily activities that would engage his attention in the areas of his life that he wanted to build, including spending more quality time with his children—all in service of moving toward his values and his true north. He found that he could go to the park with them if he did it at the start of the day. He could then rest strategically to restore his physical strength.

Bill began stretching regularly a couple of times each day to help manage his pain, even while accepting the fact that he would probably experience pain for the rest of his life. He still struggled occasionally with anger about his fate, particularly on days when his pain flared up. However, he stuck with his planned activities even when he was in pain. His relationship with his wife improved to the point that she told him he was like a new person. Bill was on the pathway out of depression!

BRAIN TRAINING EMOTIONAL ACCEPTANCE

Here are some brief, powerful brain training exercises that will strengthen your emotional acceptance skills. Try to integrate one or more of these exercises into your daily routine for maximum success! You can download all the worksheets and forms in this section at http://www.newharbinger.com/38457.

BUFF UP YOUR EMOTIONAL VOCABULARY

The more emotion words you have at your disposal, the better! Get ready to bone up your vocabulary with the list of emotion words that follows. The goal for the next three weeks is to learn and use *three* of these words each day. To reach your goal, we recommend that you use each word at least one time to describe some type of direct experience you are having.

For example, you could pick the words "frustrated," "curious," and "shy" as the emotion words of the day. During the day, you will try to use those words either together or separately to describe some type of experience you are having at work, at home, at school, or when you are on your own. If you follow this simple exercise, at the end of three weeks you will have used *over sixty* different words to describe and deal with stress-related emotions. This will make a huge difference in how you experience stress. You will notice a difference in how you understand and relate to emotions. This doesn't mean you won't have stress; it just means that you will be able to describe emotions more accurately and control urges to engage in escape or avoidance behaviors.

Emotion Words

Abandoned	Dejected	Mistrustful
Accepting	Demoralized	Passionate
Afraid	Detached	Peaceful
Agitated	Disappointed	Prejudiced
Amicable	Empathic	Restful
Angry	Frustrated	Righteous
Anxious	Guilty	Sad
Apprehensive	Harmonious	Safer
Ashamed	Hostile	Satisfied
Benevolent	Laid Back	Serene
Blaming	Let Down	Skeptical
Blissful	Impatient	Suspicious
Blue	Irritable	Tranquil
Bored	Kind	Transcendent
Calm	Lonely	Unconcerned
Caring	Loving	Vengeful
Compassionate	Melancholy	Victimized
Connected	Mellow	Warmhearted

TESTING YOUR EMOTIONAL WATERS

This exercise will allow you to better differentiate your emotions in response to everyday events that trigger them. You might think of these triggering situations as daily hassles. When you have a powerful emotional experience during the day, take time to dissect the situation, your emotions, your feeling tone appraisal, and your action tendencies. Note that this exercise can be used to dissect any situation that triggers an emotional experience, be it positive, negative, or neutral. We certainly have "helping" moments in our daily experience, and they may trigger positive emotional experience, just as "hassle" moments trigger negative emotions.

To start, first describe the triggering situation using the witness perspective. Next, check for your feeling tone appraisal. Notice cues in your body along with various mental experiences in your mind. Record the feeling tone: Pleasant, Unpleasant, or Neutral. Continue to notice your mind and body, and detect your action tendency: Approach, Ignore, Avoid. Record this and then move on to categorize your emotional experience: Are you Sad, Mad, Anxious, Fearful, Guilty, Happy, Excited, or another emotion?

Worksheet for Processing Emotions

Triggering Situation (Describe using Witness Perspective)	Emotion (Sad Mad Anxious Fearful Guilty Happy Excited Other)	Feeling Tone Appraisal (Pleasant Unpleasant Neutral)	Action Tendency (Approach Ignore Avoid)

EVALUATIONS GONE WILD

Practicing acceptance is all about creating flexibility in how you adapt to stressful situations. This exercise helps you become more familiar with the evaluations your mind tries to inject into stressful situations. When these evaluations go undetected, your responses may be more rigid and rule based. As we discussed in the NeuroNotes section in this chapter, descriptions and evaluations produce dramatically different results at the brain circuitry level, so it is very important that you develop your ability to distinguish between these.

To practice this, select a few triggering situations. Describe each one in the first column using the witness perspective. In the next column, challenge yourself to use objective descriptions about your experience in each triggering situation ("The noise was loud; I covered my ears"). Finally, write a brief description of the triggering situation using a judgmental perspective. Don't hold back! Let your mind's evaluative functions run wild ("The noise was noxious; I hated it and it nearly killed me to be near it").

Sample Evaluations Gone Wild Worksheet

Triggering Situation (using Witness Perspective)	Objective Descriptions of Your Experience	Evaluations Gone Wild

Further Exploration. How did you do in contrasting witness-level descriptions of events with an unfettered evaluative approach? Some people actually have more trouble with the objective-level description because their reactive mind is already loaded up with judgments that flow quite easily. And it's okay to have a little fun with those evaluations and make them as outlandish as possible. It'll help you build your evaluation-detection muscles so that you can accept evaluations when they appear, use them if they are helpful, and let them go if they are not, with a little smile.

OPEN AND FREE TARGETS

If the only inner or outer experiences we had to accept and make room for were mild in tone, it wouldn't cuase much stress to practice holding still and just letting these experiences show up. The unfortunate reality is that many of our inner experiences are so emotionally loaded that we struggle with them when they show up. This exercise is designed to strengthen your acceptance skills by teaching you how to lean into emotionally loaded experiences, and then release them.

To begin, on the blank lines below write down the things that you are currently struggling with in your life. This might include painful memories, negative self-judgments, thoughts about relationships problems, worries about the future, and so forth.

Open and Free Targets

1. _____

2. _____

3. _____

4. _____

When you have completed your list, lie down in a comfortable place, close your eyes, and take several deep cleansing breaths. You probably won't have much difficulty recalling items from your Open and Free Targets list! As you do, on the in-breath, silently say the word "open" and fully inhale that painful inner experience. On the out-breath, say the word "free" and fully exhale and release resistance. You are literally freeing yourself to be in the presence of this painful inner experience without struggle or evaluation. Repeat this process as many times as you need to with each particular item, until you can fully inhale your pain; then release yourself into a state of emotional acceptance.

Further Exploration. How did you do with allowing yourself to be open to and accepting of your painful inner experiences? Did you notice that some were harder to lean into? Perhaps you had more difficulty freeing yourself from certain ones? If you noticed that you got tricked into struggling with an inner experience, were you able to notice that you were struggling and return back to freeing yourself on the out-breath?

The ability to reestablish an accepting stance when you notice you are struggling is an important skill to cultivate, because we all get entangled in certain inner experiences more so than others. As you work your way through the rest of part 2, feel free to come back and repeat this exercise to see how your mindfulness muscles are developing!

IDEAS TO CULTIVATE

- One of the more difficult aspects of living a values-driven life is learning what can and cannot be changed.

- Things that can't be changed must be accepted.

- For the most part, you can't directly control internal events, like spontaneous feelings, thoughts, images, and physical sensations; you also can't control your personal history or the actions and attitudes of other people.

- Emotional resilience supports acceptance and involves being able to use words to describe and understand your experiences, without judging them.

- Willingness supports acceptance and involves voluntarily approaching situations, events, or interactions that might trigger unpleasant, unwanted emotions.

- Every day, there is a powerful relationship between willingness, depression, and vitality. The more you practice willingness in your daily life, the more vital and purposeful your life will be.

- When you practice acceptance, build emotional resilience, and make willingness moves in the service of your values, depression becomes a thing of the past.

CHAPTER 8

Step 4: Detach and Let Go

Detachment is not that you should own nothing, but that nothing should own you.

—Ali ibn Abi Talib

Depressed people tend to live in their heads. Detaching from painful private experiences is a powerful way to quickly regulate your emotions. There is a unique neural pathway in the brain that allows you to let go and stop the struggle with distressing, unwanted mental events. By practicing this key mindfulness skill on a daily basis, you can train your brain to be like Teflon. You make contact with a painful experience, but it doesn't stick to you!

In chapter 7, we introduced an alternative to the toxic, self-defeating strategies of emotional and behavioral avoidance: to accept rather than resist and struggle with inner and outer experiences that you cannot change. And acceptance of things that cannot be changed requires you to practice emotional resilience skills and to be willing to step into harm's way, figuratively speaking.

In this chapter, we move on to the fourth step on your quest to transcend depression and create a life worth living. This step is to practice *detachment*, another key mindfulness skill. Detachment involves the ability to adopt a nonreactive, disengaged stance with respect to your inner experiences. In doing so, detachment helps you avoid attaching to and overidentifying with the negative content of distressing thoughts, feelings, memories, or physical sensations. For example, let's say a friend calls to invite you to a party where there will be lots of people whom you've never met. You might notice the thought "I am such a loser; I will never find anyone who will want to be with me." You could fuse with this self-evaluation, treat it as an undisputed truth about yourself, and behave accordingly. You likely would end up making an excuse for why you can't go to the party even though you would like to make more friends.

Alternatively, you could practice detachment: just recognize you had the thought "I am such a loser; I will never find anyone who will want to be with me" and choose *not* to engage with it at the level of belief or disbelief. In other words, with detachment you neither identify with nor attach to the thought. You simply let go of the need to determine whether the thought is true or false.

You can see how important acceptance and emotional resilience are in allowing you to get to the point of detachment. You have to be willing to let this type of thought stay in your awareness without struggling to control or eliminate it. To do this, try to describe what has shown up in objective, non-judgmental terms ("I just had the thought that I am a loser and no one will ever want to be with me"), and curb your instant action tendencies ("I'm just going to sit here and allow this thought to be present rather than running from it").

The next task is to release yourself from any sense of belief in or ownership of the content of the message. Yes, the message is emotionally provocative—if you let yourself get hooked by it—but the objective is to consciously let go of any need to do anything about it. At the level of detachment, this is just a thought—nothing less, nothing more. You have bigger fish to fry in life than to get into a struggle with your reactive mind about whether you are a loser. And besides, your reactive mind has no real ability to determine your value as a person. Therefore, the message is not relevant to you. At best, it is just a distraction that is best left untouched.

In this chapter, we'll show you how to practice detachment even while your reactive mind is trying to get you to attach. This is one of the fundamental challenges you—and all of us, for that matter—will face on the journey to a vital life. To achieve this important outcome, we will teach you a new method for labeling different types of private experiences, so you can both recognize and detach from them, if needed. We will take you through a variety of self-guided brain training exercises that will strengthen your detachment muscle. Our goal is to help you develop a new relationship with your reactive mind so that you can live in the present moment, experiment with new behaviors, and attain a better quality of life.

DETACHMENT AND THE SANCTUARY OF WISE MIND

Detachment amplifies the availability of simple awareness and the influence of wise mind by creating greater *space* between you and the products of reactive mind. This makes you less likely to immediately react in ways that are counterproductive. Detachment gives you the precious time you need to connect with what matters to you in the moment, weigh your options, and eventually take action. You are then in the perfect position to act according to your values. People who live according to their values might encounter painful moments in life, but taking an accepting, detached stance turns their pain from something that is toxic and depressing into something that promotes healing and personal growth.

Although the idea of adopting an open, curious, and detached stance sounds simple in theory, it's difficult in reality. The reactive mind is not designed to promote detachment. Instead, it promotes attachment! It tries to control your attention, looks for problems, prefers evaluative thinking, and generates rules to guide your behavior. Although your mind is very useful in helping you address challenges and problems in the external world, it can be the cause of enormous struggle and suffering when applied to your inner world. In fact, your mind may be your worst enemy when it comes to addressing personal problems and dealing with personal pain. Thus, you might enter a situation with the intention of using detachment only to discover that you've been pulled back into overidentifying with your reactive mind, arguing with it to get it to change the messages it is giving you, or just trying to avoid dealing with it altogether.

For example, you might have a dream of going back to college or vocational school to get enough education or training to pursue a different career because you don't really like your current job. The last time you tried to go to school while working, you had trouble keeping up with your studies. Putting yourself back in that situation means you must risk failing again.

If you're depressed, your reactive mind will likely try to convince you to attach to the idea of playing it safe and not going to school. If you follow your reactive mind's advice, you'll end up living in a way that isn't consistent with your values. Yes, you avoid the possibility of failure, but in doing so you also relinquish control over your valued life direction. When you can't detach from your reactive mind, it's hard to respond in a flexible, values-based way.

In general, problems with detachment and problems with depression tend to go hand in hand, because the depressed reactive mind is full of well-worn negative messages about your past problems, your current flaws, and your soon-to-be unhappy future. When you become overidentified with this negative weather system, it will be very hard indeed to see the clear blue sky of wise mind awareness.

NEURONOTES: DETACHMENT IS A POWERFUL EMOTION REGULATION STRATEGY

Detachment is one of two ways people regulate powerful, distressing emotional states, according to recent neuroscience research. The other method is *cognitive appraisal*—which happens to be what psychologists have traditionally used to treat depression. Interestingly, these two methods are housed in distinctly different neural pathways.

Detachment recruits neural pathways that have been implicated in the operation of the executive control network. As we explained before, this area of the brain is directly involved in and strengthened by mindfulness practices of almost any type (Brewer et al. 2011). Detachment is regarded as an "early stage" emotion regulation system, meaning that it acts quickly and consumes relatively few brain resources. It appears that, once you learn how to do it, detachment works quicker to calm you down and leaves you with lots of leftover energy to direct toward effective problem-solving actions. Interestingly, two recent studies have shown that detachment is even more effective than cognitive appraisal in helping us deal with intense and negative emotional states (Shiota and Levenson 2012; Sheppes, Brady, and Sampson 2014; Shafir et al. 2016). Thus, strengthening the detachment circuits of your brain will make you more flexible and effective in emotionally charged and challenging life situations.

In contrast to detachment, cognitive appraisal basically involves "talking yourself down" by changing your evaluations about both the situation and the emotion that it is generating. Several traditional behavioral treatments for depression are deeply rooted in this strategy of teaching people to challenge their depressive thoughts in order to help them better control their emotions. Cognitive appraisal recruits the brain's "left sided," or verbal, semantic processing resources (Shafir et al. 2016). It is considered to be a "late stage" emotion regulation system, meaning that talking yourself down takes longer to work and consumes more brain resources.

STICKY THOUGHTS

There are certain kinds of private experiences that are harder to detach from than others. In general, the more inflammatory the thought, the more powerful the emotional experience, or the more distressing and intrusive the memory, the harder it is to practice detachment. The term we use for these higher-level provocations of reactive mind is *sticky thoughts*. These are distressing, unwanted experiences that tend to stick to you, meaning that they're difficult to let go of and detach from.

To better illustrate this concept, let's use the example of a form of identity theft known as phishing. Phishing is a practice employed by identity thieves to steal sensitive personal information over the Internet. When you are being phished, you receive an e-mail that presents you with highly distressing personal news ("We have reason to believe that your credit card has been used by someone else"). Along with this news is a request that you provide personal information. Your reactive mind instantly will evaluate this new information and produce a threat message ("You better do something right now or the thief will drain your bank account!"). You will experience a powerful emotional response in the moment (fear, anxiety). Maybe you've had your credit card information stolen before and remember what a pain in the behind it was to deal with; this memory will add to your emotional arousal. You might start to experience symptoms like heartburn and indigestion because of the stress of it all. This will add even more fuel to the emotions of the moment. The main psychological tactic in phishing is to get you to overidentify with a powerful emotional state that will make you act impulsively.

Like the Internet, your mind is a hugely positive addition to your bag of tools as a human being. A lot of what your mind gives you is instantly useful for your survival, like when it tells you to wait for a car to pass before crossing the street. If you ignore that kind of intelligence, you're going to live a very short life. This is the tricky thing about having a mind. In many real-life situations, it is important to listen to it and follow its advice, sometimes without taking the time to analyze what it's doing.

But reactive mind can operate as the Internet scammer does, sending you messages that put you in distress so you respond automatically. These sticky thoughts can be thoughts, feelings, memories, or physical sensations that lure you into a state of attachment (fusion). Usually, these kinds of experiences are potent and negative in tone, and they get you to impulsively attach to them. When you get attached to them, you may end up taking the path of aviodance that leads you away from rather than toward the things that matter to you. In the case of phishing, you might respond to the e-mail by divulging important personal information—the very thing you were hoping to avoid!

Rumination (discussed in chapter 1) is a common problem for depressed people and is a good example of how sticky thoughts work. Ruminating thoughts come from reactive mind, generally in the following order, with these messages:

1. Because you're depressed, you aren't like everyone else.

2. You should prove you're normal by consciously changing from a depressed state to a happy state—and you have the capacity to do this!

3. There must be something terribly wrong with you if you're unable to control your mood through willpower. You need to analyze where all of this personal weakness comes from.

Do these messages from reactive mind sound familiar? We all experience these self-demeaning messages from time to time, and it is easy to become overidentified with them and have them influence our behavior in ways that don't work in the long run. It will be useful to examine the mental quality of sticky thoughts in more detail so that you get better at noticing them quickly when they show up.

Qualities of Sticky Thoughts

When sticky thoughts come along, detachment is an important tool to have under your belt. Here's how it works: First, being detached allows you to step back, observe what's happening, and avoid the tendency to jump in impulsively. Then you can examine the message you've received for signs that it might be bogus. What are those signs? Here are some examples:

- Your mind is giving you a negative message about who you are as a person: "I'm a loser." "I'm fat and ugly." "I'm unlovable." "I'm defective in some basic way."

- Your mind tells you what you can and can't afford to think, feel, remember, or sense: "I can't be angry at my spouse if I want us to remain close." "I can't allow myself to think about my childhood if I want to be happy." "I shouldn't think about addressing my own needs at home because that would be selfish."

- Your mind predicts what will happen if you take a step to approach and solve a personal problem: "My kids will hate me if I punish them." "I'll get demoted or fired if I bring this concern to my supervisor." "I'll come out on the bottom end of this argument with my friend just like the last time I tried."

■ Your mind tries to compare how you're doing in life right now with how you should be doing: "With all the good things I've got in my life, I should be happier than I am." "I've wasted a lot of my life struggling with my feelings and still don't feel good." "I'm going nowhere with my career and have wasted my potential."

■ Your mind compares how you're doing in life to how other people are doing in their lives: "Other people don't seem to be depressed all the time, so why am I?" "Everyone else seems to have a direction in their life, so why don't I?" "Relationships seem to be easier for other people than they are for me."

■ Your mind focuses on mistakes you've made in the past as proof that you'll never have a meaningful life: "I can't ever forgive myself for giving my two children up to my ex-wife." "I stayed too long with my abusive husband and have been permanently damaged as far as ever finding a new life partner." "I can never forgive myself for being an active alcoholic for ten years."

■ Your mind insists that other people can tell how badly you're doing and that you shouldn't use them for support: "If I go to the party, other people will be able to tell I'm depressed." "I shouldn't go visit my friends and burden them with my problems." "It's humiliating to go to church and have everyone see how unhappy I am."

Each of these sticky messages has a set of qualities you should learn to recognize. First, the message tends to come in black-and-white terms, is negative, and is extremely provocative. Second, sticky messages encourage you to avoid dealing with your private experiences or the real-life situations that trigger them. Third, and most deadly, sticky messages come in the form of "I" statements, creating the impression that you are declaring these to be indisputable truths.

However, this is actually your reactive mind speaking to you. But when you *attach* to the message, you lose the distinction between you and your reactive mind. This is precisely what being detached allows you to avoid, because you are most likely to do what your reactive mind says when you can't distinguish where the sticky message is coming from. Unfortunately, when you're being bombarded with sticky thoughts, the distinction between you and your mind can become very unclear and will often disappear altogether. It will be helpful for you to identify some of your reactive mind's favorite sticky thoughts; this will make it easier for you to see them, even in murky situations.

IDENTIFY YOUR STICKY THOUGHTS

Take some time to think about past and present situations in which your reactive mind may have tricked you into attaching to a sticky thought. You might want to go back to the Open and Free exercise in chapter 8 and see if some high-level sticky-thoughts showed up that you could carry forward to this exercise. Write down each of these destructive messages as accurately as you can. Leave the nickname column blank for now; we'll return to it later in a few moments.

My Sticky Thoughts Worksheet

	Nickname:
My negative personal qualities and shortcomings: _____ _____ _____	Nickname:
What I should be thinking, feeling, or remembering: _____ _____ _____	Nickname:
What will happen if I try to address a painful personal problem: _____ _____ _____	Nickname:
Comparing how I'm feeling right now to how I should be feeling: _____ _____ _____	Nickname:

The Mindfulness & Acceptance Workbook for Depression

How other people are doing in their lives compared with how I'm doing: _____ _____ _____	Nickname:
Personal mistakes I've made and how they'll affect my future: _____ _____ _____	Nickname:
What other people think about me and my issues: _____ _____ _____	Nickname:
Seeking help for my problems from a spouse, partner, or friends: _____ _____ _____	Nickname:

Further Exploration. What did you discover as you worked through this exercise? Did certain themes reappear in various categories? Did you sometimes argue with yourself that certain sticky thoughts might represent the truth? This is what sticky thoughts do; they get you to swallow them, and then you're forced to struggle with them once you've been hooked. The more you struggle, the deeper the hook sets.

NICKNAMES

Part of taking a detached, accepting stance is learning to turn around and "embrace" what you are afraid of or resistant to. One way to do this is to give your sticky thoughts a nickname, as you may have done for your

168

reactive mind. Just as we use a nickname to highlight some core quality of a person we know, applying nicknames to feared or avoided experiences allows us to relate to those experiences differently. You will notice that a nickname provides some mental space between you and the thoughts, feelings, memories, or sensations you might be tempted to attach yourself to. Because they are often exaggerated terms that can actually be quite humorous, nicknames can provide some perspective on your private experiences.

When you notice that a sticky thought has shown up, you can welcome it by greeting it with its nickname. For example, a nickname for the thought "I'm never going to measure up to others because my mother beat me and my dad was an alcoholic" might be *Wack-a-mo*. Be creative as you assign your nicknames, and try to have some fun with it. Lightheartedness and humor are excellent remedies when you're in the presence of sticky thoughts.

Now, go back to your Sticky Thoughts worksheet and give each of your sticky thoughts a nickname in the right-hand column. We are going to have you use these nicknames again in the future, so take some time playing around with generating good ones!

HELEN'S STORY

Helen is a single, twenty-seven-year-old woman who lives by herself. Her mother died when she was thirteen, and she spent the remainder of her adolescence living with her father, who worked as a car salesman and had a problem with drinking. After his second wife died, he became more irritable and tended to isolate himself at home. When Helen began to gain weight at age sixteen, her father ridiculed her, often in front of family friends. He would tell her to get out and exercise like everyone else and stop eating everything in sight. Even when Helen dieted and lost some weight, he would still say things that had a critical edge: for example, that she was "built solid" and "looked stocky." Helen started to experience symptoms of depression at that time, and her struggles continue today.

Because her high school grades weren't high, Helen decided she wasn't smart enough to go on to college. She had a couple of intimate relationships in her early twenties, one with a man and one with a woman. Her male boyfriend was verbally abusive and made negative remarks about her physical appearance on more than one occasion. She had a much better experience with her female girlfriend, but Helen struggled with her sexual identity and left the relationship rather than come out to her father, other relatives, and friends. She hasn't dated in the past few years, although she has made several furtive attempts to contact other women on Internet dating sites.

Helen works as a bank teller and likes the job but is concerned that there aren't very many prospects for job growth. When Helen completed the Sticky Thoughts exercise, she made some interesting discoveries about the kinds of messages that she had trouble detaching from.

Helen's Sticky Thoughts Worksheet

My negative personal qualities and shortcomings: The hardest one for me to handle is that I'm fat and not worth much. I also get hooked on the idea that I'm not very smart. Most painful is my preference for a female partner and my being such a coward about pursuing this. I have to battle these messages all the time.	Nickname: Twinkle Toes
What I should be thinking, feeling, or remembering: I really get shaken up when something triggers memories of my childhood, especially when my mother died and all the things my father said. I try really hard to stay positive and not let myself go back there. When I fall into this pity pot, I can still see my drunk dad looking at me in disgust. I even hear his voice saying that I'm fat.	Nickname: Good Ole Dad
What will happen if I try to address a painful personal problem: Secretly, the thing I want most in life is to have a female partner who loves me for who I am. When I think about dating someone, I get hooked on the idea that either I want to be able to be proud of our relationship and take it public, or I'll be rejected or rejecting if I don't. These thoughts seem completely true and scare me to death.	Nickname: Only the Lonely (sung aloud!)
Comparing how I'm feeling right now to how I should be feeling: I get hooked on the idea that I should be confident. If I were confident, I'd have a partner and maybe even a child by now. I'm terrified of pursuing this—even just asking someone for a date gives me a knot in my stomach.	Nickname: Chicken Little
How other people are doing in their lives compared with how I'm doing: Many lesbians develop solid relationships and go on to have children and raise them in a healthy, caring environment. I don't even go to a gym or try to get in shape.	Nickname: 10th Place Wonder
Personal mistakes I've made and how they'll affect my future: I should never have left my female lover; she was kind and I just couldn't handle it. I really hurt her, and whatever comes my way I deserve it. I also haven't cared enough about my looks or, back in high school, about my grades. And one more mistake is thinking that my mother's death was somehow my fault.	Nickname: The Dis-Appointer
What other people think about me and my issues: I try not to think about this, but I guess I mostly think they think I'm sort of pitiful, like overweight and lonely.	Nickname: Only the Lonely (works here too)
Seeking help for my problems from a spouse, partner, or friends: I don't have very many sticky thoughts about this. I guess mostly just: play it safe and seek comfort in food and Internet movies.	Nickname: Chocolate Cake

Helen's responses are pretty typical of a person who's being bombarded by sticky thoughts on multiple levels. Her reactive mind presents her with gloomy predictions about her future, and as she attaches to them, she begins to experience a wide range of negative feelings, sensations, and memories. On a positive note, Helen seems to be able to see at least the dark humor in her situation, reflected in some of her edgy, satirical nicknames. Her use of the opening phrase of the song "Only the Lonely" is another example of how to completely change your relationship to a group of sticky thoughts: You can sing the thought out loud to any song you want, like the Happy Birthday song. Remember: Being able to step back and see the humor or irony of a difficult situation promotes a different way of relating to it.

PUT REACTIVE MIND IN A TIME-OUT

At times, your reactive mind can be like a child throwing a tantrum. First it gives you a sticky thought or two to get you to pay attention to it. Then, when you pay attention to it, it gives you more of that sticky thought. Your attention fuels the sticky thought, just like a parent who attempts to argue with, threaten, or persuade a child throwing a tantrum only rewards the child's behavior. This is why you might have noticed that you bounce from one negative thought, feeling, memory, or sensation to another when you're in a downward depressive spiral.

So what's the antidote for this negative cycle? When a parent responds to a child's temper tantrum, it's best to avoid a test of wills and to simply notice, maintain a sense of calm, and ensure that the child is safe. Taking a time-out allows both the child and the parent to calm him- or herself so that the parent will be less likely to act out of anger or frustration if the tantrum starts again. In this detached state, parents are still very aware of the child—and the stance is one of acceptance and kindness.

The same principles apply to dealing with the antics of reactive mind. When things go over the top, you can put your reactive mind in a time-out. As the human in the situation, you'll be aware that your mind is still blabbering at you a mile a minute (just as a child in a time-out may get a little louder for a few minutes). And while noticing this, you are able to engage in actions that are workable.

As an example, suppose you're in a disagreement with a partner over the lack of intimacy you're experiencing in the relationship. Your reactive mind gives you the sticky thought that, given all your personal defects, you're lucky to have any relationship at all. Then it threatens you with another sticky thought: that your partner will leave you if you don't quit making these unreasonable demands. Another sticky thought shows up in neon lights: if your partner leaves, you'll never have another relationship because you're ugly and unlovable.

In the midst of a tantrum of your reactive mind, you can practice detachment: pull back, create some perspective, refocus on your values about intimacy, and, when ready, assert what you want as firmly and respectfully as you can. In this example, your job is to avoid reinforcing your mind's tantrum and to take a time-out with it while the intensity of the moment subsides. The next few exercises will teach you some practical strategies to help you establish a time-out with your mind when it's throwing a tantrum.

RAILROAD CROSSING

You've probably had the experience of stopping at a railroad crossing to wait for a train to pass. Next time this happens, notice what you do. Most people fix their attention on a single car, follow it partway across their field of vision, and then drop their gaze and shift their attention back to a newly arriving car. What prompts you to give your attention to a particular car? It could be the shape or color of the car, or perhaps something printed on the side of the car draws your eye toward it. Maybe it's simply that the car looks different from those around it. When watching a train, most people just watch the cars pass by without getting locked in on a particular car.

In the exercise that follows, think of your thoughts, feelings, memories, and physical sensations as railroad cars on a train moving in front of your mind's eye. Your job is to let each railroad car pass in front of you, staying detached from the thought, feeling, memory, or sensation the railroad car carries. This exercise will help you practice the skill of just noticing the contents of your mind—being aware of mental events without becoming fused with them.

Go to a quiet place and read the following instructions. Then take a few deep breaths and allow yourself to ease into the suggested experience. Or, even better, download the audio version at http://www.newhar binger.com/38457 and just put yourself into it!

Imagine that your car is first in line at a railroad crossing and a long train is traveling very slowly in front of you. Since you're right in front of the train, it's really the only thing you can see. It's dusk and you're on your way home. You're in no hurry.

Now, imagine that the boxcars of this train are unique. They have large whiteboards on their sides that invite you to write a message. The messages you write on the whiteboards can be thoughts, feelings, memories, or sensations that you experience as you watch. They can be images that your mind offers up. When you notice any type of mental event, take it and place it on the boxcar in front of you.

Let each mental event go with the boxcar as it moves on down the track. Notice each mental experience your mind offers, and place it on the whiteboard on the next boxcar. If you notice that you're no longer watching the cars and putting mental events on the whiteboards, simply notice that you left the exercise and bring yourself back to the railroad crossing. Continue for the next five minutes, bringing your attention back to the railroad crossing as needed. When you hear the bell, return to the book to complete the remainder of this exercise.

Further Exploration. What did you notice when you tried this exercise? Most people have trouble staying with the task of simply observing mental events. Did you have a thought like, "I'm not doing this task right" or "I'm trying to put mental events on the cars, but they won't go on"? The trick is to take *those* thoughts and put them on boxcars, too, allowing them to be there and pass by just like your other experiences. Were there certain thoughts, feelings, memories, or sensations that totally drew you out of the posture of just noticing? That's what happens when your mind phishes you. When you fuse with a private event, such as a thought, memory, or feeling, you lose the observer perspective and are prone to act automatically—and often in ways that defeat your best interests.

DOWN THE TRACK

This exercise builds on the previous one and is a little more challenging. Go back to your Sticky Thoughts worksheet and write each nickname on a separate slip of paper. Now, as in the Railroad Crossing exercise, go to a quiet place, get centered, and read the following instructions (or listen to the audio version).

You are taking your time and simply watching the same slowly moving train. Now reach down and pick up a nickname. Let yourself generate the thought, feeling, memory, sensation, or image that goes with that nickname. Now place it on the boxcar in your mind. Look at it on the side of the boxcar and simply allow the boxcar to move on in its own time. The train may stop briefly and then resume a more regular pace. Respect the pace of the train and just notice it as it is; don't try to control it.

Then pick up the next sticky thought and do the same thing. If you start to experience a negative emotion, thought, memory, or sensation, simply put that experience on the next boxcar and watch it move down the tracks. Continue in this fashion until you've placed all of your sticky thoughts on the train. If you notice you're getting hooked by some other content provided by your mind, simply put it on the train as well. Just watch the train, stay in your car, and remember that your destination in life is different than the train's destination.

Further Exploration. Did you notice any difference in the degree of difficulty between these two exercises? Was it harder to put certain sticky thoughts on the boxcars? In this exercise, your reactive mind might have started a tantrum, causing you to lose sight of the task of remaining detached. Did you get lost in your own mental activity? Were you sometimes tempted to just give up?

Most people report getting drawn out of this exercise over and over again, so if that happened to you don't beat yourself up about it. Just let it serve to underscore the importance of a daily practice of exercises designed to strengthen your detachment skills. This and other types of mindfulness exercises will help you strengthen the ability to make the distinction between you and your mind. This allows you to voluntarily withdraw from an attachment when you recognize that your mind is phishing you. By the way, you'll use the index cards with the nicknames for your sticky thoughts in the next chapter, so store them somewhere you can easily find them again.

THANK YOUR MIND

Since you can't keep your mind from thinking, feeling, remembering, and sensing, learning how to distance yourself from your mind when it's provoking you is important. Our experience is that expressing gratitude to your mind—out loud—for the intelligence it is giving you is one sure way to create a more workable relationship between you and your mind. This allows you to respond in a voluntary, intentional way to your reactive mind, rather than falling for the content of sticky thoughts. This strategy also requires you to do some more naming.

Here's how it works: When you notice an unpleasant mental event unfolding, simply say "Thank you, mind, for giving me the [thought, feeling, memory, sensation] called [describe the sticky thought]." Try to get in the habit of doing this any time your reactive mind gives you a sticky thought of any kind. In Helen's case, she thanked her mind in the following ways:

- *Thank you, mind, for giving me the thought called fat, ugly girl.*

- *Thank you, mind, for giving me the thought called you come from a messed-up past.*

- *Thank you, mind, for giving me the memory called my drunk dad tells me I'm disgusting.*

- *Thank you, mind, for giving me the feelings called sad and scared.*

- *Thank you, mind, for giving me the thought about being a coward.*

- *Thank you, mind, for giving me the feeling called loneliness.*

By simply describing sticky thoughts and creating nicknames for them, you're building skills that will allow you to relate to your reactive mind in a different way. You don't have to mindlessly follow what your mind tells you to do. You are the human being; the mind is at your service, not vice versa. Learning to hold that detached posture when your reactive mind is yakking at you is an essential step toward moving through depression and reclaiming your life.

BRAIN TRAINING TO STRENGTHEN DETACHMENT

As the neuroscience clearly suggests, there are distinctive neural pathways in your brain that help foster and strengthen your ability to be detached when you need to. In addition, it does appear that detachment is a superquick, powerful way to regulate the activity level of reactive mind. You don't have to run from the chatter of your reactive mind; you can detach from it instead! In this section, we offer several brief exercises to do at home that will quickly strengthen your abilities to remain detached, even in emotionally charged situations.

CLOUDS IN THE SKY

This is a classic exercise that is used to help people learn to keep a clear mind while meditating. It is somewhat like the Railroad Crossing exercise in that you practice observing and then detaching from thoughts, feelings, memories, or sensations as they appear in your mind's eye. We recommend listening to the guided version of this exercise, as it will be a more enjoyable learning experience for you.

Imagine that you are lying on the grass on a warm spring day, looking up at the sky. As you watch the sky, different kinds of clouds appear and slowly move across from one horizon to the other. As you watch the clouds, notice any thoughts, feelings, memories, or sensations that come into your awareness. Each time you notice something, take it and put it on a cloud. If you have a feeling, put it on a cloud and watch it drift across the sky. Don't try to make the clouds move; just let them do what clouds do. Each time something appears in awareness, hold it softly and place it on another cloud. If you notice yourself getting attached to a cloud, or you are following it too closely, just release yourself from the need to do anything other than look for inner experiences and put them on clouds. Keep doing this for at least 5 minutes—or longer if you enjoy the sensation of letting inner experiences float across the sky of your awareness.

Further Exploration. How did you do at putting various thoughts, feelings, memories, or sensations on clouds? Did you find it easier to do this with some mental events than others? Did something come into awareness that pulled you out of the exercise altogether? None of these occurrences are unusual, because it is hard to keep a detached posture in the face of reactive mind's provocations! The goal is to keep practicing. Remember, practice doesn't make perfect; practice makes permanent. And you will notice over time that you get better and better at both recognizing and detaching from troublesome thoughts, feelings, memories, and sensations.

TAKE YOUR MIND FOR A WALK

This exercise (based on Hayes, Strosahl, and Wilson 2011, 161–162) helps you learn how to take personal action even as your reactive mind is throwing a tantrum or trying to get you to follow its demands. Plus, it is a physical exercise that is just plain fun—and admittedly weird—at the same time.

First, ask a friend or partner to play a game with you. One of you is going to be the human; the other is going to be the reactive mind. The task for the human is to take a walk for 10 minutes, deciding how to walk and where to go. You can walk fast, slow, or on your hands and knees if you like. You can go forward, sideways, or backward. You can randomly change direction. The goal is for the human, not the mind, to run the show.

The mind must follow behind the human no matter where the human goes. The reactive mind's task is to try to get the human to stop choosing and instead let the mind choose where and how to walk. This could involve questioning every choice the human makes or making fun of or criticizing how the human is walking—whatever it takes to get the human to argue or otherwise engage with the mind and stop walking. Any time the human responds in any way to the mind, and notices this has occurred, the mind is to say, "Never mind your mind!" After 5 or 10 minutes, reverse roles and do the same thing again for another 10 minutes.

When you've finished this exercise, it's useful to sit down and share your experiences of what each of you went through as the human and what it felt like to be in the role of the reactive mind. You may notice that you and your partner experienced some of the same difficulties in being the human. You may have stalled out momentarily when the mind hit one of your hot buttons. If so, just notice what that hot button was based in. It's a good idea to practice this exercise on a regular basis, as it's really a type of walking meditation, that is lighthearted, humorous, and instructive.

STICKY MOMENTS

This exercise is particularly useful when you have been through an emotionally charged interaction, event, or situation in which you struggled to remain detached. Get a stack of sticky notes and, thinking back through the situation, try to identify the following:

Thoughts that got me

Feelings that got me

Memories that got me

Bodily sensations that got me

Urges that got me

Write each one of these items down on a sticky note, one item per note. After you've finished writing an item down, peel the note off the pad, read it out loud, and then attach the sticky note to your clothing. Keep doing this until you've worked your way through the entire assortment of experiences that got you. After all the notes are stuck to your clothing, look into a mirror and quietly move your eyes from note to note. Read what each note says; allow whatever shows up inside of you to be there without trying to change, control, or eliminate it.

Further Exploration. As you went through this exercise, did you notice if there were certain types of sticky experiences that kept hooking you, sometimes long after the original situation had ended? Did you find that you intended to just read the sticky thought out loud and do nothing at all, only to find that all of a sudden you were off and running with your reactive mind?

As we mentioned earlier, not all sticky experiences are created equal; some are much harder than others to detach from and let go of. These are often deep-seated themes that might have played out in your life a number of times, so if you ran into them, make a mental note of what they are, because you will be running into them again as we move you down the road of mindfulness development. Remember: We all have our skeletons in the closet, so don't get down on yourself if you notice one of yours has showed up.

IDEAS TO CULTIVATE

- The reactive mind needs attachment to do its job. It will generate "sticky" thoughts, feelings, memories, sensations, and urges to get you to follow unworkable strategies.

- Learning to detach from the contents of your reactive mind is a critical feature of healthy and emotional processing.

- Neuroscience suggests detachment is based in unique neural circuitry that acts quickly and powerfully to regulate intense negative emotions.

- Detachment allows you to be aware of and in contact with distressing inner experiences without overidentifying with them.

- Brain training exercises can teach you how to notice thoughts, feelings, memories, and sensations as they appear in your awareness, while letting go of their personal relevance to you.

- The more you practice detachment skills, the stronger they will get. Pretty soon, detachment will come more naturally.

CHAPTER 9

Step 5: Don't Believe Your Reasons

Expecting life to treat you well because you are a good person is like expecting an angry bull not to charge because you are a vegetarian.

—Shari R. Barr

The brain has a complex set of neural pathways designed to help us analyze cause-and-effect relationships in daily life. This process of analytical reasoning is how we organize and understand the world around us. In depression, process takes the form of generating reasons that treat depression as the *cause* of your behavior, rather than as a *result* of it. The reasons we seize upon to explain our behavior are often arbitrary, simplistic, biased, inaccurate, and judgmental. Getting hooked by reactive mind's reasons will likely lead you in a direction that is contrary to your values. Now that you know how to detach, it's time to step back and greet reactive mind's reasons and analyses with a half-knowing smile!

In the previous two chapters, we explained how acceptance, willingness, and detachment can help you counterbalance the pull of reactive mind. If you get drawn into following the advice of reactive mind, you are likely to end up engaging in emotional and behavioral avoidance strategies that feed depression. If, instead, you practice just being open, curious, and detached, you will activate and gain access to wise mind. This will allow you to approach and take care of those inevitable challenging moments in life that we all must face.

In this chapter, we will show you how reactive mind can draw you out of your accepting, willing, detached stance and back into a pattern of emotional or behavioral avoidance. We will examine two tricky features of reactive mind:

■ Reactive mind is wired with an innate drive to make sense of the world and how we fit into it.

■ Reactive mind wants to inject its sense of moral order about how things *should* operate in the world.

The first tricky feature helps create the appearance of order and predictability that humans seem to crave. Seemingly without prompting, we develop explanations for specific things we do or don't do on a daily basis: why we didn't go to church last week, why we yelled at the kids this morning, why we're not going to work today, and so on. This is a prime function of reactive mind; its job is to identify cause-and-effect relationships that might impact our survival, such as calculating the speed of an oncoming car in relation to your current position as you cross the street in front of it.

In ACT, we use the term *reason giving* to describe this very important function of reactive mind. But, as we've pointed out again and again, the reactive mind doesn't know when, where, or how to *stop* using this linear, analytic approach. It wants to break everything down into a cause-and-effect relationship—even your behavior, your personality, your self-concept, your personal history, and so on. So the big problem here is that you have to rely on this feature of reactive mind to function in the external world, but you can't trust it to help you function in the world between your ears.

The second tricky feature of reactive mind is the tendency to apply morally charged categorical labels such as good or bad, right or wrong, fair or unfair, and so on. In chapter 7 we talked about the importance of being nonjudgmental about what shows up in awareness. The challenge in being nonjudgmental is that reactive mind believes that its main job—besides generating cause-and-effect explanations—is to evaluate events, situations, other people, and you along a moral continuum.

The ongoing processes of reason giving and moral evaluation are of tremendous importance in determining the quality of your life. When you fall prey to certain kinds of cause-and-effect evaluations combined with certain kinds of moral evaluations, your depression will be hard to control. When you buy into the content of reasons and moral judgments, it is difficult—if not impossible—to see mental processes for what they are: just antics of the reactive mind. Instead, you become attached to sticky thoughts.

In this chapter, you will take the fifth step in your campaign to transcend depression and reclaim your life: Learn to notice and be skeptical of the reasons your mind gives you so that you can put your energy into living nonjudgmentally—and with compassion for yourself and others—in the sanctuary of wise mind. We will teach you how to recognize the tricks of reactive mind that pull you out of a detached mode of awareness and cause you to suffer. We will examine reason giving in more detail so that you better understand the dangers of believing the analyses of reactive mine. We will examine four highly potent forms of moral judgments that reactive mind offers:

- Right versus wrong

- Good versus bad

- Fair versus unfair

- Responsibility versus blame

When you buy into these poisonous ways of categorizing the world, yourself included, you may act in ways that increase your depression and diminish your sense of vitality. The antidote for runaway reason giving and moral judgments is to just see them for what they are: *not* as Truth with a capital T. You can go into observer mode, accept without judgment what is currently showing on the TV screen of your mind, and let go of any need to follow reactive mind's advice. At times like this, you'll want to take the softer course of reconnecting with your values and behaving in a way that reflects positively on them. Each of these mindfulness-based actions will allow you to activate your wise mind so that you can just notice the antics of reactive mind and wait for whatever comes next. After all, life is one inner experience after another; we just have to wait for the next one.

REASON GIVING

As mentioned, *reason giving* involves the reactive mind's attempt to establish a cause-and-effect relationship between two potentially linked factors. For example, suppose a man promised his wife that he'd pick her up after work and drive her home. For some reason, he forgets that he made this agreement and doesn't show up. She's pretty peeved about this and asks him why he didn't show up. She's asking him to generate a specific kind of cause-and-effect relationship: what happened that caused him to not show up. And the husband has a desire to provide a good reason: "I didn't show up because I left my calendar at home and didn't remember I was supposed to pick you up." From an early age, we are trained to produce socially acceptable responses and to avoid using reasons that violate social norms ("I forgot" or "I thought about coming to pick you up, but I decided not to"). These are bad reasons, and you risk dire consequences if you use them.

Think of reason giving as a vehicle for both *explaining* and *justifying* your actions (and those of others) to yourself and to others. And, as we have mentioned, reason giving always originates in your reactive mind and therefore is very hard to detach from when the situation is emotionally challenging. However, as we say in ACT: *Just because you think it doesn't mean it's real.* Although your reactive mind is able to generate explanations for events and interactions in your life, that doesn't mean those explanations are necessarily accurate!

Sense making, as the term suggests, is the mental process we use to both organize and make sense of the world around us. Sense making originates in the language system of reactive mind and thus is heavily based in linear cause-and-effect thinking. It helps explain why you do what you do, why others do what they do, and why life events unfold as they do. Sense making is used to explain why you like Coke instead of Pepsi ("My parents shoved Pepsi down my throat as a youngster and now I can't stand it"); all the way up the ladder of complexity to the grand narrative of your life ("I was neglected and abused by my parents, so now I can't trust anyone"). Regardless of the level of sense making, it always operates in the same basic way: an event, situation, outcome, or interaction is explained using an analytical, cause-and-effect reason-giving framework in which one element functions as the cause and another element functions as the effect.

It turns out that the inner world of a person experiencing symptoms of depression is filled with this type of sense-making activity. The problem is that sense making tends to suggest that there's one specific cause ("I'm depressed because my job sucks"), when in reality there might be many other explanations that are just as plausible ("I'm depressed because I've stopped exercising, because I'm living on junk food, because I'm not dealing with my problems with my daughter"). In many life situations that involve personal pain, sense making can lead you down the wrong alley. Certain types of cause-and-effect explanations you may come up with, such as citing past events to explain your depression ("I'm depressed because my father constantly criticized me"), leave you with no way out. Since you can't change or undo your personal history, this type of explanation, if you buy into it, leaves you with very few avenues for overcoming your depression.

NEURONOTES: BIASES IN EMOTIONALLY BASED CAUSE-AND-EFFECT REASONING

Examining reason giving and sense making from a neuroscience perspective will make it apparent how fragile and flawed reactive mind's explanations and justifications really are. The ability to generate and evaluate complex causal relationships is a distinctive feature of human intelligence. It involves an enormously complex array of mental operations that differ widely based upon the type of causal reasoning involved.

A new model of causal reasoning, *cognitive simulation theory*, holds that the brain contains neural pathways that automatically create mental simulations of analogous physical forces that can cause small to big outcomes in the external world (Wolff and Barbey 2015). Thus, the brain will treat something big and powerful on an emotional scale exactly like a big and powerful physical force.

For example, if you have experienced an emotionally devastating event, such as physical or sexual abuse, your brain will automatically tend to attribute more "causal force" to this event when you create a personal cause-and-effect narrative. The paradox is, whereas physical cause-and-effect relationships are automatically determined by the laws of physics, the same is not true for cause-and-effect relationships in our mental world. If a car hits a tree, the weight, speed, and direction of the car will precisely determine the force of the impact; the mathematics governing this event will never change. But one victim of childhood sexual abuse might fail to finish high school, engage in child abuse, and spend a lifetime battling drug and alcohol addiction; whereas another victim might get a college degree, become a prominent member of the community, and be a role model as a parent. In short, the mathematics of human events, along with their causal impacts across time, are far less linear and predictable.

Another downside of causal simulations being applied to past or present inner experiences is that, once a specific cause acquires enough "force," it overwhelms the contributions of other causes, which subsequently get dropped from the mental simulation because they are not salient. For example, in the same car wreck example, head or tail wind speed would influence the mathematical formula determining the force of the collision, but in such a small way as to be practically meaningless. Similarly, depression might be treated as such an overwhelming cause that other meaningful causes simply drop out of the equation. This is why people with depression tend to use depression as the "causal force" to explain a wide range of depressive behaviors. Depression is a powerful emotional experience, and it can be pointed in any direction to explain why we do or don't behave in a particular way. It can be the cause of why you didn't go to work, why you stayed in your bedroom rather than spending time with your children or life partner, why you don't like to spend time with friends, and so on. As this process of causal analysis sequentially unfolds, you are likely to feel more and more powerless to do anything about this behemoth. If depression can indeed cause this many things to happen in life, it must be a force well beyond your capacity to reverse.

The automatic nature of mental simulations of cause and effect leads to another problem: The simulation is only as accurate as the information that is used to construct it. Here we run into a well-known problem in depression called *cognitive bias*. Cognitive bias occurs when some information is readily retrieved from memory but other equally relevant information is left out. This results in simulations that are overloaded, or biased, in nature. They will look exactly like a regular simulation, but they will be inaccurate.

How does this happen at the level of neural circuitry? It turns out there is great diversity in the areas of brain recruited to process emotionally salient simulations, depending upon the emotional tone of the task. When individuals create cause-and-effect relationships using evidence that is consistent with an emotional state, a network of brain regions widely associated with learning and memory is activated, including the caudate nucleus and the parahippocampal gyrus. So, if you are sad and begin thinking about all the sad things that have happened in your life, and try to estimate the causal impact they have had upon you, your reactive mind's simulator will automatically tend to screen in sad events and screen out happy events.

By contrast, evaluating information that is inconsistent with a preexisting emotional state recruits areas of the brain associated with error detection and conflict resolution, including the anterior cingulate cortex, posterior cingulate, and the precuneus (Fugelsang and Dunbar 2004). Interestingly, these areas of the brain are also core components of the executive control network. Thus, activation of the ECN is required to override the automatic and inherent bias produced in emotionally loaded simulations. As you will recall from chapters 4 and 6, these are the same neural networks of the brain that are energized and strengthened by mindfulness practice.

This pattern of differing neural activation explains why depressed individuals fall into sustained patterns of biased, self-defeating reason giving. This process is referred to as the *depressive skew* (Alloy et al. 2006). Simply put, the neural pathways responsible for running simulations that are consistent with depressed mood are habitually used and dominant compared with the pathways that run mood-inconsistent simulations. Thus, depressed people tend to develop reasons that attribute responsibility for positive (mood inconsistent) outcomes to luck, chance, or the actions of others. In contrast, they attribute responsibility for negative (mood consistent) outcomes to their own flaws, personal inadequacies, or lack of effort. The brain circuitry that supports this biased cause-and-effect reasoning involves the retrieval of biased and filtered memories, and previously generated reasons used to "explain" similar events in the immediate past. On the flip side, the neural circuitry and brain regions involved in generating reasons that short-circuit the depressive skew reside in the ECN.

THE PROBLEM WITH REASONS

By now, you might be wondering whether you can believe *anything* your reactive mind tells you. As we've said before, you can't live without your reactive mind or the simulations it produces at will. It will help you analyze and solve all kinds of cause-and-effect problems in your external world. You just have to understand when your reactive mind can help you and when it will not serve your best interests.

Generally, when you try to analyze yourself in any emotionally meaningful way, reactive mind's simulator is going to fail you, particularly if you are depressed. When you try to analyze yourself, a disproportionate amount of your reason giving will be self-focused and negative. Your reactive mind will say things like, "I didn't get the job I wanted because I'm not as smart as the other applicants" or "No one talked to me at the party because I'm not a very interesting person." In the past, you might have tried to argue with reactive mind's reasons, probably to no avail. The process of reason giving is hardwired to be structurally flawed and illogical when it comes to emotionally meaningful events in your life. You are not going to be able to change that feature of your mind.

Instead, we want you to take a deep breath, get into observer mode, and just accept that your reactive mind is giving you a bunch of reasons right now—and you can choose to not participate. You have better things to do—valuable things to do. Just hold that half-knowing smile that activates your wise mind.

The Illusion of Cause and Effect

There are times when what appears to be an obvious cause-and-effect relationship is, in fact, an illusion. One good example is sunrise and sunset. To the mind, it looks like the sunrise is caused by the sun moving up and emerging above the eastern horizon, and the sunset is caused by the sun descending below the western horizon. For centuries, people assumed this to be true and believed that the sun (as well as the moon and stars) orbited around Earth. This is, of course, an illusion. In reality, the apparent motion of celestial objects is caused by the Earth rotating on its axis and orbiting the sun. And on a cosmic scale, the entire solar system is moving through space at an unimaginable speed. However, we directly perceive none of this because our frame of reference is limited.

There are many illusory relationships in the world between the ears—a world full of symbolic activity that's constantly ebbing and flowing. As the human brain has evolved, it has expanded its ability to extend reason giving to areas of living where simple cause-and-effect explanations don't work very well. For example, if you go to a party and become extremely self-conscious to the point of choosing to leave early, you might develop a reasoning sequence along these lines: "The party caused me to be even more depressed; therefore, to prevent being depressed even further, I need to avoid going to all parties."

The tricky thing is that this cause-and-effect statement could be an illusion, just like the sunset or sunrise. There could be a multitude of other causal factors at work to produce this experience. Some could be fairly straightforward, like lack of sleep, too much coffee, or seeing an accident on your way to the party. Others might be more complex. Maybe you were afraid you might run into your ex, or maybe this was the first office party you attended at a new job and you were desperate to make a good impression. Though a list of possible factors could become quite lengthy, notice that reason giving (going to a party leads to depression) implies that there's one main causal agent. This presents a very serious problem: When the reactive mind is bent on finding a simple reason for a complicated situation, the odds of that explanation being accurate and useful are pretty slim.

Reasons Are Social Creations

In ACT, we believe that reason giving is a learned mental skill that's necessary for social order. Being able to justify your behavior is a fundamental part of your role as a social animal. For example, if one kid hits another kid in a kindergarten class, the teacher will ask, "Why did you hit Johnny?" If the kid can give a socially approved reason for why he did what he did, such as, "I hit Johnny because he took my crayons," he will get a much better response from the teacher than if he says something like "I hit Johnny because he's short and I like hitting him." This social training in reason giving begins early and continues throughout life. Suppose you miss a day of work and your boss asks you why you didn't come in. You aren't likely to say, "Because I wanted to spend the day in bed watching movies," even if that's the truth. You know you need to say something like "I was ill" or "My child was very sick with a temperature of 102 degrees."

Reasons Are Easily Programmed

As you've learned, the reactive mind is capable of generating reasons for almost anything it comes across. As one ridiculous example, the sentence "The brown grocery bag caused me to drive off the road" could function as a reason why a person ran into a tree. The minute you read that explanation, your reactive mind begins to generate various ways that a brown grocery bag could cause a person to drive off the road. Maybe his or her windows were down, the bag caught the air, and it landed on the dashboard, blocking the driver's view. Notice that as you read that explanation, your reactive mind created an image of the scenario and you may have felt quite satisfied with having been able to solve the puzzle. However, if we asked you to come up with three more scenarios explaining how a brown bag could cause a person to drive off the road, you could do that too.

Your reactive mind is designed to simulate all cause-and-effect relationships as if they were plausible. This is because the external world is full of cause-and-effect relationships, and to operate in that environment you need to have a system for constantly attending to and updating those relationships. There are often good ways to test cause-and-effect reasoning in the physical world. If you don't believe that sunblock prevents sunburn, go outside and test the idea. However, there's no good way to test this same kind of thinking when it's applied to the world between your ears.

Let's go back to the example of the kid who hit Johnny. His explanation basically boils down to "Johnny took my crayons, and this caused me to hit him." When you really look at this, you can see that this is an absurd explanation. "Johnny took my crayons" didn't actually, physically *cause* him to raise his hand and hit him, right? There might have been any number of other forces at work. He may have been tired and irritable. He might have been hungry. He might have just shared a toy with another kid, who refused to give it back. Dozens of things could have contributed to this simple act. But the child has learned, at some level, that a socially approved answer works best. As children, we quickly learn that giving an accurate account of our behavior isn't nearly as important as coming up with a socially approved reason. This raises the very real possibility that the reasons you generate to explain or justify depressed behavior, a sad emotional state, loss of motivation, or social withdrawal are little more than vestiges of your social training as a child and adolescent.

The Myth of Emotions as Reasons

Now let's complicate the situation. If you're that kid in trouble, to really get the teacher off your back you have to add a mental state that acts as the middleman between Johnny taking your crayons and you hitting Johnny. This mental state is anger. Once the teacher understands that you were angry about having your crayons taken, it doesn't make hitting a permissible response, but it does provide your teacher with an explanation for why you did what you did. But check this out: Did anger really make the kid hit Johnny, or does it boil down to a choice?

Describing an event (like having your crayons stolen) or a state of mind (anger) is not the same as explaining what caused the behavior (hitting Johnny). Although he may have experienced anger when Johnny took his crayons, there isn't a cause-and-effect relationship between either of those events and choosing to hit Johnny. A variety of responses were possible in that situation. Even as adults, we fall into the habit of using emotions as if they were physical forces compelling us to behave in some way.

Instead of a young Johnny hitting his friend, it might be a grown-up Johnny who is so depressed that he doesn't show up for work and doesn't call in sick. When his supervisor asks for an explanation, Johnny is going to say, "I was too depressed to go to work." His supervisor may in fact buy this explanation!

The take-home message is: *Emotions don't cause you to behave; you cause yourself to behave.* Once you abandon your allegiance to this destructive form of reason giving, you will be able to choose your behaviors based on your values. You don't have to let your sadness or anger make important life choices for you. You can make those choices, and sometimes you will have to work your way through not just one negative reason but a maze of them. Kevin's story illustrates how complex and intertwined reason giving, social expectations, and emotional avoidance can become.

KEVIN'S STORY

Kevin, twenty-eight, lives alone with his dog in a sober living apartment. He has been separated from his significant other for almost one year. Kevin served in the military for a four-year period, during which time he barely escaped an IED attack that left two of his buddies dead. Kevin reasoned that they walked into the ambush because he missed something that could have prevented the attack.

Kevin began to abuse alcohol after his separation from the military two years ago. He and his high school sweetheart had planned to support each other in completing their college degrees, but Kevin dropped out a year ago because of stress. He blamed himself for not staying the course and encouraged his girlfriend to move back in with her parents and get her degree. Once alone, he drank more heavily and barely managed to pay his living expenses by washing dishes in his parent's restaurant. His parents insisted that he seek help at a local veterans center and attend Alcoholics Anonymous.

After four months of sobriety, Kevin noticed his depression was getting worse, not better. Because he was alone a lot, he had plenty of time to think about his past and ruminate about his life situation. His mind worked day and night generating reasons to explain and justify his failures.

I can hardly get to work because I am so depressed.

I am depressed because I let my buddies and my girlfriend down.

I can't clean my room because I'm too depressed.

I can't see my ex-girlfriend because I'm too depressed.

Cause-and-effect explanations are often used to justify doing things that aren't socially acceptable. Since depression often involves withdrawing from or avoiding socially expected actions, it's likely that you, like Kevin, sometimes find yourself in a position where you need to justify why you did or didn't do something that was expected of you.

REASON GIVING IN YOUR LIFE

This exercise invites you to identify reasons that impact your mood and your behavior. Read through the following statements, which are often used to explain our behavior when we are depressed. Which ones have you used to explain your actions (or lack of action)? Put a checkmark beside reasons you tend to use to explain or justify your behavior. Most of us tend to fall back on using the same few reasons over and over again because they fit many different situations. We call these *go-to* reasons. If you run into a go-to reason, write "go-to" beside it.

_____ I was too tired to go walking.

_____ I didn't go to work because I was so depressed.

_____ I can't deal with my kids because I'm too depressed.

_____ I have no motivation at all, so I just sit around.

_____ I stay by myself a lot because I would just feel worse if I were around people.

_____ I would eat better if my mood wasn't so bad all the time.

_____ I can't stop smoking because my mood just goes down the toilet.

_____ I don't date because I'm still trying to get over my depression.

_____ I drink alcohol because I'm depressed.

_____ I won't argue with my partner because I just get more depressed.

_____ I didn't get together with my friends because I felt so lousy.

_____ I didn't go to church because people there don't understand what it's like to be depressed.

Further Exploration. Do any of these statements ring a bell for you? You probably recognized several statements similar to those you've used to explain your depressed behavior. Did you run into go-to reasons—the ones you tend to use repeatedly in different situations? Don't beat yourself up if you endorsed quite a few of these reasons. This is a natural part of depression—and you can do something about it! With patience and practice, you will get better and better at recognizing and detaching from reason giving when it serves no useful purpose in your life.

FOUR POISON PILLS: MORAL REASON GIVING

Moral reason giving is an especially potent feature of reactive mind. Moral reason giving helps us both explain and justify our responses according to an imaginary moral yardstick about how life should work. Assumptions about moral order in the universe are buried so deeply in our day-to-day language that we just believe them to be true. For example, let's say that during a staff meeting your boss doesn't give you any credit for your help in getting an important project done well and on time, even though you put in plenty of overtime to do so. This makes you feel victimized, and because of this you begin to act in a self-protective way at work so your boss won't do it again. You might not volunteer for a new important project because you are angry at the way you've been treated. You might begin to look for a new job on the side or look to transfer to another department. As you overidentify with your moral reason giving, your behavior becomes increasingly organized around the assumption that your boss violated an unwritten rule of life.

There are four basic categories of moral reason giving that play a major role in depression: right versus wrong, good versus bad, fair versus unfair, and responsibility versus blame. Whenever you sense the presence of any of these forms of reason giving, try to detach and take a posture of just holding your thoughts, without buying into them outright. Let's take a look at each poison pill, and then we'll explore some strategies to help you detect and short-circuit them.

Right versus Wrong

The belief that something isn't right implies that an injustice is being committed and someone is the victim of that injustice. There are some obvious examples of injustice, such as being physically or sexually abused. However, what's right or wrong is far less obvious in many situations. A prime example of this is expectations about how other people should treat you. You have your own unique set of rules about what must happen for a relationship to be right, and the other person has his or her own unique set of rules too. Deciding that an offense has occurred when your rules about moral order are violated implies that your rules are the right ones.

When you swallow the poison pill of right versus wrong, you're far more likely to act on your anger and desire for vengeance. Although you probably value being loving and respectful of others, right and wrong might lead you to say or do things that are mean and hurtful. The other side of this coin is that you'll begin to see yourself as a victim. When you look at yourself in this way, you're likely to withdraw, act in a passive way, and see the other person as having evil intentions. Be very careful when you see thoughts like "This isn't right" or "I shouldn't have to go through something like this."

Good versus Bad

Good versus bad describe the qualities of an object or event in terms of how desirable it is. If you say you're a "good person," this means you evaluate *all* of your personal qualities as desirable. When you have an evaluation like "He's a bad person," you're essentially saying that *all* of his qualities are very undesirable. One of the trickiest ways your reactive mind delivers this poison pill is through negatively charged words you might use to describe yourself or someone else: loser, defective, boring, untrustworthy, liar, hopeless, empty, unlovable, ugly, and so on.

The emotional pull of good and bad is strong, and we don't want to associate with bad stuff (unlovable, loser, ugly) because it's unhealthy to do so (another good–bad evaluation). We only want to associate with the good stuff (lovable, winner, attractive). The problem is, most of us don't fit easily into one category. We are neither all good nor all bad, and there is a lot of gray as well. Oftentimes, the same personal quality that hurts us in one life situation might be a tremendous positive in another. Reactive mind has trouble accounting for how we fit into life contexts that frequently shift and realign.

Fair versus Unfair

The moral reasoning behind fair versus unfair has a special twist to it. Fair implies that you deserve a certain outcome based on who you are or something you've done. When something is evaluated as unfair, it means you've been arbitrarily punished or deprived of something you deserve. This particular type of reason giving can be a real impediment in situations that require you to act in a purposeful way. Taking the stance of being unfairly treated usually results in a person standing still and throwing a temper tantrum at life. Unfortunately, other people involved in the situation may and often do see it differently.

Some people who struggle with long-term depression often buy into moral reasoning that life hasn't been fair to them. The problem is, just because you followed a certain set of rules about how to get a good life doesn't mean you'll have mostly positive feelings and experiences. Life doesn't work that way. Life is not fair, nor is it unfair. What's more, life doesn't care whether you think it's fair or not. The time and energy you spend under the influence of this poison pill would be better spent pursuing a valued life.

Responsibility versus Blame

This type of moral reasoning invites you to assign responsibility for an unwanted outcome to the person who caused it. The need to assign responsibility tends to be strongest when negative life outcomes are present. To illustrate the dangerous side effects of this poison pill, let's consider a depressed woman who is struggling with infertility. She thinks, "If I had taken better care of myself physically when I was younger, none of this would be happening." In essence, she's making herself responsible for medical problems that she has no possible control over.

This form of moral reasoning is toxic because it focuses your energy on determining who is responsible for what and downplays the fact that there are some things that just happen randomly and are beyond your control. When you are depressed, you might be tempted to hold yourself responsible (and to blame) for an event or life problem you have no control over: the unexpected death of a loved one, a divorce, a child's drug problems, and so on. In reality, many things happen to us that we did not want and had no say in whatsoever.

We may also find ourselves blaming someone else for our problems, and this, too, may be a trap. Whatever wrongs are done to us, we don't want to tie up too much of our energy hating the offender. Forgiveness actually benefits the harmed person more than the offender. You can't protect yourself from many things in life. It's all about how you work with the moral reasoning in your own mind; you can choose freedom from rigid reason giving. Remember the half-smile, and you are on your way.

BRAIN TRAINING FOR HOLDING YOUR REASONS LIGHTLY

Now let's turn to a series of exercises designed to help you learn to both recognize and detach from reasons. The goal is to simply hold reasons, seen as reasons, without buying into them. These exercises include practices that help you learn to play with reasons and notice poison pills at play in your life— without getting hooked by them.

PLAY WITH REASONS

Remember that, for the most part, reasons aren't accurate explanations of events and why they occur; they're just mental events. This means that none of what you write in this exercise is actually true, scientifically speaking; it will not be an accurate cause-and-effect analysis that includes all possible factors. However, you will learn something about the workability of different types of reasons. Since all reasons are arbitrarily constructed, those that produce unworkable outcomes in your life are poor reasons. Conversely, those that produce positive results are workable reasons!

This exercise gives you the chance to entertain the possibility that you're falling prey to the depressive skew of your reactive mind during important moments in your life. The first step is to choose three life situations that are bothering you right now—anything you've done that needs a reason, such as missing work, avoiding intimacy, avoiding a social opportunity, or harming your health by eating, drinking, or smoking too much. Briefly describe each situation in the left-hand column.

Now, in the middle column describe the most depressive reasons possible to account for why each problem is in your life right now. Then go to the right-hand column and describe the least depressive, most extremely positive perspective. The idea here is not to be accurate. Instead, it is to challenge your mind to be more flexible and creative in generating reasons.

Play with Reasons Worksheet

Situation	Most Depressed Perspective	Extremely Positive Perspective
Example: I am diagnosed with high blood pressure.	Now my physical health is failing too. And it's all my fault—I should have quit smoking years ago. I guess I'll just wait for the other shoe to drop.	Everyone gets old, and this is a part of my aging. At the same time, I can improve my diet and exercise more—and I will, starting right now!

Further Exploration. What did you notice as you went through this exercise? Was it easier to come up with and write out the self-blaming reasons? How did you do with generating extremely positive reasons? Did you notice that you felt differently when you went the depressive route versus the positive route? This is one way to play with reasons. When you notice the depressive skew showing up, go for a crazy-positive alternative. Push the positivity level to the point where you have to smile. This will help you strengthen the neural circuitry that both detects and counteracts memory and processing biases in the brain.

POISON PILLS

In this exercise, you'll identify a couple of your hot-button situations. You'll look at how these may be fueled by moral reasoning that might lead you into an unworkable stance. Before you start, take a look at the example from Kevin's record in the first row of the table.

Then, in the left-hand column, describe one of your target situations—an event or interaction that really sets you off emotionally. Pause, take a moment to step back, and watch your mind begin evaluating the situation. Just watch, and then decide which of the poison pills might be at play in your response to this situation: right versus wrong, good versus bad, fair versus unfair, or responsibility versus blame. Then, write the poison pill that applies in the middle column (do not swallow it). In the right-hand column, write out whatever moral reasoning your reactive mind hands you as you hang out with the poison pill. Then pause and smile at yourself. Go ahead and do another hot-button situation now if you like.

Poison Pills Worksheet

Hot-Button Situation	Poison Pills	Moral Reasoning
Example from Kevin: I go to campus to pick up a schedule of classes and see ex-girlfriend	Good versus bad	She's such a smart person, and I'm a jerk. I was wrong to drop out of school; I don't know if I'll ever go back. I'd have to measure up to all of these other people who are better than me.

Further Exploration. How did you do at detecting poison pills in your life? Most of us have been walking around with these moral reasons at the ready for many years. If you keep on the lookout and repeat this exercise regularly, you can become a poison pill cop. Pull that poison pill over and cite it for speeding. Use this approach when hot-button situations come up in your day-to-day life. Remember the steps: notice reasons (cause and effect), name them, and, above all, continue to act in ways that are consistent with your values, not with your reactive mind's biased reasons (and your depression). Push yourself to come up with ridiculously positive reasons from time to time!

IDEAS TO CULTIVATE

- Reason giving functions to explain and justify your actions or lack of action, but reasons are not the same as causes.

- Depression is characterized by biased information that leads to overly simplified, inaccurate explanations of depressed behaviors.

- Your evaluative mind weaves moral reason giving into the fabric of everything you experience—things, people, and events. And it makes assumptions about how life works seem like indisputable truths.

- Depressed individuals tend to use reasons that portray depression or lack of motivation as the cause of their problems.

- Your depression does not cause you to do anything; you are in control of your actions, or lack of action, regardless of your mood.

- Learning to notice reasons is the first step in learning to detach from them.

- You can see your reason-giving mind for what it is, use it when it pays to do so, and act in ways that build a life worth living!

CHAPTER 10

Step 6: Hold Your Stories Lightly

The real voyage of discovery consists not in seeking new landscapes but in having new eyes.

—Marcel Proust

The stories we develop about who we are and how we got to be that way don't just act as self-fulfilling prophecies—they affect our neural circuitry. Positively framed stories stimulate and strengthen the brain's reward and motivation circuitry. Harsh, negative self-stories cut this connection and stimulate threat and avoidance pathways. The irony is that self-stories are just a product of reactive mind to begin with and are just that: stories. You are free to pick any story you want to carry around, so why not pick one that's good for your brain?

In the previous chapter, we examined reactive mind's unquenchable desire to generate cause-and-effect relationships in order to help you make sense of the world. We gave this feature of reactive mind a name—*reason giving*—and showed you how the reasons used by depressed individuals tend to be both negatively biased and inaccurate. Among depressed people, biased reason giving plays a major role in triggering self-isolation, social avoidance, depressed mood, and rumination. To counteract the negative impact of reason giving, it is important to be aware of and just hold your reasons, without buying into them. This allows you to refocus your attention on the present moment and then accept and see the antics of the reactive mind for what they are. This will activate wise mind, help you reconnect with your values, and redirect your energy toward powerful, healthy life purposes.

It's one thing to explain your behavior in a particular situation, such as why you didn't exercise today or why you yelled at your kids this morning. But the reactive mind isn't content with developing reasons on a case-by-case basis; it wants to assemble all of these cause-and-effect explanations—often going back into childhood—to create a story of you. In ACT, we call this a *self-story*. The Dalai Lama calls it the *conceptual self*. This is the story that you carry around about who you are, how you got to be that way, and what is likely to happen to you as time goes by. Obviously, depending upon what is contained in your self-story, you could see yourself as anything from a broken, worthless, and unlovable person with no real future to a person full of good intentions, compassion, vitality, meaning, and purpose.

It isn't a big leap to think of the self-story as a kind of operator's manual. In that sense, we all carry around our own operator's manual. It necessarily allows us to have an overriding sense of life direction and purpose. The problem arises when the operator's manual is biased, misleading, or inaccurate, as it often turns out to be in depression. If you buy into the operating instructions of your depressed self-story, and then do what they tell you to do, you might easily find yourself not going where you would like to go in life.

Fortunately, if you pause a second and see your self-story as just that—a story—you'll be in a good position to act in ways that will promote the kind of life you want to live. Holding your self-stories lightly is the sixth mindful step on your nine-step path to living a fulfilling life. To help you take your self-story with a grain of salt, we'll expose it for what it is: an inaccurate, negatively biased, and selectively filtered narrative that's full of holes and inconsistencies. To help you learn how to do this, we will first examine what neuroscience has to say about self-stories. We will give you the opportunity to look at your current self-story with an eye toward helping it seem a tad less important than it is now. At the end of the chapter, we will expose you to some cutting-edge brain training exercises that will help you detach from your self-story, smile at it in a slightly amused and compassionate way, and connect with the positive emotion circuitry in your brain.

SELF-STORIES: REASON GIVING ON STEROIDS

Let's take a look at how self-stories work, often to the detriment of the depressed person. When a person accumulates a succession of setbacks and disappointments, the reactive mind tends to fall back on increasingly general explanations for the setbacks, such as, "I just never get it right" or "I'm the kind of person who always fails at relationships." These types of self-statements are really summaries of hundreds of reasons that have been lumped together to form a self-concept about who you are. Research into what is called *autobiographical memory* clearly demonstrates an exaggerated tendency among depressed people to retrieve emotional themes rather than specific situational events and details when recalling earlier life events (Williams et al. 2000). Interestingly enough, this memory bias basically disappears after mindfulness training, suggesting that clouded, emotionally themed memories create problems with being aware and in the moment—until the mindfulness fix is applied (Williams 2010).

As the self-story becomes increasingly theme oriented and overly general, the second part of the self-story sequence kicks in. This involves the reactive mind delving into your life history to explain how you developed into the person you are. For example, "My dad was an alcoholic and depressed, and I picked up a lot of his traits." Sometimes you'll seize upon past events, such as childhood trauma, as the cause for current setbacks ("I've always felt like I'm damaged—irreversibly damaged—since I was raped as a teenager, and it's stupid to think I could have a normal intimate relationship"). At other times, your story might suggest that you are simply imbued with a particular trait that explains why bad things happen to you ("I've never had much motivation for anything. I've always been just kind of lazy, even as a child, and I don't think I'll ever be successful at anything that requires a lot of effort").

When your self-story portrays you in flawed and broken terms, it can function as a self-fulfilling prophecy. If you think of the self-story as accurate and set in concrete, you face a very real danger of attaching to it and making it the story of "you." This allows your story to intrude into and color your experience of the present and, worse yet, to subtly or not so subtly shape your future.

NEURONOTES: NEURAL PATHWAYS SUPPORT POSITIVE AND NEGATIVE STORIES

Storytelling is of primary importance to human beings. One important thing to remember is that self-stories are not just attempts to make sense of personal history; they also serve an important social function. They help us make contact with other humans and allow us to communicate our needs in various ways. They create a high-level pathway for bonding (and mating) with other members of the social group. They allow us to compare our behaviors with others and to stop behaviors that might result in exclusion from the social group (Somerville, Kelly, and Heatherton 2010).

The area of the brain most responsible for generating self-stories is the medial prefrontal cortex (mPFC). The mPFC produces representations of the self that integrate historical and contemporary social and self-referential information drawn from other regions of the brain (Wagner, Haxby, and Heatherton 2012). Positive self-stories result in correlated activity of the mPFC and areas of the brain that produce reward sensations and motivation. Negative self-stories are associated with both decreased activation of the ventral orbital prefrontal cortex and decoupling of the neural pathways linked to the brain's reward and motivation centers (Hughes and Beer 2013). Chavez and Heatherton (2014) found that individual differences in the emotional tone of self-stories (from positive to negative) are correlated with density of white matter and heightened activation of frontostriatal circuits linking areas underlying self-related thinking to ones involved in positive self-evaluation.

It appears that frontostriatal circuits may give rise to feelings of self-esteem by integrating information about the self with positive emotions and reward. To the extent that an individual regularly experiences positive self-stories, it is possible that the repeated recruitment of the frontostriatal circuits may increase the structural integrity (density) of white matter tracts within this system over time. This, in turn, may then lead to an increase in the likelihood of positive self-stories.

The take-home message is consistent with our emphasis on brain training to promote greater levels of mindfulness: Positively framed stories stimulate and strengthen the brain's reward and motivation circuitry. Harsh, negative self-stories cut this connection and strengthen emotional and behavioral avoidance neural pathways.

HOW SELF-STORIES WORK

One important property of stories is that they condense a vast array of information into a much smaller number of simple, powerful messages. This means that your self-story is not the complete, unabridged autobiography of your life. It would be impossible for you to recall every consecutive moment of your life since you became conscious. That book would have too many pages to count. So you have to selectively remember information about events, interactions, emotional reactions, your behaviors, and so on. In order to present a plausible account of who you are, where you are in life, how you got to be there, and where you're going, your story contains a combination of descriptive elements (objective facts about things that happened) and highly selective cause-and-effect assumptions (your explanation of how these events shaped you). Taken together, these two elements form a limited set of simple, powerful, and often destructive messages about who you are.

When your self-story suggests that you are defective or flawed in some basic way, the stage is set for you to enter situations expecting to fail, be rejected, or be disappointed. You may behave like someone who is expecting bad things to happen and, sure enough, bad things happen.

Do you recall Kevin from chapter 9? His self-story was that he was a failure, and he had many reasons that he used to justify it:

I'm a failure because I let my buddies down during a mission in Afghanistan, where two died and I survived.

I'm a failure because I dropped out of school and botched my dream of becoming a nurse.

I'm a failure because I couldn't maintain a relationship with my girlfriend.

I'm a failure because I misused alcohol.

Fortunately, when you step back and look at how your story line originates and operates, you'll begin to see a lot of holes that you hadn't noticed before. Let's take a look at some of these holes.

The "Truthiness" Effect

The self-story is vulnerable to "truthiness" mistakes—mistakes we make in accepting something as fact based on it sounding right, or having a ring of truth to it, rather than it being accurate. Stories that have that ring of truth to them often do so because they capitalize on our love of cause-and-effect reason giving, a specialty of reactive mind. They seem logically organized and even plausible in tone. But, at the end of the day, they are just one of many "logical" stories that could be (and will be) spun by the reactive mind.

As you become more skillful in working with your mind, your self-story will continue to show up, but it won't command your attention with the same urgency as when you were indiscriminately buying whatever thoughts your reactive mind offered. Let's look at one self-story example: "I'll always have problems with depression because my parents rejected me when I told them I was gay. They taught me to be ashamed of myself and never accept myself for who I am." This is less compelling when seen as a part of a personal history that is just that—history—no matter how painful it seems.

The Truth Is Not Out There

This idea that the truth is not out there is a different take on the slogan for the popular TV show, the *X-Files*. We are socialized to believe that truth resides in the world outside of us and our job is to go out and find it. In ACT, we take a completely different approach to determining what is true and what is false. There is no idealized truth "out there" for you to discover. Instead, we talk about the truth value of a self-story. This means that a self-story is measured by its value in promoting your best interests in whatever situation you use the story. If the story helps you succeed in that situation, then it is a functionally true story. If you have a compelling, logical, and well-organized self-story that systematically defeats your interests, then that story is functionally false.

The ACT approach can be a challenge to grasp in this regard. You're no doubt pondering some important questions:

If I can't accurately describe the true causes of my behavior in the present moment, how can I explain cause-and-effect relationships for events that happened years ago?

How can I recognize when my self-story is operating?

How do I know if my self-story is accurate?

How can my self-story be accurate when so much information is left out of it?

In the remainder of this chapter, we'll try to help you answer these important questions and learn to relate to your self-story in a more flexible, productive way.

THE PROBLEM WITH STORIES

Memory retrieval is the core process that feeds any self-story. If you don't have a memory, you can't have a self-story. The trouble with memory retrieval, as we explained in the previous chapter, is that it is incredibly emotion dependent. In depression in particular, there is a strong negative cognitive bias leading to selective recall of negative information. This continually primes the pump with distressing memories, thoughts, sensations, and resulting emotions. This then interferes with your ability to regulate strong, unpleasant emotional states (Joorman and Vanderlind 2014). If you will recall, when we are sad, we tend to easily recall other sad events. But there are other problems with memory that are highly specific to depression that create even more cause for concern about the accuracy of a depressed self-story. Let's take a look at what some of the recent research has revealed.

Rumination and Memory Suppression

One very interesting line of study has looked at the impact rumination has on memory in depressed people. Rumination is a very unpleasant state of mind, so depressed people tend to try to suppress negative thoughts and memories as a way of stopping rumination. Unfortunately, the attempt to suppress unpleasant memories backfires; the more you try to suppress negative memories to control your thoughts and mood, the more negative, intrusive memories and thoughts you receive in what's sometimes referred to as the *memory suppression effect* (Dalgleish and Yiend 2006).

What does this mean in terms of your ability to recall your past accurately? Basically, you will remember more negative events than positive events because you artificially move negative memories up in the line of retrieval when you try to suppress them. When you're depressed, rumination, attempts to stop ruminating, and the memory suppression effect together create a self-story that includes way more negative events than positive events. The trap is that you aren't aware of this filtering bias because it operates outside of awareness. Here's another interesting fact: When depressed people learn mindfulness strategies, allowing them to detach from their self-story, they ruminate less and perform normally on memory tasks involving emotional themes (Williams et al. 2000; Williams 2010).

LET'S WORK OUT YOUR STORYTELLER

In this section, we give you multiple opportunities to become aware of how rapidly and automatically self-stories can get generated. The goal is to show you how capable this aspect of reactive mind is and why you need to be skeptical about the truth value and workability of your stories.

THE LIFE STORY WHEEL

At the end of the popular game show *Wheel of Fortune*, contestants spin the wheel to see what kind of prize they'll win. This is a random encounter with luck that significantly heightens the excitement of the game. In this exercise, we have a similar game in mind, but the prize is a little different. In this game, you get to construct a new self-story based on a random word choice. The life story wheel is loaded with evaluative words that are likely to move your mind into spinning a yarn right away.

One way to start the game is to close your eyes, put your finger on the story wheel, and start with the word closest to your finger. Alternatively, you might roll a penny onto the page, see where it lands, and start from there.

Once you have spun the wheel, so to speak, and have a word, begin your story: "I am [whatever word you landed on]" and then let your mind go to work adding details. You're likely to get the best results if you write your story quickly. If your hand stops writing, write the first sentence again ("I am _____") and continue on. Write at least one paragraph—you'll refer to it in the next worksheet. Repeat this process for four or five words. If your penny drops on the same word twice, pick it up and drop it again! Your penny isn't trying to tell you something, or is it?

I am _____

_____

_____

_____

I am _____

_____

_____

_____

I am _____

_____

_____

_____

I am _____

_____

_____

_____

Now, move on to the next worksheet. When you answer the questions, you may simply write yes or no, or you can elaborate.

LIFE STORY WHEEL WORKSHEET

Story Word	Was the Story Easy to Write?	Was the Story Familiar?	How Believable Is the Story?

Further Exploration. Were you able to construct four or five stories by just playing this little game? If you're like most people, it wasn't at all difficult, which shows you the power of your built-in storyteller. How credible did each story seem? It's usually possible to construct a story that seems very credible even though it's obviously made up on the fly. Were the stories based on negative words easier for you to believe than the positive stories? If so, you were probably being phished by your reactive mind. The real irony is you couldn't have completed this game without your reactive mind, because it handles explanations, reason giving, and storytelling. If we got you into wise mind mode and asked you to do something like this, it would strike you as an odd thing indeed! Why would anyone want to spend their precious time making up painful stories?

Kevin's Results

When Kevin dropped a penny on the story wheel, he came up with the words "inadequate," "perfect," "brilliant," and "flaky" and wrote the following paragraphs.

Inadequate

I am inadequate. I don't have what it takes to stay in a relationship. My early life experiences cost me big time. And I should have seen that ambush coming; because I didn't, my friends are dead. I am inadequate. I am not strong enough to face my fears. I am inadequate. My parents were right; I will never amount to much. I am inadequate. I am alone in life and maybe I deserve that.

Perfect

I am perfect. Right! Well, I would like to be perfect at one thing, at least, before I die. Let's see… I am a clean freak, and I do a great job of organizing my tools and other yard stuff. On the other hand, I think that might make me an annoying partner because I am uncomfortable with disorganization. I am perfect. This is hard. I feel very uncomfortable with the phrase "I am perfect." It's like my mind wants to automatically say, "Oh, no you're not!" and I start having memories of times when I've screwed up or I can hear my parents criticizing me.

Brilliant

I am brilliant. I am exceptional at making home repairs. On almost every home repair I do, I have to solve different problems. Sometimes the parts no longer exist and I have to jury-rig a new part. Brilliant. That's a strange word for me to use. It means I'm at the top, and I'm not sure I'm really at the top, or even near the top for that matter. This is difficult. Why is it so hard to write positive things about myself? I am brilliant. Once, I replaced my neighbor's kitchen faucet; she is old and can't afford to pay for a plumber. I did it for free, including buying the faucet for her. Okay, maybe that was brilliant. But I haven't gone over to see her again, and she hasn't called either.

Flaky

I am flaky. Okay, that's a tough word for me because more than one of my exes has called me that. They say I'm up and down a lot and they never know which me will be showing up. What does that say about me? Maybe I'm flaky in that I don't feel very stable emotionally at times. I am flaky. Oh, yes. Here's the story: My friends often want to introduce me to single women to date, and I pretend to be interested. However, I often make excuses at the last minute, like I have a headache, and can't go. That's flaky, I think.

Kevin's Life Story Wheel Worksheet

Story Word	Was the Story Easy to Write?	Was the Story Familiar?	How Believable Is the Story?
Inadequate	Yes, flowed from me. And no, made me feel down, so it was hard to stick with it. Kind of got lost in my thoughts.	Very familiar	Pretty believable because I think that way. But I think I question it a little more when I see it on paper.
Perfect	No. It's very hard to see myself as perfect.	No	Couldn't get myself into that story; kept having images of times when I've been a disappointment or screwed up somehow.
Brilliant	In between. I'm really interested in home repair stuff so that feels easier, but the rest seems forced.	No	It is true that I did help my neighbor just out of the goodness of my heart. Something I hadn't remembered in a long time.
Flaky	Flaky is a word I would use to describe myself.	Yes	I sort of believe the part about it being flaky to make excuses.

When Kevin reviewed his responses, he noticed it was easier to create stories using negative rather than positive words. At the same time, he was interested in the fact that even a small part of a positive story (which he rarely experienced in his internal dialogue) seemed plausible as well. He was surprised to find that he had pretty much forgotten about the act of generosity toward his elderly neighbor or that he was actually pretty crafty with home repairs.

WRITE AN AUTOBIOGRAPHY

The best way to access your whole story is to take some time and write a condensed version of your story line. Since a complete autobiography would be too big a challenge, we want you to write a smaller version. Don't do this halfheartedly. Take some time to think about everything that has happened in your life and how you feel these events have shaped you; then take a half hour or so and write a one- or two-page autobiography. You may find it helpful to first write out specific events before you go on to construct your autobiography. Here's a list of the types of things you might include:

- Formative events in your life and how they've affected you

- Things that stand out as high points in your life

- Things that stand out as low points in your life

- Relationships with parents, siblings, and other family members

- Important intimate relationships and friendships and what they've meant to you

- Specific traumas or negative life events that had an impact on you

_____

_____

_____

_____

_____

_____

_____

_____

_____

_____

_____

RUTH'S STORY

Ruth is a thirty-four-year-old single woman who lives by herself. She is a survivor of childhood sexual abuse, and she believed this would always limit her ability to have good relationships with men, a problem compounded after being date-raped in college. During college, she had dated a man for several years and had even lived with him for almost a year, but she had never enjoyed intimacy with him. She intentionally discouraged any talk of commitment, and they gradually drifted apart.

Following the predictions of her self-story, she decided that she just wasn't relationship material and stopped trying to meet men. She had very few other social connections and spent a lot of time alone, trying to forget about her misfortune and get on with the life she could create, given her losses. She began to experience more and more self-consciousness at work, where she worked with men and women and could detect flirtation and sexual interest in their interactions. She knew that the people she worked with were well intentioned when they tried to set her up for a blind date, but she didn't feel safe and planned to avoid any future exploitation. Gradually, her depression worsened to the point that she had to take a disability leave from work so she could get her life back together.

Here is the autobiography she wrote:

I was the only child in my family. My father was in sales, and we moved a lot. I think the longest I was in any school was two years. I had few close friends because I knew we would move again. I always was the "new kid," so I was often teased by my classmates. I was a pretty good student, but I never felt I fit in socially. Being alone so much caused me to be very shy and unsure of myself, something I still deal with today.

My biggest role model was my mother. I lived with her after Mom and Dad divorced. She taught me to adjust to being alone because she was alone. She had to work two jobs to support us, but she never complained about how hard it was to make a living. She just did what she had to do to support us.

The babysitter who abused me was our neighbor. He told me that I would be taken away from my mother and put in an orphanage if I told anyone. I remember wanting to tell Mom to make him stop, but I would always chicken out. I blame myself for not telling her sooner. She would have done something to stop it. Instead, it stopped when his family moved out of state. I was even more suspicious of people after this.

I went to college at eighteen and it was hard on me. I didn't feel comfortable going to social events, so I just stayed in my room or went to the library. I had an attraction to a few guys, but they didn't seem to notice me. I took a part-time job and kept a full class load, so I didn't have much time to socialize, but I still felt lonely. In my sophomore year, I went with a friend to a party where everybody was drinking. I'd never drank much before and it hit me hard. I didn't remember the end of the evening, except trying to push a guy off of me. I felt really afraid and ashamed at the same time. During my junior year, I met a man named Dave, and we became close friends. He was interested in sex, and though I wasn't, I went along with it. We lived together for a while, but relating to him just seemed to take too much time and effort, so I found a summer job in a different part of the state and left him.

Now, I just try to keep to myself and stay out of the middle of any social drama at work. My workmates are nice people, and they often invite me to social activities, but I always tell them that I have to go home and take care of my two dogs. I don't feel that social drive that other people do. I prefer to stay at home and clean or watch movies or do crafts. I don't see a relationship or marriage in my future. I'm not sure I'd be a very good parent because I would probably teach my kids to not trust other people.

With a little assistance, Ruth was able to deconstruct her story so that descriptions of objective life events were separated from arbitrary cause-and-effect, reason-giving explanations. Below are some of the results of the exercise.

Ruth's Worksheet for Deconstructing My Autobiography

Description	Cause-and-Effect Impact
I was the only child in my family.	Made me learn to entertain myself.
My family moved a lot.	Learned to not rely on friends. I could make friends quick enough and then let go and move on.
I was teased a lot in school because I was the new kid.	Made me socially anxious, I guess, but I also resolved to be okay without a lot of friends.
Lived with my mother, who worked two jobs to support us.	She taught me how to be alone. She taught me self-discipline and to work hard, to be independent.
Molested by my babysitter.	Made it difficult to trust others. Also, made me feel ashamed and different from others.
Date-raped at a party in college.	Made me feel disgusted toward men.
Left my relationship with Dave.	I don't think a heterosexual relationship will hold my interest, and I don't think I'm homosexual. Maybe just not intimate partner material.
Keep to myself at work and decline invitations to group social events.	I'm not a social person, just kind of a loner.

When you read Ruth's story, did you pick up on how few descriptions of events there are relative to the number of cause-and-effect impacts? Also, did you notice that there are only a limited number of themes appearing and reappearing in terms of cause-and-effect impacts? Her main themes are: *avoid being close because people can be cruel*, and *I am not a social person, just a loner, and probably always will be*. This reveals how Ruth's self-story has selectively included life events that represent a very simple, powerful theme: Let your guard down, and you'll get hurt.

DECONSTRUCT YOUR AUTOBIOGRAPHY

Now it's your turn to break down your self-story into its basic elements. Just as we did with Ruth's story, divide the statements you wrote in your Autobiography exercise into two categories: descriptions and cause-and-effect impacts. Make a copy of the blank worksheet (or print it from http://www.newharbinger.com/38457) before proceeding, as you'll use it again in the next exercise. (Alternatively, make a copy after you've filled in the left-hand column and before filling in the right-hand column.)

In the left-hand column, record statements that are factual descriptions of occurrences—things you did or that happened to you. This might include such things as, "My brother died in an automobile accident when I was twelve," "My parents divorced when I was two," "I was bullied for two years in middle school," or "I graduated from college with honors when I was twenty-two."

In the right-hand column, record statements that address the impacts of the events contained in your descriptions. These are the cause-and-effect explanations you give for the objective events of your life, such as, "After my brother died, my parents argued a lot, and they stopped paying attention to me or my choice of friends," "I was the oldest and took the role of parenting my brothers and sister when I was nine and my dad left," or "Once I became overweight, I felt anxious around most of the kids at school and just preferred to stay at home and read or watch movies rather than be around them outside of school."

Worksheet for Deconstructing My Autobiography

Description	Cause-and-Effect Impact

Further Exploration. Take a look at your descriptions and consider ways to work with those descriptions other than or in addition to the statements written in the corresponding cause-and-effect boxes. Are there other descriptions or cause-and-effect statements that you want to add in? Chances are you will see two or three main themes in your story. Self-stories are like that: light on objective facts and heavy on a limited number of simple but powerful (and often self-limiting) messages.

WRITE A NEW AUTOBIOGRAPHY

The themes of your self-story are usually contained in cause-and-effect impact statements within the story. But what if the impact statements of your self-story are limited by selective memory bias or your sheer inability to integrate the millions of other possibly influential experiences you've had by now?

Let's try an experiment that will involve consciously stepping outside of your existing self-story for a few minutes. You'll use the copy you made of the previous worksheet. Without changing the descriptions of actual occurrences, write out new cause-and-effect impacts of each event. We don't care what type of new impacts you ascribe to it. Your new version can increase the negative impact of an event, decrease it, or offer a different meaning altogether.

For example, Ruth's statement that the experience of sexual abuse "Made it difficult to trust others. Also, made me feel ashamed and different from others" could be revised to "made me more sensitive to others who have been victimized in some way and contributed to my interest in social work" or "made me appreciate how courageous it is to make yourself vulnerable" or "made me a feminist." Before you start, take a look at Ruth's Revised Deconstruction of My Autobiography.

Ruth's Revised Deconstruction of My Autobiography

Description	Cause-and-Effect Impact
I was the only child in my family.	I had a very close relationship with my mother.
My family moved a lot.	I learned to pack up, travel light, and keep things tidy.
I was teased a lot in school because I was the new kid.	I don't wear my heart on my sleeve.
Lived with my mother, who worked two jobs to support us.	Came to think of women as strong and self-reliant.
Molested by my babysitter.	Made me concerned about how to identify children at risk for abuse by adults and by other children too.
Date-raped at a party in college.	Made me concerned about how to prevent alcohol misuse and sexual violence.
Left my relationship with Dave.	Lead to a great job opportunity.
Keep to myself at work and decline invitations to group social events.	I'm never troubled by office drama, and I think I'm probably more respected for this.

As you see, Ruth came up with lots of new material for the cause-and-effect column. She felt empowered by this exercise. Now, rewrite your new autobiography, and then continue reading.

Worksheet for Revised Deconstruction of My Autobiography

Description	Cause-and-Effect Impact

Further Exploration. Were you able to come up with a different set of meanings for the same set of facts? Most people find that this is relatively easy to do, but if you struggled with it, just notice that you might have attached to your self-story so completely that it eliminated any access to a different set of meanings. Did you find yourself saying something like, "Yeah, I can write these other meanings, but they aren't really true. My original story is the true one!" If you went that route, here's a question to ask yourself: "How do I know that my first story is the most accurate and true?" It's probably the one you've been reciting for a long time, but that doesn't mean it's the most accurate. This fickle feature of self-stories is what we alluded to when we talked a little earlier about "truthiness errors" in self-stories. Just because a story is familiar, well practiced, and might even seem plausible doesn't mean it's true!

Is it possible that your reactive mind is similarly arbitrary in constructing your story, rather than entirely accurate? If your story is full of being exploited or abused by others, might your reactive mind filter out an event where a person respected you and gave generously to you? If your story contains one failure after another, could it be that your reactive mind has screened out the times you have succeeded?

Stories have a way of taking on a life of their own, and when they do, you can find yourself playing out the prophecies of failure, betrayal, disappointment, or personal inadequacy contained in your story. Living your life with your attention riveted on your self-story is a little like trying to drive a car by fixing your gaze on the rearview mirror, not the road; it's ineffective at best and usually downright dangerous. Although you do need a rearview mirror to profit from past experiences, you will never reach your destination if you remain focused on the view it affords. As we say in ACT: *The most dangerous thing about the story of your past is that you could make it into the story of your future.*

RUTH'S JOURNEY TOWARD A VITAL LIFE

After Ruth did the autobiography exercises, she made a conscious effort to adopt a new story about herself, one that reflected more respect for her strengths. Day by day, she began to notice the limiting effects of her old self-story and what it told her to do: remain alone and stand guard against the world. This operator instruction put her in the position of giving up on the things that she actually valued in life. She wanted to have close friendships with men and women. She wanted to invite people to her home. She realized that she needed to keep an eye out for her old self-story so that it didn't rob her of opportunities for living the life she wanted. Because she had lived with it and obeyed it for so long, she couldn't keep it from showing up in situations in which she felt vulnerable. But she did get better and better at noticing that it had been activated. She could switch her attention over to the new, more empowering story that seemed to give her better results in situations in which she felt vulnerable.

Ruth made a commitment to start with a small change: she would say yes rather than no to invitations to participate in social activities with her work peers. She used the nickname strategy (chapter 8) to name her story "Lonely Girl." This stopped her from attaching to her old self-story as she experimented with becoming a more social person. Since she valued building trust, genuineness, and candor in relationships, she committed to following those values in her social interactions: being honest about her feelings, letting others know that she cared about developing closer connections, and assuming that people had integrity and would spend more time with her if they wanted to get to know her.

Over time, Ruth noticed that, even though she had some unpleasant inner experiences in social situations, she was feeling healthier physically and emotionally. Her old self-story was still there, but not in the dark, oppressive way it had been before. Ruth noticed that she was actually having fun and enjoying herself at the exact moment her old self-story would appear in awareness and tell her to run for the hills. And, like a rebellious teenager, Ruth simply chose to disobey the toxic advice of her reactive mind and focus on her new self-story. Ruth was on the path toward living a vital life!

BRAIN TRAINING TO PLAY WITH STORIES

Strengthening the skills needed to better manage the impact of self-stories involves first learning to be skeptical of any single self-story that claims to be the true and complete version of you. In addition, since it appears that the main impact of negative stories on the brain is to weaken neural pathways that produce rewards and a desire to approach (rather than avoid) life events, you must learn to diversify your stories so that positive self-story elements get equal airtime, so to speak.

In depression, the tendency is to just pile one negative self-story on top of another so that there is no breath of fresh air. Keep in mind that we are not saying that positive self-stories are any more believable than negative ones. They are *all* stories. But at least forcing yourself to rehearse positive self-story elements will begin to strengthen those reward circuits!

TELL ME A STORY

Imagine that you are in three distinctly different types of social situations, and in each of these situations a person is going to ask you a question: "Can you tell me a little bit about yourself?"

First situation: You are at a social gathering and you are interested in getting to know a specific person better. This person might become just a friend, or you might develop a deeper relationship over time.

Write what you would say: _____

_____

_____

_____

Second situation: You are applying for a job you really want and are at an interview that will likely determine whether you get the job or not.

Write what you would say: _____

_____

_____

_____

Third situation: You are new to a church or spiritual group, after being invited to attend by one of your friends. After a brief round of introductions, the group leader asks you to tell the group a little about yourself.

Write what you would say: _____

_____

_____

_____

Further Exploration. What did you discover as you did this exercise? Did you notice that you tailored the story of yourself to fit the social demands of each situation? Is there any aspect of any of your stories that is *not* true? Which one of these stories is the "true" one? Most people are surprised at how pliable their stories are; they can change from situation to situation. That's exactly what you want: tailor your story to the context, hold it lightly, and notice how well it works. Stories that produce the outcomes you want *are* the true ones.

NARRATIVE JOURNAL

To further explore your self-story, you might want to keep a daily self-story journal. We've provided you with an easy-to-use worksheet (or you can download a copy from http://www.newharbinger.com/38457). The instructions are simple: Each time you find yourself in a new, distinctive social situation where you are required to disclose personal information about yourself, write that situation down in the left-hand column. Then, write down the contents of your new self-story in that situation in the right-hand column.

As an example, in the Storytelling Situation column you might write: "Went to the grocery store to buy some stuff, and the checker started talking about how hard it is to live with someone who is hardheaded. The clerk said, 'You know what I mean?'" In the Self-Narrative column you might write: "I said, 'Yeah, I'm one of those hardheaded types. I figure that I'm needed to balance my partner's easygoing manner. Wouldn't want too much easygoing energy in the house now, would we?' The checker laughed."

Just keep a running tab of all of the new self-stories that you generate over time. You will be mightily impressed by your storytelling abilities!

Narrative Journal Worksheet

Storytelling Situation	My Self-Narrative

Further Exploration. Remember what we said about truth earlier in this chapter? None of your stories are true in the pure sense. Truth in storyland is based in how well the story serves your best interests in each new situation. A story can be a complete success in one situation and a complete failure when applied to a different one. If you can look at your stories this way, you will be able to flexibly shift between stories depending upon your needs in each situation.

PRIMING THE PUMP: POSITIVE MEMORY REHEARSAL

As mentioned earlier, depressed individuals tend to spend inordinate amounts of time playing and replaying their negative self-stories, to the detriment of the reward and motivation circuitry in the brain. On a daily basis, give your positive brain circuitry a workout by identifying and replaying *positive* life memories. Spend at least 15 minutes practicing this exercise, maybe at the conclusion of your day or in the morning before you get started.

Use the "Life Story Wheel" exercise, but this time randomly select two or three positive words. After practicing deep breathing to get present for a few minutes, picture a prior situation, event, or interaction in which you experienced a positive, rewarding moment. The memory could be from any time in your life, from early childhood to the present. Take your time and put all the details of the memory in place so that you feel like you are right back there. Just bask in the glow of that moment.

Further Exploration. When you did this exercise, did your reactive mind show up and try to draw your attention to a negative thought, emotion, or memory? Reactive mind is like Coyote in Native American mythology: stealthy and full of mischief and dark magic. When you repeat this exercise again and Coyote appears, softly thank your mind and return to the task at hand. Pay attention to how stories propel you in one emotional direction or another. Just as negative self-story elements tend to hang out together, positive elements do the same. So you might notice that one positive memory suddenly unearths another related one. If this happens, give yourself permission to bask in as many positive memories as come into awareness, strengthening those positive emotion–producing neural networks.

A UNIQUE BRICK WALL

This story, told by physicist-turned–Buddhist monk Ajahn Brahm, offers some insight on how to gain perspective on the bad elements of your life when thinking about the whole of your life. He left his promising academic career to live in a nearby forest with other monks in his sect. Without any prior training as a bricklayer, he assembled a simple monastery with brick walls. After it was completed, and before he shared the space with fellow monks, he inspected it one more time and found two bricks that were conspicuously laid in the wrong way. The more he examined the wall, the more he was mortified by his mistake. He decided he must tear down the blemished wall before anyone saw the obvious flaw.

The next day, without warning, another monk stopped by before Ajahn could begin demolishing the wall. He said nothing of his decision to the visiting monk, who casually walked around the entire monastery and then said, "Those two bricks that protrude so beautifully give this monastery a blessed feeling, and I want to thank you for sharing this inspiration with us all!" The monk bowed in gratitude to Ajahn.

In the guided audio exercise that follows, we will help you decide what to do with the misplaced bricks in your wall of life:

1. First, list any misplaced bricks that you think have ruined your wall of life. Next, mentally bring these bricks forward, one by one. You can even put inscriptions on them if you like, just so you know they are all here.

   _____

   _____

   _____

   _____

2. Now focus your attention solely on those bricks. Try to make the rest of your wall of life disappear. Try really hard to create this image that there is no other wall at all. Your wall is completely defined by the misplaced bricks.

3. Now focus your attention on the whole of your life story, and make the misplaced bricks disappear. Try really hard to imagine that those misplaced bricks are not even part of your wall of life.

4. Now focus your attention on the whole of your brick wall of life and intentionally blend in the misplaced bricks, along with the properly placed ones. See if you can experience firsthand the beauty of this building you have constructed.

Further Exploration. What happened as you tried to change the "figure and ground" relationship between the intact parts of your life journey and the difficult setbacks or disappointments of your life? When you made the setbacks the defining feature of your journey, how did that feel inside? When you tried to make the intact parts of your journey the only story in town, what happened to the misplaced bricks? What happened when you included both the intact parts and the setbacks as core elements of your wall of life? The idea that even your flaws, setbacks, and disappointments are somehow an integral feature of your life journey is hard to grasp for most of us, but particularly so if you are harsh, self-critical, and perfectionistic. We are going to examine this fundamental reversal of perspective in much more detail in chapter 11, so read on!

IDEAS TO CULTIVATE

- The reactive mind is a natural-born storyteller; we each have hundreds of stories to tell.

- Memory bias in depression results in positive information being filtered out, leading to an artificially negative tone in your self-story.

- Your self-story contains select, highly filtered life themes and predictions about the future. It is not an accurate account of who you are.

- Buying into a compelling but self-defeating story can have a devastating impact on your behavior in situations that matter to you.

- Practiced over time, negative self-stories weaken neural circuitry in the brain responsible for producing rewarding emotions and positive motivation states.

- Practicing positive self-stories strengthens neural circuitry in the brain responsible for producing rewarding emotions and positive motivation.

- A "true" self-story is one that helps you succeed in specific life situations that matter to you. Thus, there are really a limitless number of true self-stories available for you to use.

- If you step back from your self-story and see it as a story, you can escape its toxic effects and instead act in ways that promote vitality in your life.

CHAPTER 11

Step 7: The Leap: Practice Self-Compassion

You yourself, more than anyone else in the universe, deserve your kindness and affection.

—Buddha

You have an important choice to make in your quest to transcend depression and reclaim your life. You can practice compassion for yourself or you can be hard on yourself. Practicing self-compassion not only strengthens neural pathways that regulate depression, it also stimulates areas of the brain that produce positive feelings and eagerness to live life. Self-compassion is at your fingertips, is free of charge, and has absolutely no strings attached. Go for it!

One thing we have noticed in our years of working with depressed people is that they are pretty hard on themselves, much harder than the average person, and often at points in their lives when they most need to be nurtured rather than neglected or scolded. Adopting a harsh, self-critical stance when you suffer some type of life setback not only adds insult to injury, but it also can promote long-term sadness and suffering. You'll recall that rumination is a central experience in depression that involves replaying personal failures and life setbacks over and over again, all the while analyzing your personal flaws, comparing yourself with others and finding yourself lacking, and obsessing about your inability to control your depression. In other words, rumination involves being unkind to yourself.

The alternative, as the Buddha observed, is to treat yourself with gentleness and affection. This is what we like to call self-compassion. When you treat yourself with kindness, you are more able to soften around any emotional pain you are experiencing in the moment. You can relax instead of struggle, knowing in your heart of hearts that failure is just a part of our life tapestry and that there are moments of joy and brief flashes of peace that come into our lives even when life has been very hard on us. With this stance of self-nurturing as the focus, we are more able to notice when the harsh, self-critical narratives of reactive mind show up, as they may do even when positive things happen in life.

For example, when you meet someone new and have the thought that you could become good friends, your reactive mind might immediately say something like, "You are socially awkward, so don't get your hopes up." You instantly feel a pang of loneliness and sadness inside, maybe remembering other times when you've felt left out, as the pain swells. At this exact moment of pain, you can wrap yourself in the cloak of softness, kindness, and affection for yourself. If you develop these self-compassion skills, you can respond more effectively to the provocations of reactive mind, the reasons it gives, and the familiar lines from your old self-story that could lead you down the path of avoidance. You might instead treat yourself with kindness in a situation like this and say, "Being socially awkward doesn't make me unlovable. I am genuine and that is a nice quality in a friend. Most everyone worries about being liked and accepted by others, and I am no exception."

Over and over, life will bring out your imperfections and put them on display for you and others to see. You may be irritable and short-tempered with your children, your spouse, or parents. You might find yourself making excuses so that you can avoid a family get-together, or you back out on a date night with your partner. In this chapter, we teach you to treat yourself with kindness and affection, in hard times and easy times, when you act in accordance with your values and when you do not. Treating yourself with kindness and affection is the seventh step on your journey toward becoming psychologically flexible and able to persist in pursuing the life you want.

WHAT IS SELF-COMPASSION?

The emerging role of *self-compassion* as an intervention for depression is the result of the pioneering efforts of Kristen Neff (2003; 2016). She describes self-compassion as *"being open to and moved by one's own suffering, experiencing feelings of caring and kindness toward oneself, taking an understanding, nonjudgmental attitude toward one's inadequacies and failures, and recognizing that one's experience is part of the common human experience"* (2003, 225). According to Neff, self-compassion consists of three interrelated components:

- *self-kindness,* or the tendency to treat oneself with understanding and care rather than with harsh self-judgment in moments of suffering

- *an experience of common humanity,* or the ability to recognize that all humans fail at times, rather than feeling cut off from others when we fail

■ *mindfulness*, or being aware of present-moment experience in a balanced way rather than overreacting to emotions associated with failures or setbacks

The Benefits of Self-Compassion

A self-compassion practice is the perfect antidote for depression. In fact, there are so many benefits to self-compassion (Neff, Rude, and Kirkpatrick 2007) that we recommend you adopt some type of regular self-compassion practice as a long-term feature of your lifestyle, depressed or not. People who practice self-compassion tend to experience lower levels of depression and anxiety (Leary et al. 2007; Neff 2003; Neff, Rude, and Kirkpatrick 2007). Higher levels of self-compassion reduce the frequency and intensity of rumination in people experiencing symptoms of depression (Raes 2010). This is great news because, as we have repeatedly mentioned, rumination—brooding, or pondering personal flaws and failures in a self-focused, negative, judgmental way—is responsible for both producing and maintaining depression.

People with high levels of self-compassion also tend to be more motivated to learn about themselves, are less fixated on gaining the approval of others, and are less afraid of making mistakes (Neff, Hsieh, and Dejitterat 2005). In a highly influential article reporting on five different studies of self-compassion, Adams and Leary (Leary et al. 2007) showed that self-compassion:

■ Reduced the level of negative emotional and cognitive reactions to negative events in everyday life

■ Buffered people against negative self-judgments and resulting painful emotions when recalling distressing social events

■ Moderated negative emotions after people received unpleasant social feedback, particularly in those who struggled with low self-esteem

■ Led people to acknowledge their role in negative events without feeling overwhelmed with negative emotions

The last bullet point turns out to be an important factor in determining how we respond to the need for positive lifestyle behaviors to promote our health and manage chronic disease. Sirois, Molnar, and Hirsch (2015) showed that self-compassion buffers the negative mental effects of chronic disease by increasing the use of adaptive coping responses such as acceptance and positive emotional framing of health problems. In a study involving more than three thousand adults, Sirois, Kittner, and Hirsch (2014) showed that higher levels of self-compassion were linked to positive lifestyle behaviors such as healthy eating habits, exercise, regular sleep, and use of day-to-day stress-management strategies.

In general, these studies suggest that self-compassion buffers our reactions to negative life stresses or interpersonal events in ways that are distinct from, and possibly superior to, other coping strategies.

In addition, self-compassion—due to its association with a nonjudgmental, self-accepting attitude, as well as positive emotional coping strategies—seems to promote positive, healthy lifestyle behaviors, a topic we will examine in some detail in section 3 of this book. In this chapter, we will help you begin to practice new skills that will quickly strengthen your self-compassion muscles!

NEURONOTES: SELF-COMPASSION REGULATES DISTRESSING EMOTIONS

For well over a decade, neuroscientists have been examining the effects of compassion and mindfulness-based training on neural structures and mental efficiency. One exciting discovery is that practicing compassion for self and others reduces activation of the amygdala, the brain center involved in producing negative emotions (Schuyler et al. 2014). In other words, being compassionate toward self or others down-regulates neural pathways in the brain responsible for producing negative emotions. When you put yourself in a space of compassion toward self and others, your emotional experience will soften.

Another exciting finding is that compassion training increases the density of gray matter in those areas of the brain involved in learning and memory processes, as well as emotional control, self-awareness, and perspective taking (Holzel et al. 2011). Interestingly, social self-awareness (seeing yourself as affiliated with others) appears to be supported by a set of neural circuitry that's distinct from, yet overlapping with, the brain circuitry that supports empathy. This is so in regard to the ability to mentally visualize and compare different problem-solving approaches that have social consequences (Quirk and Beer 2006). In other words, when you practice compassion, it influences the amount of weight you give to social considerations in attempts to solve personal problems. As you become more self-compassionate, you are more likely to be tuned in to the impact your problem-solving actions have on others.

Research also suggests that, with practice, you can develop greater skills in this potent area of psychological health in a fairly short period of time. After brief self-compassion training, participants in a recent study demonstrated more altruistic attitudes toward the suffering of others and less impairment from their own negative emotions in response to suffering (Weng et al. 2013). In this study, participants practiced only thirty minutes daily for two weeks, with the support of a mindfulness-based compassion exercise on the Internet. The participants who exhibited the most significant changes in altruistic responses also showed the greatest changes in brain activation in response to suffering. In the most altruistic participants, activation increased in the inferior parietal cortex (a region of the brain involved in empathy and understanding others), in the dorsolateral prefrontal cortex (a region involved in emotional control), and in the nucleus accumbens (a region involved in producing rewarding emotions). These unique patterns of neural activation suggest that compassion practice increases detection of others' suffering through neural circuitry involved in empathy and imagining the perspective of others.

If you are interested in downloading a free guided audio version of the compassion training exercise used in these studies, go to http://centerhealthyminds.org/well-being-tools/compassion-training. We also provide downloadable guided self-compassion brain training exercises at the end of this chapter.

ASSESS YOUR SELF-COMPASSION SKILLS

Now it's time to take a look at your self-compassion skills. Fortunately, there have been substantial advances made in both defining what self-compassion is (and isn't) and developing ways to measure it (Neff 2016). In this section, you will complete a shortened version of the Self-Compassion Scale originally developed by Neff (2003) and revised by her and colleagues (Raes et al. 2011).

First of all, before your reactive mind gets on its high horse, remember that this is not a test. There are no good or bad scores on this scale. The assessment is meant to give you a baseline of where you are now. As we mentioned, low levels of self-compassion tend to be associated with higher levels of depression, so if you discover some low spots in your self-compassion profile, don't be surprised—and don't beat yourself up for it. With practice, you will notice that your score improves and, even more important, that it is easier and easier to be gentle with yourself.

How I Typically Act Toward Myself in Difficult Times

Please read each statement carefully before answering. To the right of each statement, indicate how often you behave in the stated manner, using the following scale:

Almost never				Almost always
1	2	3	4	5

For the six items with a "6-": subtract the score associated with your answer from 6. The result will be your score for that item. For example, if your answer to item 1 using the scale is 4, then subtracting that from 6 would equal 2 as your adjusted score for item 1. You do not need to record anything in boxes that are shaded, as higher numbered responses indicate increased levels of self-compassion in those cases.

	Your Rating	Your Score
1. When I fail at something important to me, I become consumed by feelings of inadequacy.	6-	
2. I try to be understanding and patient toward those aspects of my personality I don't like.		
3. When something painful happens, I try to take a balanced view of the situation.		
4. When I'm feeling down, I tend to feel like most other people are happier than I am.	6-	
5. I try to see my failings as part of the human condition.		

6. When I'm going through a very hard time, I give myself the caring and tenderness I need.		
7. When something upsets me I try to keep my emotions in balance.		
8. When I fail at something that's important to me, I tend to feel alone in my failure.	**6-**	
9. When I'm feeling down I tend to obsess and fixate on everything that's wrong.	**6-**	
10. When I feel inadequate in some way, I try to remind myself that feelings of inadequacy are shared by most people.		
11. I'm disapproving and judgmental about my own flaws and inadequacies.	**6-**	
12. I'm intolerant and impatient toward those aspects of my personality I don't like.	**6-**	
Total score (add items 1–12)		

Total scores range from 12 to 60, and higher scores indicate greater skill in self-compassion. Make a note of today's score on your smartphone or daily planner. If you can, set a reminder for you to repeat this assessment in two or three weeks to see if your score has improved. Yes, that's right—you can change your level of self-compassion in a very short period of time with regular practice! That's how the brain works; if you ask it to do something over and over again, it will get better and better at doing what you ask it to do.

JOAN'S STORY

Joan is a thirty-six-year-old divorced single parent of three children. She works as a manager at a local bank. Joan was one of three sisters who grew up on a wheat farm in the Midwest. The family heritage she grew up with emphasized not showing emotions openly and being a person of few words. From early childhood, she heard comments from friends, family members, and teachers about her quiet, reserved personality. Over time, Joan felt more and more self-conscious and ashamed of this feature of her personality. Social situations were always her least favorite activity, because making small talk and social chatter was not her forte. Although she did well in school, she never really joined a social group, preferring to focus on her studies and piano lessons.

Joan didn't think she would have a relationship until she met Sam in college. He was much more socially inclined than she was and enjoyed being the talkative one in social settings. After college, they eventually married and had three children. Sam was absent from the home frequently for job-related travel. When he wasn't working, he didn't spend much time around the house. He was an avid golfer and had a lot of male friends he liked to hang out with.

Five years ago, without any warning, Sam told Joan that he was leaving her, packed up his stuff, and left the area. Joan later discovered that he had been having an affair for several years and was now living with his new partner in a nearby city. She replayed pieces of their relationship over and over again in her mind, wondering what she did wrong. This played into her self-story about being a "plain Jane" and not entertaining socially. She thought a lot about this and worried about her children and finances. She focused on her job and being a good mother to her kids.

Sam only saw the children every couple of months during the first year after he left the marriage. Then he announced that he was starting another family with his new partner and, although he would continue to pay child support, he would have very little time to be involved in the lives of their children. He insinuated that the children weren't really that entertaining to be with and made a snide comment that the "nut doesn't fall far from the tree." Joan took this to mean her children were also going to have bland and uninteresting personalities. She felt even worse thinking that maybe her flaws might be damaging her kids' social development. This left her lying awake at night trying to figure out some way to become more dynamic and engaging as a person. She also spent a lot of time blaming herself for choosing a guy like Sam, who could be so heartless.

Joan's Results

Joan completed the Self-Compassion Scale and was concerned about her relatively low score. She talked to a friend about it, and the friend stated that Joan was a very caring friend and that she saw her as a kind and thoughtful person. Joan considered this and reviewed her answers again; she saw a pattern of being pretty intolerant of making mistakes. She decided to focus her attention on practicing kindness and acceptance toward her flaws, rather than getting lost in her attempts to analyze and eliminate them. She realized that trying to criticize herself for her weaknesses really wasn't helpful and, at this point, really hurt a lot.

WAYS TO CULTIVATE SELF-COMPASSION

In this section, you will practice a series of exercises designed to strengthen your self-compassion skills. We invite you to test-drive them all to see what skills benefit you the most. Like most people, you will likely have several areas in need of greater attention—definitely focus on the exercises that target those areas. But don't overlook exercises that help you grow stronger in areas where you already have some strength, as all of the skill areas are highly connected.

Practicing Self-Kindness

Supporting self-kindness involves enhancing your ability to take a loving, caring stance toward yourself all of the time, particularly when the chips are down, so to speak, and you are feeling a lot of emotional pain. This can be difficult to do, particularly if you didn't receive this kind of acceptance and encouragement from a nurturing parent during your formative years. Moreover, if one of your parents suffered from depression, he or she may not have noticed your pain or may not have had the energy or skills to respond with concern and encouragement.

LOVING-KINDNESS PRACTICE

There are a variety of meditation practices associated with the development of compassion, and these are sometimes referred to as *loving-kindness meditation practices*. We recommend that you start with a brief daily practice. The following table outlines the key components for a practice, phrases (or *compassion wishes*) that may be helpful, and the amount of time recommended for practice.

Typically, your first practice efforts will be in using key compassion phrases directed toward a benefactor, or someone who showed a strong interest in you and went out of his or her way to help you learn and grow—someone who was gentle with you when you made mistakes and curious and encouraging about your potential as a human being. Not everyone can identify a benefactor, so you might select a friend instead. It's best to choose one with whom you do not have a sexual relationship and one who is generous and loving toward you. It is best to choose someone who is alive, but it is okay to choose someone who has passed on as well. Spend a few days or up to a few weeks practicing the compassion wishes for this chosen person.

Next, begin directing statements toward strangers. You might try the first person you see on a morning walk. Do this for several days. Finally, direct compassion statements toward yourself.

Whoever is the focus of your compassion (benefactor, friend, stranger, or self), always try to conclude your brief practice by directing your wishes for compassion to a larger group (the people on your block, the people in your city, all beings in this world). For most people, it is easier to be compassionate toward others, so this approach helps you take advantage of that.

Practice daily at whatever time is convenient and for 5 to 30 minutes, focusing on the wishes and the target of those wishes. Concentrate your efforts on creating images, emotions, and sensations consistent with your wishes. And feel free to use your own words to express your love and kindness!

Focus of Compassion Wishes	Compassion Wishes	Length of Practice
Benefactor	*May you be safe.* *May you be healthy.* *May you be happy.* *May you have ease of being.* *May you know peace.*	1–2 days to 1–2 weeks
Friend	Same as above	1–2 days to 1–2 weeks
Stranger	Same as above	1–2 days to 1–2 weeks
Self	Same as above	1–2 days to 1–2 weeks
Larger groups	Same as above	1–2 days to 1–2 weeks
All in combination	Same as above	5–30 minutes daily for the rest of your life

SELF-KINDNESS SKILL BUILDING

The following two-part exercise will help you develop strength in self-kindness. It involves learning to be intentionally kind to yourself when you are suffering, to be tolerant of your shortcomings, and to be patient with parts of yourself that you do not like.

To build skill in these areas, stay mindful of your day-to-day painful inner experiences. The goal is to identify specific events and times when you are self-critical. Use the form below to track your results. We recommend that you keep a copy of this worksheet with you and review it three to four times per day so that you can catch the contexts where you could really use self-kindness but usually don't provide it.

Kindness and Criticism: When and What

When do you feel the most kindness for yourself? What is the target of your kindness? When are you most critical of yourself and for what?		
Time of Day	Context Most Kind	Context Most Critical

Further Exploration. After doing this for a few days, can you identify patterns in the time of day when you are triggered to be either kind to or critical of yourself? Do you see patterns in various social contexts, like being at work, at home with your partner, or during interactions with friends, people at church, and so on? Do you notice whether the triggering events for kindness or criticism center around a theme? You may be able to identify daily behaviors that function as a pathway for self-criticism or self-kindness. For example, you might realize that you actually experience feelings of kindness toward yourself at night when you apply lotion to your feet. Alternatively, you might notice that you are highly critical of yourself every Thursday afternoon before a weekly meeting at work. Your goal is to build on your kindness and let it spill over to the moments when you need more love and patience.

JOAN'S RESULTS

Joan was intrigued by the idea that she had moments of both kindness and criticism in her day. She found it helpful to look for moments of kindness, as she really wanted to grow these moments. Below are the results of her work on the Kindness and Criticism worksheet.

Kindness and Criticism: When and What

When do you feel the most kindness for yourself? What is the target of your kindness? When are you most critical of yourself and for what?		
Time of Day	Context Most Kind	Context Most Critical
Morning	Ever since my children were born, I wake up and say a prayer for them and a prayer for me to be a good mother.	On nights I sleep poorly, I wake up tired and start in on myself. I blame myself for worrying too much!
Afternoon	I'm usually tired, and I go and fill my water bottle and get a cup of coffee at break. I tell myself I can make it to the end of the day.	Usually busy with work and children; hours fly by—even though I'm tired.
Evening	After I put the kids down, I make a cup of herbal tea and take it to my room and think, "It's my time."	Pushing to get the day wrapped up—just looking forward to having some time alone when I don't have to do anything.
Before going to sleep	Not sure I show myself kindness at night—I just try to make my bed comfortable. Sometimes, I'll light a candle and pray.	Before bed, I think about missed moments during the day when I could have stepped up and put myself out there but didn't. I criticize myself for having married Sam and blame myself for how he has hurt our kids.

BUILDING MORE MOMENTS OF KINDNESS

Another way to create more moments of kindness involves developing a plan to practice specific self-compassion actions. To do this, start with identifying one or more contexts where you want to practice more kindness, and then develop a cue to prompt you. The cue could be a written note, a photograph, or even a special alert on your phone—anything that will serve as a signal to be kind to yourself. Place the cue in situational contexts that might trigger self-criticism *and* be an opportunity to practice self-kindness instead. It's fine to also target a moment when you already show kindness toward yourself, with a plan of embellishing the kindness or spending a little more time savoring the moment.

It's important that your new plan involves a behavior that you or someone else could observe. This doesn't mean someone has to observe it—the action just needs to be something you do in the world, as opposed to something you think in your head. The rationale for this is that we exert *far more* influence on our thinking and emotions when we vary our behavior.

Kindness Behavior Plan

Take a moment to think about a few situations in which you will practice self-kindness, and describe them in the first column. You may use examples listed in the Kindness and Criticism worksheet. Next, describe what cue you will use as a reminder to behave differently when you want to show more kindness to yourself. Finally, list what your new kindness behavior will be.

Context	Cue	New Kindness Behavior

JOAN'S RESULTS

After she had identified several ripe moments for practice in her daily routine, Joan was ready to develop a plan to bring more kindness into her life. This was her plan.

Context	Cue	New Kindness Behavior
Waking up	Picture on bedside table	Say the Four Compassion Wishes and direct them to my children and then myself.
Bedtime	Sticky note on the bathroom mirror that says, "I love you, especially your quiet nature."	Read the "I love you" note and then write in my respect journal for a few minutes.

Joan had been practicing the loving-kindness meditation for a few days, with a focus on a college professor who had been a very helpful mentor. She liked the practice and decided she wanted to add an element of it to her morning routine. Joan had enjoyed painting as a hobby before she had children, so she decided to paint a picture for her bedside table to serve as a cue for her new kindness behavior upon waking.

For her nighttime practice, Joan decided she would briefly write about positive aspects of her quiet and reserved personality for a few minutes. It was the single moment during the day when she practiced loving her reserved, low-key nature. She painted a cover on an old notebook and then wrote, "May you give and receive respect; may your mind be open." She placed the journal by her bedside table.

Her "I love you" note on the bathroom mirror would be her cue to spend a few minutes writing kind words to herself about herself. She persevered in both changes and noticed more spontaneous moments of self-kindness in her days during the following two weeks.

Softening Self-Judgment

Judging ourselves comes naturally for most us, beginning early in our lives as children. We judge ourselves a lot in social situations ("Was I thoughtful? Did she think my responses were helpful?"). It's a pretty automatic behavior for us, so it's challenging to change. Our self-judgments often reflect our experience with significant individuals who were important in our upbringing. For instance, if you had a parent who was critical of you, or who tried to motivate you by always finding some fault with your performance, it is highly likely that you will use that same approach with yourself. The good news is that you can change this. Here are several strategies for addressing runaway negative self-evaluations:

- **Ask yourself, "Am I a good person?** When we invite our clients to answer this question, almost all answer with an affirmative. You do have kindness in your heart; you are well intentioned. But you're struggling right now and don't *feel* good, even though you know deep inside you *are* good. To bolster your belief that you are a good person, place little reminders in your environment, like posting sticky notes with positive messages on your toilet seat or refrigerator. Remember: the love of your life is the person you see when you look in the mirror.

- **Address your problematic behaviors.** Come up with a new protocol for addressing behaviors that are ineffective. This involves being able to respond to a list of standard questions, even while your mind is scolding you. Ask yourself: "What was the behavior? What was my intention? Did the behavior produce the results I hoped for?" Many times, when we answer these questions, it is clear that we meant no harm and that our behavior was simply ineffective. The goal is to eventually be able to identify alternative behaviors that might work better.

- **Develop a new perspective on making mistakes.** One vulnerability that contributes to depression is having exceedingly high standards or being perfectionistic. But even if you aren't a perfectionist, you can still be hard on yourself when you make mistakes. If you have this vulnerability, then think of an alternative perspective on the situation. For instance, instead of judging yourself harshly, cultivate a sense of humor. Keep in mind these aphorisms: *Perfectionism is perfectly silly. Make mistakes perfectly. Fail often and early.* The idea is to add in new ideas that lighten the impact of failing to meet your high standards. In addition to adding in lightness, we recommend that you develop an attitude of curiosity about your mistakes. When you are curious about something, your interest will often result in a slight smile. That slight smile can change what's happening in your brain and promote a sense of calm—a state from which it is easier to see what you did and what else might have been possible.

SOFTEN SELF-JUDGMENT

This exercise will help you formulate a plan for treating yourself with kindness in the face of a future triggering situation. The objective is to come up with a *soft statement* that you can say to yourself in place of a judgment.

In the space provided, first describe a situation in which you are likely to start judging yourself. Include the key features of the situation that are likely to provoke self-criticism. Second, check in on how you are feeling. To do this, it is important to get in the present moment. Imagine the feelings you might start with, then write them down. Third, imagine what behaviors would help you to soften and treat yourself with kindness. Write down what you could say to yourself; this is your soft statement. Next, write down how your feelings might change with this new self-compassionate approach.

Once you have formed your plan, take a few minutes to mentally rehearse the entire sequence as if you are actually in the situation. Think about the intentions you have as you enter into this situation. Now that you are free of the need to judge yourself, what values are going to guide your actions? What do you want to do differently, if your behavior is not being controlled by fear and self-judgment?

As you go through this mental simulation, can you think of other behaviors that might promote an even greater posture of self-kindness? Write down your answers, and don't hesitate to modify your plan if you discover something new that tickles your fancy. Consider downloading the worksheet from http://www.newharbinger.com/38457 so that you may revise and adjust your approach as you discover new ways to promote self-kindness.

Soften Self-Judgment: Skill Practice Plan

1. Describe a situation that is likely to trigger a self-judgment.

_____

_____

_____

_____

2. What would my immediate feelings be?

_____

_____

_____

3. What could I do differently that would promote self-kindness? What would my soft statement be?

_____

_____

_____

4. How might my feelings change after softening self-judgment?

_____

_____

_____

5. Would my behaviors be consistent with my intentions and values?

_____

_____

_____

6. What behaviors might promote greater self-compassion?

_____

_____

_____

Further Exploration. Were you able to work through this exercise in a way that might prepare you to act with self-compassion in an upcoming risk situation? The more you mentally prepare yourself to be self-compassionate, the easier it will be to get into that mode if the difficult situation materializes in your life. Stay with this practice, as you can add in one soft statement after another, building up your kindness reservoir for tricky situations. Of course, the next step is to enter into tricky situations and practice soft statements in the heat of the moment. In time, your softening self-judgment plan will help you love yourself even when you are making mistakes.

JOAN'S RESULTS

For her plan to soften self-judgments, Joan decided to start with a small but persistently troublesome situation at work. Because she is usually quiet, the other members of her team at work would complete projects without really seeking her input. This fed into her narrative that she didn't have much to contribute. She would then get frustrated and angry inside and blurt out some type of criticism that would catch her coworkers by surprise. She would then feel bad about coming in at the last moment and changing things.

Joan decided to take a few minutes for the next few days around 6:00 p.m. to develop her softening self-judgment plan. She chose this time because it was when she tended to obsess about her personality shortcomings. Joan's plan for addressing the problem at work involved curbing her impulse to blurt out a negative judgment of the team, because she actually liked them and respected them. Instead of judging herself, she decided she would show kindness to herself when she was frustrated. She would remind herself that it was okay to feel the way she felt and that it was understandable.

She also planned to think through and identify the value that she wanted to inform her behavior when she was angry. This involved showing respect for her team by asking questions, rather than making judgments, and letting them draw their own conclusions about how to finish the project.

Joan's Soften Self-Judgment: Skill Practice Plan

1. Describe a situation that is likely to trigger a self-judgment.

Finally getting up the courage to speak out at a meeting at work and then saying something critical about a decision made by the team. My supervisor looks hurt. I start thinking, "I've really blown it this time. I should just keep my opinions to myself like I always have. Maybe I really don't have anything to add anyway."

2. What would my immediate feelings be?

I am feeling tired, angry, and frustrated with myself.

3. What could I do differently that would promote self-kindness? What would my soft statement be?

I could tell myself that it is natural to feel angry or frustrated at times because I care about the results.

4. How might my feelings change after softening self-judgment?

This would leave me feeling calmer and less on edge.

5. Would my behaviors be consistent with my intentions and values?

I want to help my team make the best decisions possible because they affect a lot of people. I care about my coworkers, and I care about my supervisor too. She has been there for me in my darkest times. My value is to show respect to her and everyone else on the team. They are all very dedicated to doing a good job. So, being critical isn't really where I want to go with this.

6. What behaviors might promote greater self-compassion?

I can think that it's okay for me to feel uncertain about my role in the group, and that is one way to improve my contribution to the group. It helps me do my job better, not worse. Uncertainty is not the problem; it is what I do when I'm uncertain that I can improve at. This is one of the challenges of working with a group of people.

A couple of days later, Joan ran into the same work situation that she had developed the plan for. She noticed feeling much calmer and more centered inside. She also felt less of a need to express her skepticism about how the project was going. Instead of being bombarded by self-criticisms from her reactive mind, she had a sense of clarity and could more easily relate to others' points of view. After the meeting, a team member remarked that she seemed to be more supportive of each person's efforts.

Connecting with Common Humanity

The world is full of suffering, and it can be difficult to keep that in mind when we are suffering from depression. The result may be that we may not see how our suffering connects us with others; you may recall that about one in ten people in America is depressed. There are many things we might share in common with others that depress or challenge us: problems with our loved ones, financial problems, drugs and alcohol, poverty, unemployment, currently living in danger, and so forth.

The well-worn saying "Life is a vale of tears" suggests that suffering is a necessary and normal part of life. It is resisting suffering, and failing to see its potential for strengthening our bond with others and its changeable nature, that limits our self-compassion. Knowing that we cannot make our suffering last any more than we can make it go away, and that we are a part of a world where many suffer, contributes immensely to our ability to care for ourselves.

There are several strategies for strengthening your connection with humanity:

- **Understand that suffering is not failing.** Suffering is actually proof of your humanity. At any given moment, you and many others are in pain. Rather than criticize yourself for suffering, try acknowledging it and recognizing its impermanence. Say to yourself, "I am suffering and this will change… I am suffering, along with millions of others… I acknowledge my suffering and release it." Pema Chödrön (2012) said it well in her book, *Living Beautifully with Uncertainty and Change*, "When we resist change, it's called suffering. But when we can completely let go and not struggle against it, when we can embrace the groundlessness of our situation and relax into its dynamic quality, that's called enlightenment."

- **See suffering as helpful to your evolution as a person.** In implementing this strategy, it is important to recognize that you are like many others in learning life's lessons through suffering. Truly, it is not possible to learn some lessons without feeling sad, frustrated, or fed up. Putting these lessons in the context of "being a part of being human" puts them in a whole new light.

- **Our failures are not proof of our aloneness but of our common humanity.** This is a key principle of self-compassion, because we tend to feel alone and cut off from the world when we fail at something or run headlong into a painful personal flaw. Because we are taught that failure is abnormal, the corollary idea is that we must be different from others if we fail. But failure need not cut us off from the world—it can actually strengthen our connection with others. An example of this is the Alcoholics Anonymous program, where fellowship is central to the work of addressing the problematic use of alcohol. Another example is various weight-loss groups, where fellowship is a critical aspect of releasing a painful relationship to the body and embracing healthier lifestyle behaviors.

COMMON HUMANITY SKILL BUILDING

The worksheet below invites you to explore your suffering in a broader context than might be familiar for you. The objective is to identify ways to connect your suffering with others and to see it as purposeful and temporary as well. If you tend to minimize your connection with humanity and have a difficult time seeing suffering as a part of life, we recommend that you use this form daily or several times a week to develop stronger skills for accepting pain as part of the human condition.

First, describe a life event, situation, or interaction that causes you to suffer. Then, broaden your perspective on this situation by trying to imagine all of the people in the world who, at this very moment in time, are struggling and suffering in this same type of situation. If your suffering is not an aberration and actually serves a purpose in your life, try to describe what that purpose is. Finally, instead of seeing suffering as unending, try to think of it as occurring at a fixed point in your life journey. See if you can put yourself in the mindset of "This too shall pass." Describe how that mindset might alter how you currently react to this difficult or challenging life issue.

Common Humanity: Skill Practice Plan

Develop a plan to behave differently when you are hurting and not feeling connected to your common humanity. Ask yourself, "What is it that I am suffering with?"

1. Describe the painful event, situation, or interaction.

_____

_____

_____

_____

2. Do other people in the world suffer in this way?

_____

_____

_____

_____

3. Can my suffering teach me something?

_____

_____

_____

_____

4. Will this suffering pass?

_____

_____

_____

_____

Further Exploration. How did you do with this exercise? The idea that you are part of humanity can be a little hard to get your arms around at first. It is challenging to imagine that others are suffering from the same types of flaws, disappointments, life setbacks, or failures that you are, but it's true. And once you realize that everyone has a burden to bear, you can bear yours in the context of being a part of humanity.

When we have no choice but to live with a challenging situation, such as having a child with a health problem, we may find value in connecting with others who are suffering from challenging situations too. At times, we may find meaning in volunteering to work with others who suffer from problems similar to our own—or different from our own. For example, you may struggle with caring for a spouse with dementia but find that volunteering at a food bank or tutoring at an elementary school gives you a huge sense of connection with the challenges of being human and being together. You don't have to work directly with people who are suffering in the same way you are in order to reap benefits. You can build your connection to humanity and your skills for seeing your suffering in the context of being human by offering your help to people who suffer in a completely different way.

JOAN'S RESULTS

While Joan did not identify this area as a priority, she used the Common Humanity worksheet to further develop skills in acknowledging shared suffering. She found value in being able to use the word "boring" and to see it as a word rather than a sentence to misery. Joan also liked the sense of connection she felt with others who struggle in a similar way. She was able to see some choices she could make in response to her suffering and to connect with its impermanence.

Joan's Common Humanity: Skill Practice Plan

1. Describe the painful event, situation, or interaction.

At a social gathering after work with a colleague and couldn't engage in small talk. Eventually, colleague started talking to a person right next to me. I had the thought, "I'm dull and uninteresting." Like so many other times, I had this feeling of being alone and disconnected.

2. Do other people in the world suffer in this way?

Of course, lots of people like to keep to themselves and probably feel like a fish out of water in social situations. I imagine being there to comfort them.

3. Can my suffering teach me something?

My suffering is teaching me to be okay with my differences. I am different in how I react to things. When I try to be the same as others, then I suffer.

4. Will this suffering pass?

I can let go of thinking that I have to talk more. If and when I do that, I will find more peace.

The Middle Path

A cornerstone of self-compassion is the ability to walk a middle path—the perspective from which you can see yourself and what has happened in your life in a balanced way. On the middle path, when something happens that upsets you, you see it from a perspective that promotes mental and emotional balance. Rather than exaggerating the significance of a problem or mistake you make, you simply describe the problem and let it be. Cultivating this middle-path perspective strengthens the neural circuitry of your wise mind and helps you see life with soft eyes. If we are all swimming in the same river of life, and we all possess an assortment of positive and negative qualities, there is no reason to get bent out of shape when one of your negative qualities shows up. As the title to the popular self-help book by Richard Carlson so poignantly states: "Don't sweat the small stuff...and it's all small stuff" (Carlson 1997).

Strategies that help you build a middle-path perspective may include mental exercises that foster psychological flexibility as well as lifestyle practices that enhance your sense of mental balance. The worksheet that follows provides structure for an exercise that helps you curb the impulse to overreact when you are faced with an emotionally charged situation. Often, all that is needed is for you to recognize the impulse to overreact—and then be able to imagine what the overreaction would look like, along with what the middle path would look like. By seeing the difference between the two, you can wisely choose to travel the middle path.

MIDDLE-PATH SKILL BUILDING

This exercise invites you to identify an activity that you believe will support you in developing less reactivity and more balance in your day-to-day perspectives on life.

First, describe a recent emotionally triggering situation or event. Then imagine what an overreaction to that event would look like. Next, report from the perspective of the middle path—describe just the facts in a nonreactive way without injecting or attaching to your judgments. Finally, think about a lifestyle activity that would act as a regular cue for you to practice taking the middle path. These types of activities may include becoming a part of a spiritual community, such as a church; joining a yoga or meditation group; or participating in a sports activity involving self-discipline and mental focus.

Middle Path: Skill Practice Plan

Develop a plan to take the middle path when you are triggered to overreact, whether toward yourself or others.

1. Describe the challenging event, situation, or interaction.

_____

_____

_____

_____

2. What would it look like if I overreacted?

_____

_____

_____

_____

3. What would it look like if I took the middle path?

_____

_____

_____

_____

4. What would promote better middle-path perspective taking in my life?

_____

_____

_____

_____

Further Exploration. What happened when you tried to imagine taking the middle path, instead of being emotionally reactive and judgmental? Did you feel the burden of suffering lift a little bit? Did you feel a sense that it might be easier to roll in this situation if you stayed focused on the middle path? After all, if it is all "small stuff," then you can conserve a lot of your mental energy by going to the middle!

JOAN'S RESULTS

Joan wanted to strengthen her ability to take a middle-path perspective, because she felt that she often overreacted—not just in relation to her insecurities about her work performance and value, but also in other social situations in which she felt like a fifth wheel. One situation that stood out for her was being more socially integrated at her place of worship, where she had met a lot of people she liked but with whom she didn't initiate any follow-up contact.

Middle Path: Skill Practice Plan

1. Describe the challenging event, situation, or interaction.

Performance evaluation from my supervisor. She was positive, but I did not receive a raise or a promotion.

2. What would it look like if I overreacted?

They don't value me. They think I'm a social misfit and are just being nice to me. I should get a new job.

3. What would it look like if I took the middle path?

It's been a tough year for the company, and they still got me a better benefits package than last year. It could have been worse; it could have been better. No need to overthink it.

4. What would promote better middle-path perspective taking in my life?

Try to join a women's group at church, just to give me a chance to take some social risks.

JOAN'S JOURNEY TOWARD A VITAL LIFE

As Joan continued to practice self-compassion in daily living, she noticed that she was not as preoccupied with her quiet, reserved nature as she used to be. She received social invitations from several members of her women's group, took advantage of the opportunities, and soon was drafted as chair of one of their charity events. Her anxiety level during performance reviews at work steadily decreased, and she received feedback that she was being more of a team player who contributed value to her work group. One particularly powerful exercise she developed on her own was to stand for a few minutes in front of the mirror every morning. When her reactive mind would show up with harsh evaluations of her being dull and uninteresting, Joan would soften her focus and connect with her innate goodness as a person.

During one of these morning moments, she had a thought about her ex-husband and his seemingly insatiable need to point out her supposed personality flaws. She realized that he too must be struggling with his own fears, inadequacies, and imperfections, and perhaps it was fitting that they had ended up on separate paths. Joan decided it was time to close this chapter of her life and open a new one—one that included the possibility of finding a new life partner. Joan was on the journey to living a vital life!

BRAIN TRAINING EXERCISES FOR SELF-COMPASSION

Of all the mindfulness skills we have taught you so far in this book, practicing compassion for self and others is one of the quickest ways to promote a positive emotional aura in your life. We normally don't take the time in daily life to work out the brain's reward and positive emotion circuitry, and so we forget how powerful these particular mindfulness muscles are!

FEELING LOVED

Can you remember a time in your life when you felt totally loved and cared for? Can you remember what it felt like to bask in the warmth of being accepted for who you are? In this audio-guided exercise, we want you to put yourself in full contact with a moment when you truly felt loved.

To start, see if you can recall and describe some peak moments in your life when you felt really loved. Then, choose perhaps one or two of these moments to use during this exercise. We will help you re-create the actual physical, emotional, and mental experience of receiving love.

Now, get seated comfortably, close your eyes, and take a few deep cleansing breaths. Let your breath get both longer and deeper with each cycle of inhaling and exhaling. Get your mind clear, focused, and ready to imagine the moment in time when you truly felt loved. Put yourself into it; don't spare any details about the various feelings, thoughts, memories, or physical sensations that this experience created in you. You might remember being held or gently touched by a parent when you were small. Or you might recall moments with a partner, such as holding hands and watching a beautiful sunset. Perhaps you have a memory of being hugged by someone who was very glad to see you after a period of time apart. Feel the warmth in your heart and mind as you just let yourself bask in love as it washes over you.

Try to keep those sensations present. Notice the unconditional quality of this love; it isn't something earned; it is given freely. Your imperfections are part of this experience of love. Now, try to see if you can shower yourself with this same feeling as was shared with you by someone else. See if you can make that slight U-turn and start reflecting that positive energy on yourself. The experience of loving yourself may come in many forms: it may lie more in the realm of sensation or perhaps color. Let whatever inner experiences show up just be there, and attach your loving energy to them. If you run into a moment of doubt, try to shower that doubt with love as well. Anything that comes your way is perfect; you can let your love wash over it.

When you hear the meditation bell, you can slowly bring yourself back into the present. And when you are ready, move on to the next brain training activity.

Further Exploration. What happened when you just let yourself be showered with love? Did it feel awkward at first, like you didn't deserve it or that it seemed artificial? That is a pretty common experience, which speaks to how as adults we gradually learn that we must earn love from other people. How sad, when you think about it, that you somehow have to prove that you deserve love. Love is the most powerful expression of human attachment there is! This quote by Steve Hayes, one of the cofounders of ACT, says it best: *Love isn't everything; it's the only thing.* However you experience it, love is love, and it primes our brains to be compassionate toward others as well as toward ourselves.

YOU ARE FLAWSOME!

This exercise requires you to practice self-compassion for your personal flaws, both real and imagined. There are two basic types of flaws that figure prominently in our negative self-stories that we tend to beat ourselves up about. The first is some attribute we have that we find unacceptable, be it a receding hairline, stuttering under stress, or not being as interesting as other people. The second type of flaw is something we believe we lack, like good looks, confidence in social situations, or public speaking ability.

Take a few minutes now to identify the flaws you most dislike about yourself in both areas. Try to clearly describe the flaw and what you don't like about it.

My Flaws:	Why It Bothers Me:

Now that you have identified your flaws, it is time to practice being flawsome! Read each of your flaws out loud, and at the end of each statement add in "and I love this part of me too!" As you recite this statement, put yourself into it.

Further Exploration. Were you able to genuinely extend loving energy toward those things you dislike about yourself? If your reactive mind tells you that your flaw can't be accepted, practice detachment and gently redirect your attention to loving yourself. You could even take what your reactive mind told you and write *that* down as a flaw and make that part of your flawsomeness! The fact that you have a reactive mind that is unwilling to stop judging you is also a part of your flawsomeness. How cool is that? During this practice, try to create a mental space in which you relax, let go of attachment to self-rejection, and truly love what you dislike about yourself.

EXPRESS GRATITUDE

One way to experience self-compassion is to make contact with and express the experience of gratitude or thankfulness. One exercise we like to use is called One in the Beginning and One in the End. Upon waking, express gratitude for whatever enters your awareness. If you hear a dog barking, your beginning line might be, "I am thankful for dogs." Or you might become aware of the feeling in your eyes—that they are rested and ready to begin the day—and say, "I am thankful for my eyes."

"One in the End" refers to the same practice when you lie down at night to sleep. If your awareness is of a soft, favorite pillow, express gratitude by softly saying, "I am thankful for my pillow" or simply "I am thankful for the end of the day and the opportunity to lie down. While you may benefit from simply thinking these thoughts of gratitude, you may also want to experiment with saying them aloud or writing them in a gratitude journal.

PROMISE YOURSELF

Practicing self-compassion is not an accident; it is an intention that you need to reaffirm every day. Try starting your day by repeating this simple affirmation to be self-compassionate:

When I experience suffering today, I will acknowledge the moment of suffering.

I will remind myself that suffering is part of being human.

And I will treat myself and others with kindness in this moment of suffering.

WISH YOURSELF WELL

Another way to cultivate compassion each day is to wish yourself well in the most important areas of daily life: physical safety, physical health, mental health, and ease of being. This short audio-guided exercise will help you connect with your most self-compassionate intentions.

Get comfortably seated, close your eyes, and take several deep cleansing breaths. Allow your breathing to get longer and deeper with each breath cycle until your attention is completely focused on the here and now. Don't rush yourself; just take the time to be with yourself and come into full contact with your consciousness. Now, to start with, you will slowly repeat each phrase softly and out loud. Take your time and really ponder each word in each phrase.

May I live in safety.

May I have physical health.

May I have mental health.

May I have ease of being.

Each time you repeat this sequence, try to form a deeper and deeper, earnestly felt self-compassionate intention. You truly wish yourself the best. Continue softly repeating this sequence until you hear the meditation bell.

Further Exploration. How did it feel to wish yourself the very best in today's life? Did some part of you think that you don't deserve any of these things? Reactive mind is capable of putting you into a space where that can easily happen. If that showed up during this exercise, make a self-compassion game plan for what you intend to do the next time that happens…and recommit to practicing this brain training exercise as often as you like!

IDEAS TO CULTIVATE

- Self-compassion is the perfect antidote to the harsh, self-critical, self-rejecting chatter of the reactive mind.

- Self-compassion involves being kind and affectionate toward yourself, even when your flaws or imperfections are exposed, or when you are in a moment of inner pain.

- It is easier to be self-compassionate when you remind yourself that all humans have flaws, that all humans have moments of suffering, and that you are not alone in your suffering.

- Practicing self-compassion skills on a daily basis will allow you to short-circuit the tendency to be hard on yourself when you run into inevitable life disappointments or setbacks.

- Being self-compassionate also promotes your ability to be compassionate toward, and to improve your connection with, others.

CHAPTER 12

Step 8: Live with Vision and Intention

Vision without action is a daydream. Action without vision is a nightmare.

—Japanese saying

Depression often is the result of living on autopilot, in which you follow other people's rules or simply try to avoid being exposed to failure, setback, or rejection. One mindful alternative is to create a powerful life vision and the corresponding intention to follow it. Developing daily routines that require imagination, vision, and intention stimulates and strengthens the emotional reward centers of your brain. You will find that the combination of living with intention linked to your values and a clear vision of the life you want to live is powerful medicine indeed!

Up to now, we have introduced you to several mindfulness skills that you can use to address the assortment of mental barriers that reactive mind throws in your way as you make your journey toward a vital life. These are undeniably important life skills, and, just used on their own, would probably improve your quality of life. However, at heart, ACT is a behavior therapy. We are in the business of helping people create radical change in their lives. So, there is a little more work yet to be done, if you will bear with us. This involves helping you accomplish the eighth step on your quest to transcend depression: forming a powerful life vision and developing your intention to live according to that vision. If learning to live mindfully is the means to the end, then being able to live your life vision is the end.

Think of your life vision as the amalgamation of all of your values projecting out to the end of your life. In this sense, your life vision is the "grand plan" that you intend to follow in your life. This important and often overlooked aspect of mindfulness is experienced as a dreamy quality of knowing something without your being able to readily explain how you know it. It doesn't come from your verbal, reactive mind. This sense of life mission is anchored squarely in the wise mind and is associated with intuition, premonition, preconscious awareness, and inspiration. It's a kind of awareness that allows you to see the future not in the rigid, evaluative terms of your reactive mind but rather in an idealistic, positive, and intriguing way. In contrast to the quest for the illusion of control over life that is the hallmark of reactive mind, the visions, intuitions, and premonitions of wise mind can draw us into an unknown future with a sense of curiosity and eagerness. On more days than not, this allows you to wake up to a distinct feeling of being alive and well!

To achieve this positive state of mind, we'll help you envision the life you want to live, first at the level of basic qualities and then at the level of intention. This involves developing a life vision based upon intuition and inspiration with the aim of defining the themes for the rest of your journey through life. Then we'll help you plan the actions you intend to take to realize that vision. Taking specific steps to live out your vision is done with full knowledge that your reactive mind will undoubtedly attempt to stop you in your tracks with those all-too-familiar emotional barriers. When it does, your wise mind will tell you what to do: *Be willing to accept these barriers for what they are and keep moving in the direction of "true north."*

As you work through this chapter, we have an important request: The vision exercises we will take you through require you to leave the familiar, day-to-day world and let your mind travel to places you may only know in your imagination. We'll ask you to be open to a metaphorical world, where you can listen for pieces of wisdom to help guide you on your life journey. Accept any gifts you receive the same way you would an unexpected birthday present. Be amazed and thankful for wonder in the universe. Accept what comes to you with grace.

WHAT IS A LIFE VISION?

A life vision involves having a clear, consistent image of your overall purpose in life. While it doesn't usually include a step-by-step guide, it does provide a sense of continuity and direction as you proceed through the typical stages of life: birth, childhood, emancipation from your parents, formation of a family of your own, aging, health problems, and death.

So how do the concepts of true north, life vision, and intention connect with each other? To create a memorable life journey, you need both a destination, which is what goes into a life vision, and a course to follow, which you create on a daily basis by sticking to your true north. Intention, as we use it, is the act of being and acting in the present moment each day, keeping in mind your life's destination and the true north course that will take you there. Intention guides you through the seconds of your life, and as the Buddhist saying goes: *If you take care of the seconds, the years will take care of themselves.*

In contemporary society, we often develop a life vision in a haphazard way, if we develop one at all. A variety of factors may contribute to this clouding of life vision, including messages received from relatives, teachers, and other authority figures. As we grow up, most of us receive a mixture of optimistic and pessimistic predictions from various authority figures, and many of these people may not be purposeful in their delivery of these messages. Various personal qualities may create an imbalance in feedback that favors negative predictions about what a child can expect from life, often creating a self-perpetuating cycle. This unfortunate experience makes forming a vision of a meaningful life particularly challenging.

Many of the messages originating in contemporary society about how to live "the good life" are often just socially inculcated rules about how to live without upsetting the tribe. We are promised rewards if we follow the "rules." Unfortunately, all of the reactive mind power of the entire tribe doesn't eliminate the basic flaws of reactive mind; it just enhances them. So, while some socially transmitted rules are helpful, others are problematic. We recently asked several college students about their visions for their life at this early stage in their life journeys. Here are some of their responses:

I don't know what to do. I know I have to go to college because everyone in my family does, and I know that I'd better get good grades.

Go to school, get good grades, and then get a job being the boss.

Get a degree in business, then get a good-paying job and buy a nice car.

Rules about acquiring things that symbolize success are common in modern society, but as the Dalai Lama notes, attachment to worldly things also can be the source of great suffering (Dalai Lama, Lhundrub, and Cabezon 2011). It creates the illusion that the roots of happiness lie outside of us, not inside of us. And, in the world of worldly things, bad things can happen just as easily as good things. What happens when the Great Recession hits and you get laid off from a job that you've had for twenty-five years, and you suddenly discover that the company pension plan is bankrupt and your retirement savings have vanished? Even if you pass the cultural litmus test and become a "success," a nice car, a nice house, and a good job may not translate into a vital, purpose-driven life. Even with all the trappings of a "good life," many people feel empty and wonder why their lives lack substance and a deeper sense of purpose and meaning.

If you developed a vision about your life when you were young, think for a moment about that vision. Would the people around you now recognize that vision being actualized in your daily activities? If you didn't have a life vision when you were younger, do you have one now? If you do, who in your life supports your efforts to live according to that vision? Has your vision for your life changed over time? How? Why?

All too often, people climb the tall ladder of socially defined success only to find that the prize at the top isn't really what they set out to attain. Don't worry if a vision for your life has not yet come to you. You aren't alone. Right now, many others like you are trying to form a life vision, while others are seeking to clarify, refine, or revise their vision. Life takes many unexpected twists and turns, creating a need to evaluate and update your vision on a pretty regular basis. In truth, pursuing your life vision is something you'll do every day for the rest of your life. The fact that you're reading this now means you're ready to come closer to a more meaningful and deeply experienced vision; it means you're preparing yourself to live the life you want to live.

NEURONOTES: IMAGINATION IS THE MOST COMPLEX OF ALL BRAIN ACTIVITIES

A life vision necessarily involves using the imagination to assemble mental representations of the future, creatively develop different means to imagined ends, and problem-solve imagined barriers via different brain simulations. As might be expected, imagination is an extremely complex brain activity. One recent study found that no fewer than eleven distinct regions of the brain become sequentially involved during an imagination task. This broadly distributed pattern of neural activity—involving the perceptual, memory retrieval, and self-referential processing areas of the brain—has been called the "mental workspace" (Schlegel et al. 2013).

Another recent study showed that imagination tasks activate a unique neural pathway in the hippocampus, the area of the brain most implicated in memory retrieval and mental rehearsal (Kirwan, Ashby, and Nash 2014). Remember also that activation of the hippocampus is one distinctive feature of the default mode network (DMN). Although overactivation of the DMN is related to failures of present-moment awareness, mind wandering, and depression, appropriate levels of DMN activation are associated with imagination, social reasoning, self-awareness, and creativity. It appears that in daydreaming and mind wandering, the coordinated sequence of brain activity that leads from memory retrieval to formulating and testing new mental representations of future events stalls out. In this sense, you might think of rumination as your imagination gone bad.

Imagination relies on using perceptual information, such as visual and spatial inputs, to create mental images that often are analogies for physical relationships (Schlegel et al. 2013). Coming full circle, this is why the visioning exercises in this chapter ask you to physicalize your life vision rather than think about it in the abstract. It is easier for the imagination network of your brain to develop a vision of the future this way.

VISION PLATEAU

This exercise invites you to use your imagination to clarify your life vision at this point in your life and to generate information that will help you make plans that support that vision. We recommend that you download the audio version from http://www.newharbinger.com/38457 so that you can close your eyes and be guided through the exercise. Before starting, find a comfortable place to either sit or lie down, like a quiet place at home, or at a local park. We want you to be in a state of mental quiet, so you can stay focused on this guided meditation, which will take 15 minutes or so.

At this moment in time, you are going to take a journey to Vision Plateau. Inhale deeply and allow yourself to relax as you exhale slowly. As you breathe, prepare yourself to receive something important. Breathe in the air you need to sustain you, and breathe out any reservations. Feel your body as it warms and becomes heavy and soft. This is the nature of relaxing and a helpful way to prepare to receive something you need. Breathe in and out, and know the breath for what it is—a bridge between your body and mind. Walk that bridge and strengthen the connection. Be here and be now.

As you are ready, begin to imagine that you're walking on a path. Everything is new on this path, yet it seems familiar. It is as if you've been here before, but you have no conscious memory of it. The path goes through the woods and comes out at a river. The river is wide and the current swift. You sit down to watch the water. You wait and watch and breathe. The sun is high in the sky and it warms you. The sunlight plays on the water, and the current takes the light, and together they create shapes. While you don't understand this, you sense that the sun and the water are working together to give you something, something to take with you. It may be a shape, a texture, a sound, or a color. You will know it when you see it. Name it and take it, because it is for you.

When you're ready, you can leave the river. It will be time to move on. Now you're going to Vision Plateau, where someone is waiting for you—a special person who has known you all your life. This person has heard every affirmative statement made to you. This person knows your strengths, your vulnerabilities, and your values. Breathe in and out, and know that you will soon shake hands with a person who understands and loves you.

The plateau is only a few hundred yards ahead. Take your time. There's no need to rush as you climb to your final destination. When you reach the top, you sense the presence of another being. You sit down on the plateau. It feels good, solid, and warmed by sunlight. This is a good place to rest and wait. Your back is straight, and you feel relaxed, almost like you're floating. You can see a long way in every direction from Vision Plateau. You stand up so that you can turn in all directions to appreciate this extensive view. You look to the east, to the south, to the west, and then to the north.

Having taken in so much, you are satisfied, and you sit down again, now facing north. You close your eyes, and you can easily see moments from your life, from the beginning of your consciousness to this very moment. Some are pleasant, some less so. They are all just moments, memories, and images. Take them in and let them go. Breathe in and breathe out. Walk the bridge of the breath, connecting mind and body.

As you watch the picture show of your life and breathe, someone approaches you. You sense the presence of a friend and feel no need to open your eyes or stand. You wait for this friend's touch, and you know that it will be a loving, gentle touch. You feel soft, warm fingertips on your forehead, and you know that this person is here to help you see your life vision clearly.

Remember the gift the sun and river gave you, and tell your wise friend about it. This will strengthen the work you do together now. Talk it over. Breathe in and out. Allow silence. Pay attention closely. What does your friend do with the shape, sound, or image you were given? Does your friend change it or simply mirror it back for you to see? How does this relate to a vision for your life? Accept anything your mind says about your vision—good or bad, desired or not desired. Accept it as mental activity; then accept your evaluation of mental activity and return to the moment and your friend and your work together on Vision Plateau.

When your friend is ready to leave, stand and express your gratitude. After your friend departs, look to the east and imagine a future that includes your past. Then look to the south and imagine a future that includes the present and the courage to pursue your life vision. Then look to the west and imagine a future that includes the present and the ability to plan activities that fulfill that vision, even when there is no specific reward for doing so, and perhaps no end to the suffering of pursuing your vision. Finally, turn to the north and see that wise people are there to help you now and always with your life vision. Look into their eyes and thank them.

You can now prepare to leave Vision Plateau. This is a place you can return to. Your experiences will differ each time you go. Say good-bye and take the path down and around, back into the forest, past the river, and back to the place where you live day to day and where you are resting and using your powers of imagination to create a vision for planning a vital life. Breathe in and breathe out, walk the bridge between your body and mind, and when you are ready, open your eyes. You are seeing a new world now—seeing a new world with new eyes.

As soon as you complete the Vision Plateau visualization, answer the following questions. You can also record them in your journal or download the worksheet from http://www.newharbinger.com/38457.

Vision Plateau Worksheet

What did the river and sunlight offer you? Was it a shape, an image, a group of words, or something else?

_____

_____

_____

What does the gift mean to you?

_____

_____

_____

What do you recall seeing from your past as you waited on Vision Plateau?

_____

_____

_____

What did you feel when your friend touched your forehead on Vision Plateau?

_____

_____

_____

What happened to your life vision as you talked with your friend about your gift from the river and the sun?

_____

_____

_____

What did you say in expressing gratitude to your friend?

_____

_____

_____

What did you see when you looked to the south and saw courage to pursue your life vision?

_____

_____

_____

What did you see when you looked to the west and saw the ability to plan activities consistent with your life vision?

_____

_____

_____

Who did you see when you looked to the north and saw wise people ready to support your life vision?

_____

_____

_____

Further Exploration. How did you fare during this exercise? Were you able to put yourself into the images that were created? Were you able to stay present with the guided journey? Did you profit in some unexpected way from just allowing yourself to roll along with the exercise? For many people, this is a very powerful experience that produces a wide range of emotional reactions. So if you experienced a mixture of sadness, curiosity, regret, or anticipation along the way, that is pretty commonplace. If you found this exercise emotionally meaningful, you'll want to save your responses and review them from time to time. You may find that you understand your answers differently as you go further with planning directions and changes in key areas of your life.

EXAMPLE: RUTH'S EXPERIENCE

Remember Ruth from chapter 10? A survivor of sexual violence, she had struggled with forming a close and lasting intimate relationship. Although she wanted a lifetime partner, she eventually concluded that this simply wasn't in the cards for her. After all, her parents spent most of their relationship in a cold war and finally ended their marriage when Ruth was fourteen. Even if she could get over the trauma of sexual abuse, how would she ever learn the skills needed to stay in a close relationship?

Ruth's life vision included being an artist: a person who could arrange colors and objects in ways that were esthetically satisfying. As a child, she had shown talent and found that drawing helped her escape from the silent suffering she sensed in her home. She downplayed the fact that she drank a little too much in the evenings when she was feeling particularly blue and reasoned that it was okay because she could stop drinking if she wanted to and had few other bad health habits.

Ruth was a little apprehensive about the Vision Plateau exercise, but she truly wanted to deepen and expand her vision for her life. She decided to take a walk to the park to settle her mind and connect with nature before doing the meditation and answering the questions. Here's what she came up with in response to the questions above:

Ruth's Vision Plateau Worksheet

What did the river and sunlight offer you? Was it a shape, an image, a group of words, or something else?

I saw a rainbow.

What does the gift mean to you?

It means good luck to me. It also means diversity and unending transitions.

What do you recall seeing from your past as you waited on Vision Plateau?

I saw myself standing alone in a room with a lot of people who were talking to each other. It was kind of loud and I wanted to leave.

What did you feel when your friend touched your forehead on Vision Plateau?

I felt relieved, like I had been waiting for her forever. And strangely, I didn't feel like we needed to speak.

What happened to your life vision as you talked with your friend about your gift from the river and the sun?

I saw myself being in a group of people—artists with things they were making. They were interested in each other's work and committed to their own; they were serious but fun-loving artists. I felt like I belonged.

What did you say in expressing gratitude to your friend?

I said "Namaste," meaning "peace for both of us," and told her I would return.

What did you see when you looked to the south and saw courage to pursue your life vision?

I saw a little girl holding up a picture she drew; she was proud of it and wanted people to see it.

What did you see when you looked to the west and saw the ability to plan activities consistent with your life vision?

I saw myself taking an art class and meeting people who were artists. I saw myself supporting their work and taking chances in showing mine.

Who did you see when you looked to the north and saw wise people ready to support your life vision?

I saw people who didn't shame me for using alcohol to escape my pain, but who instead wanted me to treat my body and mind with respect and kindness. They wore blankets the color of golden corn, and they had green eyes and sweet smiles.

Ruth felt that the exercise helped her expand and clarify her vision. She felt more optimistic, and she decided to spend a few minutes every morning drawing with charcoals and considering her life vision further. She bought a new journal with a warm yellow cloth cover and named it her rainbow journal. In addition to drawing, she planned to make notes each morning about her life vision and her plans for that day.

FORM YOUR LIFE VISION

Elements of your life vision often come from your wise mind and may appear in many different forms: images, pictures, gut-level feelings, intuitions, or sudden insights. Similarly, values originate in your wise mind. They aren't derived logically; rather, they are more like intuitive ways of knowing where you want your life to head and what you want to stand for in your life. When you express your values with words, the words are typically action oriented; for example, to be a *loving* partner, to be a mother who really *listens,* or to be someone who is *devoted to helping* those in need. Your values, which we helped you identify and describe in chapter 5, can serve as the framework for establishing a life vision; they reflect what matters to you, and acting according to them can help create a sense of life purpose.

Remember that values typically manifest themselves in the life domains of relationships, work/study, leisure/play, and health. In order to create your life vision, it's important to revisit your values in these areas. As a reminder, think of *health* broadly: a state of physical, mental, social, and psychological integrity supported by skills that help you deal effectively with the ongoing stresses in life. The area of *relationships* involves the way you interact with people—an intimate partner, family members, coworkers, neighbors, and so on—and your ability to be present, honest, and authentic with them. Engagement in *work or study* activities looks at the specific qualities you bring to the process of working, whether through a job, school, or regular volunteering. Engagement in *leisure or play* activities concerns qualities you bring to whatever you enjoy: hobbies, sports, leisure activities, and so on.

Now you will create several life vision statements from the information you received in the Vision Plateau exercise. You'll also identify the underlying values that form the foundation of your vision plan. Before you get started, take a bit of time to review the work you did on defining your true north, in chapter 5. For example, you might benefit from a review of your responses to the Bull's-Eye exercise. Spend some time contemplating your responses. Make any additions or modifications to your values statements that seem appropriate at this juncture of the self-help program. You may wish to write out more detailed descriptions of your values before distilling them into more concise statements in the worksheet below. If you're having difficulty linking the vision exercise below to your previous values work, take a look at some of the examples that follow the written exercise to help guide you.

CREATING YOUR LIFE VISION

This exercise builds on the previous exercise, Vision Plateau, and asks you to connect your visualization with your values. Life vision (the destination) and values (the direction to be followed) are highly personal, reflecting your unique life experiences and knowledge up to this moment in time.

1. To begin, in the "Life Vision Gift" column describe what you saw or received on Vision Plateau that gave breadth or depth to your vision for your life. Do this for each life domain.

2. In the "Life Vision Statement" column write one sentence that describes your vision for your life. Do this for each domain.

3. In the "Values" column describe your values in each of the life domains at this point in time. Each description need not be comprehensive; just write a concise statement that's representative of your current perspective on what's important in each domain.

4. In the "Vision and Values Statement" column integrate your vision and values into one statement of purpose and intention. Do this for each of the four life domains.

Life Vision and Values Statements Worksheet

Life Domain	Life Vision Gift	Life Vision Statement	Values	Vision and Values Statement
Relationships				
Work/Study				
Leisure/Play				
Health				

Further Exploration. How did you do with this exercise? Was it hard to come up with a combined vision and values statement in some areas but not others? This might suggest you have more clarity about your life mission in one life domain over another. You can sometimes use the confidence created by having clarity in one life area to try some new and bold statement in an area where you are not necessarily clear. It's important to avoid rushing through this exercise; if it takes you more than one sitting to get it fleshed out, that's preferable. In particular, the vision and values statements can be quite challenging to put into words. Indeed, it took Ruth several days of thinking and contemplation to eventually complete that portion of the exercise.

Ruth's Results

When she reflected on her inner experiences with the Vision Plateau meditation, Ruth had new ideas about how to better address health, work, leisure, and relationship issues in her life. She spent considerable time writing the following responses on her worksheet, and as she did, the process helped her better understand the gifts she received when she arrived at Vision Plateau.

Ruth's Life Vision and Values Statements Worksheet

Life Domain	Life Vision Gift	Life Vision Statement	Values	Vision and Values Statement
Relationships	A rainbow	Many kinds of people come into my life. I respect their differences and the impact those differences have on me.	I value courage.	I will make courageous, bold moves in pursuing meaningful relationships.
Work/Study	A rainbow	I will always have meaningful work opportunities.	I value respect and diversity.	I will show respect for my work and the work of others.
Leisure/Play	The little girl	I have a gift for making things beautiful.	I value self-expression and being a part of a group.	I will share my creativity with others.
Health	Loving green eyes seeing me, understanding me.	Other people love and support me.	I value recognition of support from others.	I will look for love in people's eyes, and I will treat myself with kindness.

Again, we understand that identifying something as basic and important as a life vision can be daunting partly because, as we mentioned before, we are not taught to think big about our lives. We are taught to think small, to conform to social standards, and to wait for the promised rewards if we don't rock the boat. It is in this spirit that we offer these examples from a variety of people who've completed the exercise, not to tell you what would be appropriate for you but rather to help you grasp the spirit of the exercise.

RELATIONSHIPS

Listening with all my senses, just like my wise friend on Vision Plateau

Accepting my lack of control over my husband's struggles (the man with the rope I couldn't reach in my vision) and filling that space between us with love

WORK/STUDY

Being mindful in my work activities (like the sun on the water in my vision, which always found a new place to connect)

Connecting and cooperating with my coworkers (accepting that we can't all be like the monarch in my vision)

LEISURE/PLAY

Taking my pain with me into my play (knowing it for what it is, hot and heavy like the piping-hot biscuit offered in my vision) and letting it, too, be a teacher

Laughing with abandon like my great-aunt, now passed on, but present in the group of wise people I saw when I looked north.

HEALTH

Using the gracefulness of the bird I saw in my vision to surrender to sleep so that I approach life with more rest and better balance

Using my cane to help me dance and play at the park with my grandchildren

CULTIVATING INTENTION

Now let's learn about the important skill of being intentional. *Intention* helps us find a balance between imagining and doing, between seeing possibilities and executing various actions. Intention is not the same as action; it normally will precede action. As such, forming intentions involves learning to use your imagination to generate alternative paths you could walk down; to go through a mental rehearsal of the actions needed to go down each path; to conduct a mental evaluation of the different consequences associated with each path; and then to choose a preferred course of action. As this description suggests, intention is a very complex mental process, and it requires you to be present and aware, and make voluntary choices. You can't be intentional when you are living on autopilot. You need all of the brain resources at your disposal to consistently be intentional.

One of the biggest threats of modern culture is that many aspects of daily living have been made so easy that we don't really think about what we are doing as we are doing it. Then, when we run into a challenging life situation that requires us to exercise the intention circuitry of the brain, our intention muscles turn out to be weak and flabby from lack of use. We would argue that depression and intentional living are stationed at opposite ends of the life vitality pole. Many depression-producing behaviors are done without any intention. They just happen automatically and with minimal self-awareness.

For example, procrastination, a common problem in depression, appears because there is no intention formed to follow a vision path. You didn't procrastinate because you were depressed; you failed to follow through on a planned action because you did not generate a strong intention to follow through. The following exercise offers a strategy for becoming more flexible and mindful in planning and living a vital life.

KEEPING THE BEST OF INTENTIONS

This exercise will help you form the intention to do something that's consistent with the vision and values statements you came up with in the preceding exercise. You will go through the entire sequence of steps involved in forming an intention:

- Linking vision and intention

- Mentally rehearsing acting according to your vision

- Mentally evaluating possible outcomes

- Imagining barriers to intentional action

- Imagining your responses to barriers when they show up

The goal is to stay present and keep your intention flexible but unwavering. If you have any difficulty with this exercise, take a look at the example from Ruth that follows.

1. To start, copy your vision and values statements from the previous exercise into the first blank column of the provided worksheet.

2. Now think about something you can do this week that supports your vision and values statement in each life domain. Write it in the "Intention" column.

3. Now take a minute to imagine that you're implementing the plan and things are going well. However, something negative and unsupportive happens as you implement your plan, and you feel discouraged. Visualize the details of what's happening and watch what your mind has to say about them. Write that down in the "Negative Barrier" column.

4. Now, and this may be the most difficult part of the exercise, imagine that you react to barriers in a way that is positive and supportive of your vision and values statement. It may be that you use one of your mindfulness skills to undermine the barrier, or you enlist the support of someone else if it is an external barrier, or you find a creative way to overcome that barrier on your own. Write down whatever your imagination gives you in the far right-hand column.

Good Intentions Worksheet

Life Domain	Vision and Values Statement	Intention	Negative Barrier	Positive Outcome
Relationships				
Work/Study				
Leisure/Play				
Health				

Further Exploration. What was your experience with creating an intention? Was one kind of intention easier to visualize than another? Were you able to watch your reactive mind come up with barriers? Did you let your wise mind intervene with some kind of positive or reassuring image of an alternative response to overcome barriers? Did your intention remain solid throughout the exercise or did it waver at certain points? We encourage you to use this exercise on a regular basis, as it can help you develop deeper and more "wind resistant" intentions to carry into your future.

Ruth's Experience

Ruth started this exercise with a great deal of enthusiasm. Having clarified her vision and values, she intended to begin making changes in her life. Here's what she came up with.

Ruth's Good Intentions Worksheet

Life Domain	Vision and Values Statement	Intention	Negative Barrier	Positive Outcome
Relationships	I value courageous, bold moves in life.	Go to a new gallery exhibit.	A man starts talking to me and I feel uncomfortable and want to leave. I'm thinking, "He's going to try to hit on me."	I ask the gallery owner about the featured artist and she tells me about an upcoming talk by the artist, and I say, "I'll be there!"
Work/Study	I will show respect for my work and the work of others.	I will bring one of my paintings to work and hang it in my station.	Someone says, "Where did you get that?" and I'm afraid they are going to criticize it.	I tell a couple of people that I painted the picture and that it's one of my favorites because it shows two people who are different from each other really listening to each other.
Leisure/Play	I will share my creativity with others.	I'll volunteer to decorate the bulletin board in the staff room once a month.	My manager will say no, that I'd have to get my decorating plan preapproved.	I ask the manager whom I should talk to about decoration ideas. The go-to person is another art lover like me!
Health	I will look for love in people's eyes, and I will treat myself with kindness.	Go to a beginning yoga class on Saturday morning.	I feel nervous when I get there. I think, "I don't know enough about yoga to go to a class."	After the class, the teacher invites us to come to a picnic later that day, and I say, "Yes, I'll be there."

While this exercise was more difficult than Ruth thought it would be, it helped her anticipate the negative thinking that surfaced as a barrier when she began to implement an important change in her life. It also helped her stretch her imagination in the direction of seeing unanticipated positive events that could support her efforts. She decided that this exercise would be worth integrating into her weekly goal-setting routine.

BRAIN TRAINING FOR VISION AND INTENTION

Like any of the mindfulness skills we have looked at in section 2, the more you practice them, the stronger they will become in real-life settings. Here are several brief vision and intention exercises that you can practice at home. It doesn't take much time to see positive results, if you just stick with it. Remember that the beneficial effects of mindfulness training occurred in research participants with only two weeks of brief daily practice!

LIVE WITH DAILY INTENTION

The main reason we lose contact with the ability to be intentional is because of all the small daily things we do unintentionally and by force of habit. This practice allows you to both form intentions each day and then close the loop on them at night. It will teach you how to use your intention on both a small and a large scale in your life. We promise you: This exercise will make waking up a whole new experience for you!

When you wake up, take a few minutes to formulate your intentions for today. Start by asking yourself:

How do I intend to conduct myself as a person today?

What values do I intend to display in my actions today?

How do I intend to treat other people at work, school, and home today?

What self-care behaviors do I intend to practice today?

At night, before you go to sleep, go back to each intention and put a mental checkmark beside each one you followed through on. If an intention escaped you today, maybe it'll be better for you to focus on one rather than all four areas tomorrow. In that case, choose one for tomorrow and see how that goes.

AWAKENING AND RETIRING WITH LOVE

This meditation exercise, inspired by Ajahn Brahm, is a slight variation of the preceding exercise. It involves focusing your intentions on being present and acting with love and compassion. When you awaken, and again when you retire for the evening, softly and repeatedly recite the questions and your own answers. The answer to question I will always be "now," but we invite you to vary the rest of your responses based on whatever your intentions are in that moment in time.

1. What is the most important time in my life? [*Now*]

2. How do I intend to make now the most important time in my life today? [*Pause and find joy in a little act, be attuned to and aware of my senses, etc.*]

3. Who is the most important person in my life? [*Name of person, myself*]

4. What will I show this person? [*Love and compassion, honesty, support, etc.*]

DELIBERANCE

Deliberance is a funky derivative of the word "deliverance" that a depressed client once used to describe his daily habit of singling out seemingly mundane tasks and doing them very slowly and mindfully. In this exercise, you will mindfully engage in routines that you don't pay much attention to…but perhaps should!

Targets for deliberance training include routine daily tasks like getting out of bed in the morning, chewing the first bite of a meal slowly, washing dishes, doing laundry, taking breaks at work, gardening and yard work, fixing stuff around the house, and so forth. To do things deliberately requires you to show up, get into the moment, and then pay attention to what you are doing as you do it. Listed next are some possible areas in your daily routine that might need the deliberance fix applied to them. Using the Deliberance Planning worksheet below, pick at least one or two routine daily tasks that you will do deliberately and mindfully.

Deliberance Planning Worksheet

Deliberance Activity	Practice Plan (What will I do differently, when, how often, and for how long?)
Getting out of bed in the morning	
Taking the first bite of a meal	
Taking a shower	
Washing breakfast dishes	
Starting a load of laundry	
Taking a 5-minute break at work	
Drinking a cup of tea after lunch	
Tending a houseplant	
Weeding a small area in a garden	

Sweeping the floor in the kitchen	
Changing a lightbulb	
Taking 10 relaxation breaths while sitting up in bed before going to sleep	

TAKE TWICE AS LONG

When you are depressed, you will tend to do daily activities automatically and without much awareness. This exercise requires you to break up this behavior pattern by showing up and being intentional. Pick any of the routine activities listed in the Deliberance exercise and try to do it at half speed; this means it will take you twice as long. Your intention while slowing down is to make conscious contact with each action you engage in while you are completing the task. If you pick taking the first bite of a meal as your target, then you would focus on consciously choosing each behavior you engage in to take a bite (reaching for a fork, lifting the fork, opening your mouth, chewing, tasting, and so on). See if you can get into that zone where you are aware of and can study each action, almost like you are becoming aware of the action for the first time.

These slow, intentional movements are quite likely to trigger the chatter of reactive mind, so you might hear messages like, "Hurry up and get this task done so you can get on to the next one!" If you notice this happening, detach from that message and just see it as a message. You can always speed up again in a few minutes after completing this task. However, you might notice that it is actually kind of fun to slow down and get into doing things with more awareness and intention!

SAY IT OUT LOUD

This is a slight variation of the Live with Daily Intention exercise. At the beginning of your day, pause for a few minutes and try to visualize opportunities for enhancing something that brings you joy that you want to do more often. You would say out loud, "Today, I'm going to talk with [name] about what brings me joy and how I can do it more often."

For example, you might have an opportunity to talk with your spouse or life partner about something that made you feel closer and that you would like to cultivate in your relationship. You would say out loud, "Today, I'm going to talk with [name] about how we can create more opportunities to do this together."

IDEAS TO CULTIVATE

- The quest to build a life worth living requires you to develop a clear vision of the direction you want to head in, based on your values.

- Rehearsing your life vision on a regular basis stimulates and strengthens multiple regions of the brain linked to the experience of creativity, imagination, inspiration, problem solving, and positive motivation.

- Using your imagination to envision the life you desire activates your wise mind, reduces the dominance of your reactive mind, and allows you to see new and different opportunities.

- Intention helps you walk the walk of your life vision while being linked to your values on a day-in, day-out basis.

- Cultivating your ability to act with intention allows you to show up and experience the simple joy of being.

CHAPTER 13

Step 9: Make and Keep Promises to Yourself

Energy and persistence conquer all things.

—Ben Franklin

You have at your beck and call the ability to make powerful, values-based choices that will help you reclaim your life. This involves strengthening neural circuitry responsible for choosing actions that are geared to produce more sublime long-term enrichment over the short-term rewards that come from emotional and behavioral avoidance. Making and keeping promises to live by your values is how you create a life with vitality, integrity, and meaning. Your depression doesn't stand a chance when you commit to taking this high road!

First of all, congratulations on reaching the ninth and final step on your quest to transcend depression and live the life you want to live! To get here in the midst of battling your depression symptoms and your reactive mind is a great achievement, and you should pat yourself on the back for sticking with it.

Thus far, we have introduced you to powerful mindfulness skills that will help you live a vital, purposeful, meaningful life. Being squarely anchored in the present moment of life allows you to see the world as it is, not as what your reactive mind says it is. The twin anchors of acceptance and nonjudgmental detachment keep you from overidentifying with the distressing, unwanted private experiences that can be triggered in the course of daily living. When you hit a rough patch, you can just notice (and be skeptical of) the constant flow of reasons and moral judgments pouring out of your reactive mind. You can be aware of your self-story without having it dominate your perspective on things. You can then clearly see what's working and what isn't from the viewpoint of self-compassion rather than habitual self-criticism. This puts you in a perfect position to go back to wise mind mode, connect with what matters to you in life, and form a clear intention to live according to your values.

There is one central idea that we want you to grasp: We have never met anyone who wanted to be depressed or enjoyed feeling sad, numb, or empty inside. Depression is an awful place to be. And so the question is: How do people end up in a place they don't want to be? Part of the answer is that depression is cunning and persistent. It plays into our basic desire to avoid emotional pain, even though doing so just makes that pain worse. Equally important, though, is that the forces that lead to depression slowly break down our resolve to do things that we know are good for us. When you battle low motivation and the feeling that you are walking through mud for days, weeks, or months on end, it is easy to see how your spirit could get broken.

Throughout this book, we have discussed a lot of different mindfulness strategies that, if used regularly, will create a meaningful, purposeful life. The question confronting you now is this: Will you hold yourself accountable to using these techniques, even while the forces of depression are trying to drag you down? Or to put it in even simpler terms, will you use your energy and persistence to conquer all that you can?

In this chapter, we share with you what might be the most important skill of all: making promises to yourself and following through on them. It's very easy to make empty promises to yourself—most of us routinely do just that. Just think about the millions of people who every year make a New Year's resolution that is all but gone and forgotten by the tenth of January. Learning to keep promises is vital to your success in the quest to transcend depression, particularly when those promises involve promoting your health; improving relationships that are central in your life; contributing to your community through work, education, or volunteerism; and developing growth-producing, restorative patterns of leisure and play. These are the core areas of living that ultimately determine your quality of life—and they will be the arenas in which you execute your most powerful life choices.

Making and keeping a resolution to engage in valued actions in these life domains, even when the temptation to avoid difficult emotions is present, takes courage. Be forewarned: Your reactive mind will work overtime to get you to stop and leave the field. You'll have to stare down your demons and keep moving in the direction you want your life to go, even if you still see those demons on the sidelines.

The life you would like to live is out there waiting for you, and you can claim it. However, it won't be handed to you on a silver platter. Life can be fickle at times, and you can engage in positive, values-based behaviors only to be cut down by factors you have no control over. But we will teach you how to be persistent and stay true to your values. You'll have to do some difficult work to get there, work that won't always be successful, but the rewards more than compensate for the challenges.

In this chapter, we will examine another central concept in ACT called *choice*. Choice is the act of persistently holding yourself accountable to a promise because that promise involves living up to your values and life vision. This is not done to get praise from others or earn a certificate of achievement from life; it is a pact between you and yourself. We will look at some mental and situational barriers that you can anticipate arising as you enter into this pact with yourself, as well as how to address and overcome them. In particular, we will teach you to deal with instances in which you break promises you have made to yourself. We'll also show you how to convert broken promises into opportunities to grow more mature and wiser as a human.

NEURONOTES: CHOICE, FREE WILL, AND FREE WON'T

The issue of human choice and free will has been a source of intense controversy and debate among neuroscientists. A classic research study published by Libet and others (1983) started the controversy by suggesting that unconscious brain impulses typically precede subjective reports of a freely initiated act. The implication is that the brain is preparing us to act even before we know it is, and our experience of choice is an illusion. More contemporary accounts have modified this rather extreme point of view to include the possibility that the experience of free will is part of a complex feedback loop between the brain's motor cortex and the areas of the prefrontal cortex responsible for self-awareness (Haggard 2008). Human choice and decision making are part of an incredibly complex process, requiring multiple neural systems responsible for planning, prediction, mental rehearsal, reward salience, motivation, and moral judgment.

If, indeed, our brain is silently rehearsing options and actions, what is the basis for the options it is considering? One clear answer is the short-term versus longer-term reward value of the behavior. This process of valuation, or *valuing*, seems to originate in the orbital medial prefrontal cortex. Activation of this network is associated with decisions that involve delaying immediate gratification in return for much larger long-term rewards. Patients with brain damage to this area of the brain are typically unable to make this type of choice. Instead, they will impulsively choose an immediate small reward over a much greater long-term reward (Peters 2011).

We think of values as an intrinsic but longer-term source of personal reward. Thus, from a neuroscience perspective, choice is best thought of as an act of *free will* and *free won't*. The free will part is choosing a course of action that might not produce immediate positive results but will result in personal gratification over time. The flip side, free won't, is choosing not to engage in a strategy that is solely designed to produce immediate rewards (such as avoiding painful inner experiences), even though those rewards are palpable and tempting.

LUKE'S STORY

Luke, a twenty-six-year-old single man, lives by himself. He's been chronically depressed since childhood, and as an adolescent he slipped into a pattern of meth addiction. He entered drug treatment two years ago, and although he's had a few slips, he basically hasn't been using drugs or alcohol since starting treatment. His depression has steadily worsened since he stopped using drugs and alcohol, though, and he admits to thoughts of suicide on an almost daily basis. He works part-time as a night janitor and frequently gets to work late because no one is there to know whether he has arrived or not. He enrolled in a local trade school to study computer repair but dropped out because he was failing. While he liked the classes and was academically and intellectually capable of doing the work, he didn't complete required assignments.

Luke hasn't been on a date for several years and avoids any activity that might lead to that, having convinced himself that he probably couldn't follow through on even the simplest commitments in a relationship. Although he purchased a health club membership three months ago to get in shape, he has yet to go to the club. He has a few friends from his drug rehabilitation program, but he doesn't get together with them often. Some of them are using drugs again, and he doesn't want to relapse. He smokes about a pack of cigarettes a day and doesn't exercise. He doesn't attend church, but he is interested in Buddhism. Luke wants to follow through on things that are important to him, but so far his only success has been in staying off drugs.

THE POWER OF CHOICE

Luke hasn't followed through on many promises he's made to himself in recent years. Consequently, his life lacks the meaning he desires. Living this kind of story line is inherently depressing because it precludes taking risks in the pursuit of vitality. Luke is so sold on his sad self-story of defeat that he has voluntarily withdrawn from the world of relationships. Luke's life is going nowhere fast, and although he believes his depression is what keeps him from a better life, in reality the problem is his inability to make and keep his promises to himself.

In ACT, a *choice* is a pact you make with yourself—a promise to take a specific action in a specific situation regardless of what shows up inside your head. In all likelihood, your reactive mind will show up and make its best effort to get you to stop. Even as you read this, your reactive mind might be telling you that this approach will never work for you, that you're too weak to pull it off, or that it will just provide you with another opportunity to fail. Your reactive mind is probably feeling fairly threatened right now, because *committed action* is to the reactive mind what the sunlight is to Dracula. Committed action spells the end of your reactive mind's reign of terror and opens the door onto a new day where your wise mind can prevail. Committed action allows you to stop following rules and instead do what works in your life. So if you notice any kicking and flailing on the part of your reactive mind as you read any of this, simply thank your mind for these thoughts and come back into the present moment with us so we can get to work on banishing that vampire who's been sucking you dry.

Choice Originates in Wise Mind

Making a choice is the ultimate act of free will, and free will is a distinctly human trait. Whereas we can train animals to behave in highly predictable ways, it is much more difficult to achieve that outcome with humans. This is because humans can reflect back on their behavior and relate it to such things as their values, a desired outcome, or its impact on others.

A choice means you are free of having to choose an action because of social expectations or the programming of your reactive mind. You choose because you have a vision of what you want life to be about, and this vision originates in the sanctuary of wise mind. This makes choice a very powerful tool in your campaign to reclaim your life. Choices are often the most powerful when made in murky situations in which there are lots of reasons for going in many directions. In these types of conflicted situations, it is easy to fall into a state of "analysis paralysis" if you rely on your reactive mind for guidance.

In Luke's case, he constantly had to battle his reactive mind's predictions of failing at anything that mattered to him. Given these constant predictions of failure, it actually seemed logical to him to back out of a promise at the last minute in order to protect himself from the pain of yet another broken promise.

Choices Originate in Your Values

The most powerful choices are rooted in and reflect your deeply held values. This is partly because values, like choices, are not creatures of logic. They just come into being.

Let's take the example of Susan, a forty-two-year-old woman who struggled with depression on and off for years. Over time, she gained a lot of weight and got out of shape. She had always been athletic as a teenager and young adult, loved sports, and encouraged both of her teenage daughters to play soccer. She volunteered to be an assistant coach for her youngest daughter's soccer team but began to make excuses for not showing up at practices because she was so self-conscious about her weight and lack of physical conditioning.

As a result of going through the Life Vision and Values planning exercise in chapter 12, Susan made a promise to herself to change her diet and get in shape, because she valued her health and wanted to coach her daughter's soccer team. This value motivated her to run with her daughter and teammates during soccer practice—and she stuck to it. A few years ago, she had joined a gym to keep her husband off her back, but she didn't keep her promise. This time around, Susan realized that the constant visual reminder of her daughter engaged in something that they both enjoy doing was what kept her on track.

EXERCISE: CHOICE IS ALL IN

A choice is measured not by the size of the action it generates but rather by the quality of you being "all in." Whatever you choose to do, aim to do so in full measure. This exercise (based on Hayes, Strosahl, and Wilson 1999) will show you what we mean. For this exercise, you need a piece of paper; a large, thick book; and a chair.

1. First, you must choose to complete this exercise, which involves jumping off a piece of paper, a book, and then a chair. Are you willing to make that promise to yourself? (If you're physically unable to jump, simply commit to imagining yourself jumping.)

2. Next, stand solidly on both feet atop the piece of paper. Ready? Jump off the paper and onto the floor!

3. Now you're ready for the next step: Put the book on the floor and stand on it with both feet. Then jump off the book and onto the floor!

4. Finally, stand on the chair with both feet, and then jump off the chair and onto the floor!

Further Exploration. What did you observe as you went through this simple exercise? You probably noticed that there is indeed a difference in the magnitude of the action needed to jump off a piece of paper, a book, and a chair. There's a difference in height, and jumping off a chair feels like a bigger act than jumping off a piece of paper. If we asked you to jump off of your roof, you would probably choose not to, correct?

Notice something else though: The choice to jump is *always* the same, regardless of the height you jump from. You have to choose to bend your knees and use your muscles to propel you up and forward. That is the essence of jumping; it is all in, or it is something else (like falling forward). The difference between the paper, the book, and the chair has more to do with the size of the act and, as often occurs in the real world, the things your reactive mind chatters at you about ("Be careful—you could hurt yourself," "This is stupid," or "You've never been good at sports!"). Having heard your reactive mind's analysis and warnings, you then choose to jump or not.

The beautiful thing about choice is that it has a mentally freeing quality that is present even when the choice involves a very small promise. Let's consider Lisa, a single woman in her thirties, who was painfully shy but wanted to have an intimate partner. She first chose to join a book club that included men and women. Choosing to leave home where she felt safe (and lonely) and go to the book club was a choice, nothing more. She couldn't go halfway to the book club; that would be a different choice, just as choosing to say yes rather than no to an invitation from a man at the book club to have a cup of coffee was a choice. That choice involved being willing to have any thoughts, sensations, feelings, or memories in awareness, while at the same time saying yes. Getting comfortable with this all-in quality of choice can be a huge step forward in your campaign to live the life you want to live. There's a Zen Buddhist saying that makes this point far better than we can: "You can't jump a crevice in two steps."

Choice Is a Process, Not an Outcome

Another key element of choice is that no matter how much choosing you have done, there is always more choosing ahead of you. You'll never reach the end of this process. If you value being a faithful, affectionate partner, for example, you don't finally reach a place called "faithful and affectionate"; you don't get a certificate from the universe announcing that you have achieved this value and that you no longer have to make choices. There is always more faith and affection to act on. As long as you are alive and hold this value, choosing to act on this value is an important part of your life. And, if you can manage to hold that value, really keeping to your promise of, for example, being a faithful and affectionate partner, you will be as faithful and affectionate a partner at age eighty as you were at age thirty.

In many life endeavors, it is what you run into along the road that you choose that's important, not whether you arrive at a specific destination. At times, when you're very close to achieving a particular life outcome that reflects your values, such as getting a long-sought promotion or running your first 5K race after months of training, you may notice that the journey has changed you and that the goal no longer seems to be an end point at all; rather, it's just a milepost on the path toward your values.

We Don't Choose Perfectly

Because choice happens every day and is an ongoing process, you can operate comfortably with the knowledge that if you screw up, you will most certainly get to choose again. You will make mistakes, and you will choose, perhaps impulsively, to act in ways that aren't consistent with your values. This happens to everyone; it's the human condition. The bright side of this is that after every choice to act comes another choice to act. If you choose to act in a way that isn't in accordance with your commitment or your values, just notice that and then turn your attention to the next choice that awaits you. If you choose to say no to a social invitation from a friend, and this turns out to be a form of self-isolation that only increases your depression, you will get a chance to remedy that error in short order. The goal is to be able to say to yourself, "Most of the time I choose to do things based in my values, and most of the time I keep the promises I make to myself.

Choice Doesn't Give You a Hall Pass!

As we mentioned before, the most meaningful choices in life will be made in the presence of a lot of mental chatter from reactive mind. If we had a magic wand that would allow us to install an on/off switch for your reactive mind, we would do so in a heartbeat. But the reality is that your reactive mind will come along for the ride and will try to get you to choose what it wants you to choose. That could involve you choosing to follow the same old rules for living that put you in a depression in the first place.

In a way, learning skills such as being in the present moment, practicing acceptance, being nonjudgmental, remaining detached, holding your self-story softly, practicing self-compassion, and staying in contact with your values allows you to maximize your freedom of choice in challenging life situations. This path involves choosing to walk the path of your values and being willing to steer clear of the influence of reactive mind while doing so. The journey to a vital life requires you to hold yourself accountable for follow-through on your promises, to be self-compassionate when you fail, and to remain resolute even when life fails to cooperate.

HIDDEN BARRIERS TO PROMISE KEEPING

Throughout this book, we've helped you identify some of these barriers: life issues you might be avoiding; the thoughts, feelings, memories, and sensations that are scary to you; and mental tricks that your reactive mind might play on you. So, at this point, you're quite clear about what some of the barriers will be; unfortunately, you can't anticipate all of the barriers that your reactive mind will raise once you start to act. We'd like to help by alerting you to some hidden hazards that could surface in your journey toward a vital, purposeful life.

"I Lack Self-Confidence."

Unfortunately, because you've struggled with depression in the past, you're prone to having feelings of low confidence, and this could keep you stuck in not making promises at all or not following through on the ones you have made. The word "confidence" hails from Latin and literally means "acting with fidelity" to yourself. When you act with confidence, you take valued actions even when you aren't feeling confident. You aren't sure what will happen, and your reactive mind might even be giving you negative predictions. Acting with fidelity to yourself means you stay true to your values even in the midst of uncertain thoughts and feelings. Ironically, this is the only way you can ever feel confident: by entering situations in which you're uncertain and *still* acting in ways that are consistent with your beliefs. The goal isn't to acquire the feeling of confidence; the goal is to learn to *act* confidently even if you don't *feel* confident.

"I Need Justice in Order to Move Forward."

What if you were sexually abused as a child, but no one in your family ever acknowledged that someone hurt you? What if a parent or sibling did this, but no one is willing to fess up? Would you still be willing to make and keep promises to yourself that will help you transcend depression and reclaim your life, knowing that the person responsible for this outrage is still at large?

Often, a life story of victimization has a secret clause in it: you cannot be or act in a healthy way until the person responsible for what happened to you is singled out and punished. If this is a self-story you tend to buy into, it could become a major obstacle on your journey to a vital, purposeful existence. Fortunately, you have an equally powerful force at your beck and call: *forgiveness*. The modern meaning of this word is actually a distortion of its original meaning and suggests that to forgive someone is to let that person off the hook, so to speak. But when you consider the original meaning of the word "forgiveness," you can instantly see that another course of action is available to you. The Latin root of the word "give" means "grace," and the prefix "for" means "that which came before."

Thus, the act of forgiveness can be viewed as giving yourself the grace you had before you were victimized. Forgiveness isn't about freeing someone who hurt you from responsibility for horrible actions. That person will have to face the universe eventually, and it won't be pretty when it happens. But that isn't your job; that's the universe's job. Your job is to live your life as best you can and in a way that reflects your values.

One of the values-based promises you might make to yourself is to stop the cycle of abuse in your family by being a loving and devoted parent to your children. Why not take this stance, which is positive and points you toward your true north, instead of a stance in which you wait for justice to be served while your life spirals downward? Practicing forgiveness will allow you to take back your life and reclaim your grace!

"I've Wasted My Life"

Another way the reactive mind can trick you into breaking promises is by drawing you into a cycle of self-blame for not having used mindfulness principles earlier than you have. According to your reactive mind, it is your fault that you have let your depression go on as long at it has! You can't rewind the videotape of your life and start again at the beginning. Your life is what it is, and you *can* live with it.

And you could also soften into the journey and realize that you are in the perfect spot you need to be in at this very moment in your life. Everything you have gone through, including your suffering, has prepared you to create the life you want to live, free from the tyranny of reactive mind and the depression it breeds. The forces in your life that led you to pick up this book are exactly what needed to happen for you to pick up this book. There is no such thing as a wasted life. Every moment of your existence, including the painful ones, is precious. You only get to do this once (unless you believe in reincarnation), so don't look backward—look forward!

WHEN PROMISES GET BROKEN

News flash: We are not gods! We are imperfect beings, and we make and break promises to ourselves and to others. That is inevitable. What happens next is critical. Will you use your energy and persistence to get back in the groove and fulfill your promise to yourself? Or will you get lost in self-analysis and self-criticism, and give up on the promise to yourself? We know this for certain: Reactive mind will not be your friend at such times. It will attempt to come up with some type of bogus reason for why you did what you did (or didn't do what you should have done).

Can't versus Won't

When you don't follow through on a promise to yourself, you can be certain that reactive mind has played a big role in the outcome. You might notice thoughts like, "I just can't do this; it's too hard," "I don't have the time to do this the way I want to do it," or "I can't make any more commitments like this because I feel like a failure when I don't follow through." When this happens, your reactive mind is saying that you lack the ability to keep your promise. Indeed, there might be situations when life intervenes and you really don't have the ability to follow through on a promise. For example, you might promise to reach out to an adult child you have been alienated from for years and who refuses to answer your e-mails, phone calls, or letters. In this case, you simply don't have the ability to make that child behave in a more conciliatory way, in spite of your choice to continue trying.

What we are most concerned about are situations when you have the ability to keep a promise, but you simply don't follow through. This is when reactive mind might be playing word games with you. Notice the word you ordinarily use in such circumstances: "can't," which literally means that you don't have the ability to choose. While it may be true that you lack the means needed to succeed at following through on a promise, the likely cause is being tricked into not doing what you promised you would do. Reactive mind showed up and created the impression that you don't have what it takes to follow through, usually because of the mental or physical barriers you might have to deal with.

A much more objective way to respond is to state out loud that you presently aren't *willing* to follow through on your promise because of the barriers you will run into. This means that you could keep your promise (you have the ability to) but that you won't keep it in this situation. The word "won't" means you "will it not," and since willingness is a voluntary action involving choice, you are actually *choosing* not to keep your promise.

Thus, when you find the word "can't" showing up in your reason giving about a failed commitment, we want you to replace it with the word "won't." This will signal that you've encountered some barrier that you aren't willing to confront and move through. This happens all the time to most of us; a new or more powerful barrier shows up that we hadn't anticipated and it stops us in our tracks. The key here is not to get into a cycle of excuse-making but instead to reanchor the situation in the language of choice.

For example, Luke routinely promised himself that he would go to the health club and work out several days each week. But then he would sleep in, get distracted with menial household tasks, and then tell himself that it was too late in the day to work out now that he was tired. When he examined this behavior, he realized it was not a matter of not being *able* to work out when he was tired. Rather, he acknowledged that he was not *willing* to deal with feeling fatigued and to work out at the same time. This made it much harder for him to back out on a promise by claiming he didn't have the ability to follow through. Sometimes, simply acknowledging that you are a choosing being—and at this moment your choice is what it is—leaves you with many cards to play when the next opportunity to choose rolls around.

Make Another Promise

Instead of beating yourself up for not following through and making this into yet another trigger for more depression, we want you to try another strategy. When you first make a promise to yourself, try to make another promise at the same time: Tell yourself that if you don't follow through on the initial promise, you promise that you will choose to be self-compassionate at that exact moment. You pledge to acknowledge the personal value that you wish to live by and acknowledge that you have chosen to act in a way that is not consistent with your values.

We then want you to restate your choice to follow through on the initial promise the next time it becomes available to you in a life situation. Notice in this moment that all you are doing is holding yourself "response-able." You aren't blaming yourself or trying to motivate yourself with guilt; you are reminding yourself that you can control most of the choices you make (sometimes life will hit you with something unexpected that might throw you off course), and you are willing to be accountable for your actions.

The great thing about choosing is that you will most certainly get to choose again within a matter of seconds, minutes, or hours. If something is valuable enough for you to choose it at all, it's probably still going to be valuable the next time that choice comes around. Not living up to a promise does not change the fact that it was your values that led you to make the promise in the first place!

Broken Promises as Opportunities

As the old saying goes, *What doesn't kill you makes you stronger.* Although we've encouraged you not to mindlessly fuse with such sayings, and we don't want you to take this saying too literally, it does offer some wisdom about embracing the moment when you fail to live up to your expectations. It acknowledges that such instances are indeed difficult and painful, but, at the same time, they allow you to learn a lot about who you are as a person. You can put this perspective into practice when you find that you've broken a promise to yourself by seeing this moment as an opportunity to learn something new about yourself. This, too, is part of what living a vital life is all about: taking the good, the bad, and the ugly in stride and using each life setback as an opportunity to choose actions that reflect your values and allow you to grow as a person. You don't have to do this perfectly either; you can, and will, make mistakes. When you do, the most workable response is to get back on your feet and resume your journey. That's where all of the life learning is—in the journey.

LUKE'S JOURNEY TOWARD A VITAL LIFE

Luke did a lot of work on clarifying his life vision and his intention to follow it. He realized he actually had a lot of things that mattered to him in life. He wanted to get into an interesting, fulfilling line of work that would challenge him. He wanted to have a family, and he really wanted to be a devoted, caring father. He wanted intimacy in his life. He valued taking care of his personal health; that was the main reason he had stopped using drugs in the first place. The problem wasn't that he lacked values; the problem was that he wasn't following through on choices that would make his life more meaningful. Luke realized that buying into his self-story of perpetually failing in life had probably planted the seed for most of his failures.

Luke created a plan for a vital life by promising to engage in several seemingly small actions. The first was to go to his health club and exercise once a week. The morning of the day he planned to go to the gym, he felt lethargic; he had the thought that he should put off exercising until he felt better. Luke thanked his reactive mind for that thought, reminded himself of his promise, and went to the health club anyway. As it turned out, the exercise really helped his energy level and mood.

Luke's next promise was to apply for admission to the trade school he had dropped out of. Despite the predictions of his reactive mind, he was accepted. He next promised to attend all of the project meetings in a course he was taking. Within the first week, he missed a project meeting. But rather than throwing in the towel, as he might have done before, he simply owned up to his broken promise as something he didn't value and recommitted to attending all project meetings.

Before long, his instructor noticed how gifted Luke was and asked him to tutor students who were having trouble in the class. Luke noticed that he enjoyed tutoring and that he had a knack for it. He decided to apply to a local community college and work on getting a teaching certificate. In his first class, he met a woman he was instantly attracted to. His reactive mind kicked in big-time and reminded him that he would eventually disappoint her, drop out of sight, and be rejected. Luke pushed right back and made a promise to continue dating her even though he was afraid of rejection, and soon their relationship became serious.

Luke also learned to participate in social activities even if his mood wasn't perfect, and a lot of times it wasn't. However, he also noticed that his mood was less of a factor in his daily activities than it had been for a long time. The more Luke learned to make and keep promises, the more motivated he was to engage in other activities outside of his comfort zone. Luke was on the journey toward a vital life!

BRAIN TRAINING FOR PROMISE KEEPING

Just like with every other mindfulness skill we have introduced you to in part 2, consciously practicing the skills we share here will make it easier for you to use them when the time comes. These simple exercises will strengthen the reward-anticipating circuitry of your brain and help you follow through on your values-based choices.

ROLLING DOWN THE RIVER

Choosing a valued course in life does not guarantee you an easy journey or freedom from setbacks that you have no control over. You must be persistent and pursue your promises—even when you feel as if life has treated you unfairly (or your reactive mind tells you that).

Here's a brief mental exercise that will help you see this point. The best way to approach this exercise is to download the guided audio version from http://www.newharbinger.com/38457. Then then find a comfortable place to sit, and close your eyes for a few minutes. Really try to get yourself into the sensations of traveling down the river of life on an inner tube.

Imagine that you've been set on the river of your life and are asked to float the river to its end. You haven't been given much instruction on how to do this; all you have is the assurance that this river will end in the ocean. Soon after you begin your trip, the river begins to meander back and forth, almost coming to a standstill at times so that you stop making progress. You begin to wonder whether the river is somehow coming to an end. It doesn't seem to be going anywhere, it just meanders back and forth with hardly any force. It's frustrating and you feel you have to walk in the river just to make the kind of progress you think you need to make.

A little while later, the current quickens. All of the sudden you are in very shallow rapids. You are bouncing along with the river and hitting rocks and boulders. You're splashed in the face, and then splashed again repeatedly until you're soaked through. The rapids go on and on, and you begin to feel tired, bruised, and disheartened. After one particularly hard jolt, your raft flips and you frantically swim over to the riverbank and begin cursing the river.

If life were fair, this river would go straight down to the ocean—no meandering, no rapids. If the function of rivers is to deliver water back to the ocean, why are there so many rocks and twists and turns? What do rocks have to do with getting water to the ocean? It isn't fair that rivers are made the way this river is made! You decide that if this river doesn't change its character immediately, you aren't going to float in it.

But as you stare at the river in disgust, you notice that the water didn't decide to go ashore and complain about its journey. It simply does what water knows how to do. It understands what the nature of a river is. How can you get to the ocean if you stand on the bank looking at the water flowing by?

Further Exploration. What went through your mind during this mental exercise? Could you relate to the outrage of being asked to float on a river like this, without any notion of what lies ahead of you? You didn't ask for the boulders. You didn't ask for your life to be hard like this. Even so, what choice is required if you are to get to the end of your journey? Sure, you have to get back on the river and start floating again. You have to accept that this is how rivers are. They don't follow your reactive mind's specifications of how a river should behave. Rivers have their own nature and you can't change it. Your job is to reaffirm that you value floating the river of your life and that you will choose to let the river take you where it will.

THE GARDEN OF CHOICE

It is easy for emotionally loaded life situations to divert our intentions from being positively focused to becoming negatively charged. This guided meditation, inspired by Ajahn Brahm, allows you to see how easy it is to shift back and forth between positive and negative intentions, and how to use values to bring you back into contact with what is important.

To start with, find a comfortable place to sit, close your eyes, and take several deep cleansing breaths. Try to clear your mind of any cares and concerns of the day. Imagine that you have just moved into a residence with a large garden in the backyard. The garden has a beautiful flowering plum tree and several shrubs with blooms and flowers. There are even some tomato plants with ripe tomatoes.

But you also notice that the garden is full of weeds. You are really put off by the prospect of dealing with those weeds. Your first temptation is to just forget the garden and go inside and watch some TV. Next, you generate a long list of things you would need to do to get the garden in shape. You find yourself wondering if it wouldn't be better to just let the garden go. It feels like there are just too many weeds in it to deal with. Then you realize that if you don't water anywhere in the garden, the weeds will stop growing, but the plants and trees will stop growing too. Finally, you consider just sitting in the garden and allowing the plants, trees, and weeds to do what they naturally do. You smile as you realize what type of gardener you are.

Further Exploration. As you participated in this exercise, did you feel your own urge to react in a specific way? Was that urge based upon a positive value or a reflection of your desire to control something that you found unacceptable? What happened when you allowed the flowers, plants, trees, and weeds to just coexist? Did your reactive mind show up and push back? Like many choice points in life, there is not a right and wrong choice, so the important thing is to be fully aware that you are the one making the choice. You are the one who is playing in the garden.

BROKEN PROMISES AS TEACHERS

One good way to capitalize on a broken promise is to approach it with gratitude. Because, painful though broken promises can feel, they are also opportunities to learn more about yourself—and because your life vision, shaped as it is by the values you hope to live by, is always there to be pursued. To practice gratitude in this way, you might think or say aloud, something like:

Thank you, life, for giving me the opportunity to learn to live with the money I have.

Thank you for helping me learn how to bounce back from arguments with my spouse.

Thank you for helping me to learn how important agreements with my friends are.

I'm grateful for the opportunity to recommit to promoting my health today.

I'm grateful for the opportunity to promote my ease of being today.

Thank you, life, for helping me learn how to accept failure gracefully.

Rolling with broken promises while reaffirming the choice you intend to make the next time around helps you accept your imperfections, and thus you can learn from them. It is important to remember that you learn as much about yourself in moments of failure as you do in moments of success. We often tell clients that the goal of living every day is to end it as a new person!

IDEAS TO CULTIVATE

- The road to a vital life involves choosing to make and keep promises to yourself.

- Powerful choices can be made when there are conflicting urges to act in healthy or unhealthy ways.

- Choice involves strengthening neural pathways responsible for choosing longer-term enrichment over short-term relief from inner pain.

- Choice has an "all in" quality that isn't defined by how big the choice is. Small choices require the same level of commitment as big choices.

- Because a choice originates in your values, any failure to follow through doesn't alter the fact that you have values. You will get to choose again soon enough!

- When you make a promise to yourelf, make another promise to keep trying if you don't follow through.

Creating the Life You Want to Live

We are what we repeatedly do. Excellence, then, is not an act but a habit.

—Aristotle

In this section, we'll teach you how to use all of the mindfulness skills you have learned to build a positive, intentional, and depression-busting lifestyle. This is not going to be easy; like life itself, the road to living a vital life is full of unexpected twists and turns. You will come to forks in the road where the signage is confusing, incorrect, or perhaps entirely absent. At moments like this you'll have to let your wise mind be your travel guide!

The lack of certainty and constant change involved in values-based living is scary and can stop you in your tracks, so it is best to plan for this likelihood. There is a well-known saying that applies here: *The best defense is a good offense!* Rather than wait for challenges to arise and then react to them, we are going to teach you how to develop a positive emotion lifestyle that will protect you when you sail into troubled waters. Another antidote for dealing with challenging life situations is to develop daily habits that allow you to protect yourself against the impact of unexpected depression-triggering life events. It is easier to breed these habits when you already are busy developing an active sense of positive emotional momentum, which is where we hope you end up by the time you finish this section!

You have been on a mission since you started working on this program: a life-changing quest to transcend your depression and live a meaningful life. Below you'll find a worksheet to help you keep track of your intention to use the ideas presented in this part of the book. After you finish reading chapter 14, come back to this worksheet and use a scale of 1 to 10 to rate your intention to practice the positive emotion lifestyle and depression prevention strategies listed in that chapter. Note that we use the verb "practice." We don't expect that you'll apply any of these strategies perfectly. As the saying by the great philosopher Aristotle suggests, vital actions are not isolated moments of excellence; rather, they are the result of habits you create through repeated practice. You never arrive at a vital life; it's a direction you head toward each and every day.

PART 3 INTENTION WORKSHEET

Not Likely to Practice				More Likely to Practice				Extremely Likely to Practice		
1	2	3	4	5	6	7	8	9	10

Lifestyle Strategy	My Intention Level
Identify positive emotion–producing activities that I can perform on a regular basis.	
Practice savoring the positive or pleasant moments I encounter in my daily life.	
Set important lifestyle goals for myself using the SMART goal approach.	
Identify upcoming life situations, events, or issues that pose a depression risk for me.	
Regularly monitor my mood and behaviors to detect early warning signs of depression.	
Form and post in a conspicuous place a written plan with strategies I will use to short-circuit a developing depression.	

Further Exploration. If your intention level for any item is at a 5 or less after reading chapter 14, we recommend that you reread that section or consider sharing it with a friend or partner. Ask the person to read it and discuss it with you. Having another person to bounce ideas off of might give you some fresh ideas about ways to put these important concepts into practice on a daily basis. If you find you're having trouble sticking with these strategies, consider increasing your support level, perhaps seeking an ally in a health care professional, a therapist, or a priest, minister, or rabbi.

CHAPTER 14

Promote Positivity, Prevent Relapse

If you learn to take care of the minutes, the years will take care of themselves.

—Buddhist saying

Congratulations on reaching the point where you can go out and live the kind of life you want to live! It has a taken a lot of time, persistence, and energy to get to this point. Take a moment to feel proud of yourself for doing this. We give you complete permission to attach to any positive self-stories that show up!

In part 2, we taught you nine powerful mindfulness strategies to use on your quest to transcend depression. And, hopefully, you are seeing the benefits already. This last section of this book is going to help you design a permanent way of living that promotes a sense of vitality, purpose, and meaning. In this chapter, we will introduce you to some cutting-edge concepts from the field of positive psychology that bear directly on your quest to build a life worth living and reduce your risk of falling back into a depression.

Positive psychology, as the term implies, is an arm of psychological science that investigates how human beings flourish. *Flourishing* is a state of consistent emotional well-being and growth that is driven by active participation in a variety of positive life activities. You may have met a person or two who were really flourishing. They typically participate in lots of activities that interest them; they look at life challenges as opportunities for self-discovery; and they typically have a very positive life outlook. For all intents and purposes, people who are flourishing are "playing" the game of life and loving it, even when the going gets rough!

There is also a very important neuroscience detail that we want to bring back for consideration: the brain's reward- and punishment-anticipating functions exist in separate neural pathways. Therefore, while it is important to decrease behaviors that strengthen the avoidance circuitry of your brain, it is *equally important* to increase behaviors that strengthen the brain's approach circuitry. Put in real-life terms, getting your depression under control doesn't automatically guarantee that you will burst onto the scene of a life filled with positive emotions, growth, and personal meaning.

Admittedly, you don't have much of a chance to flourish if you're battling depression. You know that as well as we do. Living a fulfilling life according to your values is incredibly hard to do consistently over time. Because life happens! You are guaranteed to have setbacks. The trick is to have the right tools in place so that when a difficult life challenge falls in your lap, you are well prepared to *continue* flourishing with intention—so that you don't fall back into a depressed state.

As the saying goes, *life is just one damn thing after another.* No matter where you are in your life right now, there is more life to go, and therein lies a potential threat to your emotional health and sustained freedom from depression. What if something bad happens, as it surely will? What if you lose a job, or one of your children gets really ill, or a relationship you had hoped would work out doesn't? Will you be ready to use your newly learned skills to keep yourself on steady ground? How do you intend to keep yourself focused on using those powerful mindfulness skills to help you cope with what Shakespeare called "the slings and arrows of outrageous fortune"?

In the spirit of preparing you to weather life's challenges and to help you develop a vital life at the same time, we will teach you how to build and maintain a positive emotion lifestyle in the four important areas of daily living we've dealt with in earlier chapters: your relationships, your work or studies, your leisure and play time, and your health. The best defense against the "slings and arrows of outrageous fortune" is to build positive emotional momentum through your daily routines so that you are ready, willing, and able to mindfully respond to life's challenges.

The challenge we help you address in this chapter is how to get a positive emotion lifestyle ramped up to begin with. Fortunately, all of the mindfulness strategies we taught you in section 2 will be of immediate use to you in this quest!

POSITIVITY RESONATES

The heading for this section encapsulates the single most important concept you will need to keep in mind as you develop a depression-busting lifestyle. *Positivity* involves actively and intentionally engaging in behaviors that generate positive emotional feedback loops on a daily basis. The concept of *resonance* means that positive mood states create self-sustaining feedback loops that generate what are called *positive emotion spirals* (Garland and Frederickson 2013).

Positive emotion spirals are self-sustaining systems that affect every aspect of your mental life. They create a "savings account" of positive coping resources that builds over time and buffers you not only from the daily hassles of living but bigger life stresses as well. To illustrate this, imagine that you really enjoy yourself on a weekend camping trip with your partner. You take a couple of nice day hikes in the woods. You and your partner have several interesting conversations and snuggle a lot. You have a nice campfire and roast marshmallows. You sleep peacefully in your tent listening to the sounds of the forest and a nearby lake. The chances are very good that some of that positive energy will carry over to your work on Monday morning. You might invite some of your favorite coworkers out for appetizers and some schmoozing. You will be in a good mood, and that mood will make you want to seek out more activities that produce more good mood.

The self-generating quality of positive emotional experience is one of the most consistent and important findings of positive psychology research. For example, research on happiness shows that, over time, positivity builds durable coping resources that can be applied to decrease the intensity and duration of subsequent negative emotion spirals (Cohn et al. 2009). In short, if you learn to build positive emotion spirals in daily living, you will have a heightened ability to not only survive but thrive in times of emotional distress.

By now, you might be wondering if a positive emotion spiral is, in effect, another way to access wise mind…and the answer is yes. Read on, and you will see that there is a distinct similarity between a positive emotion spiral and the mindfulness skills we introduced you to in section 2.

Hedonic and Eudaimonic Pleasure

Another important discovery in positive psychology is that pleasure actually exists on a continuum. At one end of the continuum is *hedonic pleasure*. This is positive emotion produced by activities that are typically short term and self-focused, such as going tailgating with friends at a sporting event. The goal of these activities is to have fun and make yourself feel good. At the other end of the continuum is *eudaimonic pleasure*. This involves positive emotion produced by activities that benefit others or involve the expression of deeply held personal principles, such as volunteering at a local animal shelter or participating in a prayer or meditation group.

Interestingly, the impact of hedonic activities on positive emotion spirals is less durable than the impact of eudaimonic activities. In other words, when you derive pleasure by being altruistic toward others, or by connecting with deeply held spiritual or personal values, the positive impact on your mood state will be more enduring than if you just did something fun and enjoyable. In addition, the experience of eudaimonic pleasure is often more sublime than hedonic pleasure. And keep in mind that many of the mindfulness skills we have taught you (values, visioning, being present, compassion for self and others) are more likely to produce states of eudaimonic pleasure. Thus, a basic feature of a positivity-based lifestyle is to create a strategic blend of daily activities that produce both eudaimonic and hedonic pleasure.

Anatomy of Positivity

Garland and Frederickson (2013) assert that there are three basic components of a positive emotion spiral:

- **Mindfulness.** As you already know, mindfulness means being anchored in the present moment while steering clear of attachments and judgments that can lead to downward-spiraling patterns of rumination and worry. Whereas present-moment awareness is a temporary and often transient state, when it is practiced over time it can become a dominant form of paying attention (Chambers, Gullone, and Allen 2009). And, consistent with what we have taught you already, being in the present moment brings your senses alive, broadens your perspective, and puts you in direct contact with your values, life vision, and positive intentions. In a state of present-moment awareness, you are a kid in the candy store of life.

- **Reappraisal.** This involves assigning a new, health-promoting meaning to a stressful life experience. We will inevitably run into painful experiences, and we need to use our perspective-taking abilities to convert personal pain into personal strength. In a state of mindfulness, individuals are more likely to assign benevolent, constructive meanings, or *positive appraisals*, to painful emotional experiences (Garland, Gaylord, and Frederickson 2011). Positive reappraisals are associated with activation of the parasympathetic nervous system, which regulates stress responses and is linked to positive emotional states. Thus, even the physical impact of life stress can be limited through the use of positive appraisal. For example, you might hear from a longtime friend that he or she is moving out of state. Your first reaction might be imagining being alone and not having someone who understands you to lean on during difficult times (negative appraisal). On second thought, you might feel happy for your friend because the move is a good thing for him or her, and this will be an opportunity for you to learn how to form new close friendships (positive reappraisal). Notice that a positive reappraisal bears a certain resemblance to the ability to come up with a more workable self-story.

- **Savoring.** This skill involves practicing intentional self-focused awareness of pleasant experiences or values-consistent actions and events (Bryant, Chadwick, and Kluwe 2011). You literally are savoring the joy of the moment! Savoring has been shown to be one of the most powerful ways to amplify a specific positive emotional event as well as to strengthen positive emotion spirals (Quoidbach et al. 2010). Pleasant experiences can range from mundane but positive behaviors, like taking your dog for a walk in the park, to more intense positive emotions such as those produced when you are sharing an intimate moment with your spouse or partner. Especially potent forms of pleasant experience involve actions or events that connect you directly with your values. For example, singing a good-night song to a young child at bedtime while you consciously connect with the reality that you are being the kind of parent you want to be, at this exact moment, is savoring. You are not off in the future thinking about work tomorrow; you are squarely anchored in the here and now and being aware of and appreciating the positive emotions associated with living according to your values in the moment.

The Principle of Emotional Inertia

One of the most basic principles of Newtonian physics is the principle of *inertia: Bodies at rest tend to stay at rest; bodies in motion tend to stay in motion.* The principle of inertia also applies to how to cultivate positive emotional experience. Since life is a mixture of movement and rest, it is very important that you work both sides of this equation. Whatever emotions you put into play will develop their own momentum until they encounter an equal or greater counterforce. This is the first side of the equation: You must respond to a depression spiral with a positive emotion spiral of equal or greater force. This is where daily lifestyle planning comes in. If your routines produce positive emotion on a daily basis, you will be far more likely to counter any negative spiral that comes along.

The other side of this equation has to do with what we call your *resting emotional state.* This is the emotion that shows up in the present moment, when you are doing nothing in particular, when you are at rest. This is your default mode of emotional experience. If you struggle with depression, when you are at rest you might start recalling negative memories, analyzing your past, worrying about your future, experiencing apathy and emotional numbness, or focusing on physical aches and pains in your body. Recall from part 1 that these mental activities are the result of overactivation of the default mode network. These activities can produce a low- to high-grade depression spiral, depending on how long you let yourself continue in the default mode.

Right now, you are on your way out of a depression spiral. Just like being in the middle of a negative emotion spiral depletes your resilience, being in the middle of a positive emotion spiral both generates and strengthens your emotional resources. This is important to understand, because if you enter into a depression-triggering situation already emotionally depleted, it will be much more difficult to consistently use the mindfulness skills we've taught you. Your emotional energy level will become an issue in its own right—something you will want to avoid.

When you come to your senses and practice any or all of the mindfulness skills we have taught you when you are idling along in a mild depression spiral, you *will* notice an *immediate* change in the quality of your emotional experience. You will have followed the principle of emotional inertia by inserting a powerful counterforce of positivity. At first, you will need to frequently use mindfulness skills to offset any problematic aspects of your resting emotional state. This is because you might spend a fair amount of time in depression-spiraling activities, and the routine has become second nature for you. Turning your resting emotional state around is a little like turning a huge cruise ship around at sea. You have to continually apply force to the rudder and then, ever so slowly, the ship will turn to the new heading.

If you keep practicing the strategies we have shown you in part 2, you will begin to notice something different: Your resting emotional state will be characterized by pleasurable and reinforcing memories, daydreams, thoughts, and physical sensations. This is what we call *trait mindfulness*. Think of a trait as the habitual way that you roll when you are just being you. The research on positivity suggests that the more you invoke mindful awareness in daily living, the stronger the positive emotion spirals become and the more trait mindfulness you develop (Chambers, Gullone, and Allen 2009).

SAVORING IN DAILY LIFE

The concept of savoring shows that it really is the little things you do in life that create a foundation for vital living. Taking time to slow down, be mindful, and savor rewarding moments in daily life broadens awareness, tamps down your nervous system, and makes you less reactive to stress. Just as one example, simple daily compassion practices, similar to the ones we have introduced you to, are associated with development of durable positive emotion spirals and increased coping resources (Frederickson et al. 2008). You can think of the task of creating positive emotion spirals as the boots-on-the-ground version of living mindfully. In this section, we will help you develop a daily approach to living that will create positive emotion spirals in your health, relationships, your work, and your leisure activities.

Quoidbach and colleagues (2010) point out that savoring does not come of its own accord. You must consciously make an effort to savor a positive event, just like you would take the time to savor a really good meal. They suggest several tactics to elevate how much you savor a positive moment in time:

- Share your good feelings with others by communicating your joy.

- Take a moment to create a vivid memory of right now so that you can recall it later.

- Sharpen your sensory experiences by being attentive to everything around you.

- Allow yourself to be absorbed in the moment.

- Experience and express gratitude for this moment of positivity.

- If the experience is bittersweet, avoid killjoy thinking by focusing on the sweet side.

- Generate positive facial expressions that will bring others into your experience.

- Don't try to forecast how long the positive feelings will last— just embrace them.

As should be obvious, positive emotion lifestyles don't appear out of the blue. They take forethought, planning, and follow-through over time. Consider this: The rewards you will reap if you do this far outweigh the amount of energy needed to create durable positive emotion spirals on a regular basis.

Given the emphasis on "all work and no play" in modern society, it can be surprisingly difficult for us to generate a positivity plan rich and diverse in activities. In addition, clients often tell us that they don't have the time or money to engage in a lot of pleasurable activities. So we set out to build the List of Positive Emotion Activities: pleasurable pursuits that don't cost a lot and are not all that time-consuming. Look at the list below to see if there are any activities you might be interested in trying.

List of Positive Emotion Activities

Rearrange or redecorate a room

Listen and dance to music

Get involved in a charity group

Go for a walk in the park

Go to a play, concert, or musical event

Plan a trip out of town

Buy something frivolous like a toy

Do artwork or crafts

Read spiritual works that inspire you

Wear clothes that make you feel good

Read an interesting book or magazine

Attend a community lecture series

Listen to a relaxation tape

Go out to a local pond and feed wild birds

Fix something that you want to repair

Play a board game with someone

Solve a sudoku or crossword puzzle

Take a long bath or shower

Write a story, poem, or music

Sing or play an instrument

Go to a church or temple function

Spend time with a friend

Bake a pastry you like

Work in the garden

Sit in the sun

Go to a street fair, zoo, or museum

Plan a social event

Play with your animals

Listen to music

Give someone a small gift

Take pictures

Watch or participate in sports

Help someone in need

Hear comedy (go to a comedy club or watch funny movies)

See beautiful scenery

Go window shopping

Go for a drive to someplace peaceful

Ride a bike along a mountain or river trail

Enjoy a sauna or hot tub

Buy some watercolors and paint a picture

Be with friends or relatives

Join a political party or social interest group

Talk on the phone with a person you like

Go to a movie with someone you like

Cook a tasty meal

Do odd jobs around the home

Go out to eat with your partner or a friend

Reminisce or talk about old times

Go outside early in the morning and awaken your senses

Volunteer at the local animal shelter

Write in your diary

Say prayers

Meditate for 10 minutes

Read the comics section of the newspaper

Go for an early-morning walk or run

Walk barefoot in the house and yard

Toss a Frisbee or football, or play catch

Spend 5 minutes doing deep breathing

Sew or do needlework

Organize your day so you can spend quality time with someone you love

Rent a movie

Go to the library

Go people-watching in the mall

Sit in front of a fire

Volunteer at a food bank

Buy some flowers

Play video games

Care for houseplants

Work on or start a collection

Play a game with your children

Go to a garage sale

Introduce yourself to someone new

Go swimming at the local pool

Read cartoons or comic books

IDENTIFY YOUR POSITIVE EMOTION TARGETS

In the worksheet below, we have grouped positive emotion activities into several savoring categories for you to consider. You might naturally gravitate toward one or two categories and be less interested in the others. Or you might be interested in trying all of them! Whatever the case, use the List of Positive Emotion Activities to identify some positive behaviors you are interested in experimenting with on a regular basis, just to see how they impact your mood. Identifying positive emotion targets in different areas of life will let you diversify the ways that you induce positive emotions in your daily routine. Keep in mind that you don't have to choose something that will be done every day at the same time. You can vary the time, frequency, and type of activity as you like.

Positive Emotion Worksheet

Area of Positive Emotion	Savoring Target	When, Where, with Whom, and How Often?
Awakening Senses (for example, smelling a rose, eating an orange slowly, watching the sunset mindfully, belly breathing for 5 minutes)		
Gratitude (for example, thanking someone for doing something nice, spending some time with mental images of things you are grateful for in your life)		
Generosity (for example, opening a door for someone, buying a coworker a latte just to be nice)		

Connectedness (for example, going to church or a spiritual meeting, going to lunch with a friend, holding hands with your spouse while walking together)		
Compassion (for example, doing a 5-minute compassion meditation, helping someone who needs help, forgiving yourself for a recent mistake you made—however small—and savoring it)		
Play (for example, taking kids to a playground or running around with them, going to a movie with your partner, getting into a tickling game with your partner or children)		
Valuing (for example, sitting down with your partner and sharing how you've been doing today, exercising 20–30 minutes, preparing a healthy meal for everyone in the family)		

Further Exploration. How did you do at identifying positive emotion–generating actions that you could savor? When you imagined doing them, did you notice a feeling of positivity inside? If so, that's a good indicator that you're likely to experience positivity if you select that behavior. Were you able to figure out when would be the most convenient time to engage in an action? It's okay to fit these things in around your existing lifestyle. Sometimes though, you have to prioritize between something you are *used* to doing and something you would *like* to be doing in your daily routine. Often, we are taught that it is only after we complete everything on our to-do list that we get to do something fun, relaxing, or enjoyable. Try not to get drawn into that trap; it's just reactive mind giving you more rules to follow!

YOUR POSITIVITY LIFESTYLE PLAN

Now let's take the results from the previous exercise and embed them in an overall plan for generating positive emotional experience on a daily basis. On the worksheet below, identify your positive emotion goals in the four major life domains: relationships, work/study, leisure/play, and health. Then rate the intensity of the positive emotion you are likely to experience if you achieved your positivity goal. Obviously, activities that are likely to produce higher positivity scores are to be desired. If your projected positivity rating is only a 1 or 2, consider looking for another positivity goal in that life area.

Next, list the steps you intend to take that will produce a positive emotional experience. Be as concrete and specific as possible when outlining your plan so that you can follow through on your positive emotion target behavior. For example, if your positive emotion target is to exercise three times a week, your action plan might include joining a local gym, hiring a personal health trainer, finding a friend to go to the club with you, and so forth. As another example, a plan to "eat mindfully at eight o'clock each morning" is specific, whereas a general statement that you plan to "eat better" isn't. The more specific you are, the better you can assess whether you're acting as planned—and the better you can evaluate how your actions are affecting your sense of vitality.

Positivity Lifestyle Plan

RELATIONSHIPS

Positivity goal: _____

_____

Positive emotion rating (1 = weak; 5 = strong)

Action plan

1. _____

_____

2. _____

_____

3. _____

_____

4. _____

_____

WORK/STUDY

Positivity goal: _____

_____

Positive emotion rating (1 = weak; 5 = strong)

Action plan

1. _____

_____

2. _____

_____

3. _____

_____

4. _____

_____

LEISURE/PLAY

Positivity goal: _____

_____

Positive emotion rating (1 = weak; 5 = strong)

Action plan

1. _____

_____

2. _____

_____

3. _____

_____

4. _____

_____

HEALTH

Positivity goal: _____

_____

Positive emotion rating (1 = weak; 5 = strong)

Action plan

1. _____

_____

2. _____

_____

3. _____

_____

4. _____

_____

Further Exploration. Any time you set out to change your lifestyle, your new behaviors will take time, practice, and some troubleshooting to take hold. One good way to see if your changes are moving you toward your goals is to conduct a lifestyle review. How? Simply repeat the Positivity Lifestyle Plan a few times. You might do this monthly for the first six months as you are sorting out the mindfulness strategies and positive emotion targets that work best for you. Once you have a handle on the situation, you could lengthen the test period to quarterly or every six months.

Use the results of these periodic self-assessments to make course corrections so you can continue traveling toward your true north. If you ever feel overwhelmed, select just one or two life areas to focus your work on, based on your priorities. You will likely notice that the type of life activities that produces positive emotions will shift over time; this is to be expected when you live life intentionally and according to your values. Different activities that float your boat will suddenly appear on the horizon and, when they do, go for them! However, we do recommend that you address all four life domains at least once a year, as each usually has an important role to play in generating the positive emotion reserves needed to weather the hard times that life will surely offer.

Compare your scores across time. Is your positive emotion score going up, even slightly? If so, your plan is bringing you closer to the goal of positive, values-based living. If your score is staying the same or getting lower, consider whether you need to change the plan. You can't always be sure how a plan will work out when you're creating it, but you can have an open mind and change the plan when your experience tells you it isn't working. This review is important, so record it on your calendar, just as you would any important activity.

If you've chosen a particularly challenging area to work on, you may want to review your plan more often at first—perhaps once a week.

The simplest way to see if your Positivity Lifestyle Plan is working is to look at each of the statements below and check off any that are true of you at this moment in time.

☐ In most ways, my life right now is close to my ideal.

☐ The conditions of my life right now are excellent.

☐ I am satisfied with my life just the way it is right now.

☐ I am getting the important things I want in my life right now.

☐ If I could do anything in my life over right now, I would change almost nothing.

If several of these items describe your life right now, way to go! Keep it up! If none of the statements describes your life right now, go back and review your current Positivity Lifestyle Plan to see if there might be a new positive emotion target that would work better for you.

LIFESTYLE CHANGE POINTERS

Your eventual goal is to make a habit of engaging in positive emotion–producing behaviors on a daily basis. When you make a behavior into a habit, it becomes automatic and will still work even if you run into external or internal barriers. We know that habits are formed by repeated practice in different settings and circumstances. The more you practice mindfulness and positive emotion strategies in different settings and life circumstances, the more likely they are to become automatic responses.

The term *habit strength* refers to the degree to which a well-learned behavior is likely to keep showing up in different situations. There are both negative and positive examples of habit strength that are pretty common in daily life. You bathe and groom yourself every morning because it makes you feel awake, refreshed, and ready for the day. You've practiced these behaviors so many times that you don't even have to think about them as you do them. The downside of habit strength is just that: You might not even be thinking about what it feels like to bathe in warm, relaxing water and then to treat yourself kindly by practicing good grooming and hygiene. We want you to take the positive side of the habit strength idea and apply it to your positive emotion lifestyle campaign. These tips will help you do that.

Be SMART

You may be familiar with the concept of SMART goals. If not, it's an easy sequence to understand and follow as you attempt to change a lifestyle behavior. SMART stands for goals that are:

Specific—It's clearly defined

Measurable—It can be observed

Attainable—It is within your grasp

Relevant—It is important to you

Time-bound—You set a timeline for achieving it

The SMART goal approach requires you to think about your lifestyle goals ahead of time, being as concrete and specific as possible. Avoid forming vague or subjective goals that are hard to measure, or setting unrealistic standards. Setting a goal like, "I just want to be more positive about my leisure-time activities" sounds nice, but it is not going to contribute much to lifestyle planning because it's not specific enough.

Instead, you want to specify what behaviors would indicate that you are achieving this goal. For example, you might plan to spend five minutes every morning after you wake up thinking about what you are grateful for that day. You might set a goal of looking at someone at work, smiling at him or her, and offering some type of compliment.

We have a saying about setting goals that makes this easy to understand: *If you can't count it, it doesn't count.* If your lifestyle goal can't be converted into a behavior that someone else could observe, then it isn't a workable goal. Focus on setting lifestyle goals that reflect your values and that really would be gratifying if you achieved them. Don't set goals because other people want you to. Do it for yourself!

Finally, define a realistic time frame for achieving your goals. At a certain predetermined point in time, you will sit down and review your goals to see if you've accomplished them. This gives you the opportunity to troubleshoot unexpected barriers that might arise after you've implemented your plan.

Create Behavioral Intention

Behavioral intention is a state of mind in which you are mentally committed to following through on a promise. People who experience high levels of behavioral intention are much more likely to succeed at making complex lifestyle changes. One way to strengthen behavioral intention is to mentally rehearse the new behaviors you want to engage in. Mental rehearsal can be even more powerful when you first imagine being tempted to do an old, unworkable behavior, followed by imagining that you correct that tendency and go on to successfully practice the new behavior.

Expressing promises out loud is another powerful way to strengthen your intention. For example, when you first wake up, you could say, "Today, I intend to sit down over breakfast with my partner and talk about the things I like about our relationship." The more you prime the pump of behavioral intention, the stronger your action tendencies will become.

Learn Bit by Bit

Another important aspect of learning habits is the process of *shaping*—practicing parts of a larger habit and then beginning to piece the parts together. For example, if you are shy and one of your goals is to be more socially outgoing, you might first stand near the edge of a social conversation and listen (and learn) to how people make small talk. The next step might be to practice small talk with just one person, outside of a social setting.

Each little behavior is a piece of a more complex chain of behaviors that will allow you to overcome shyness and succeed in social situations. The benefit of shaping is that, whereas engaging in the entire chain might seem overwhelming and stop you in your tracks, each individual piece feels more doable and less threatening.

Develop Cues

One of the main obstacles to starting new lifestyle behaviors is that your current social context will tend to elicit the old behaviors that you want to change. For example, you might want to practice relaxation and deep breathing right after you wake up in the morning, but everyone else in the household is racing around trying to get ready for work or school. They are not going to tell you to sit down and practice deep breathing!

Cue-controlled behavior involves developing your own reminder system so that you are on your own practice schedule. Here are some very popular cueing strategies:

- **Pneumonic:** using a particular word, phrase, or quote to trigger the new response. "I will use the phrase, *may you have ease of being*, as a signal to look compassionately at myself in the mirror for 2 to 3 minutes."

- **Pairing:** pairing the new behavior with a well-established daily habit. "I will practice looking compassionately at myself in the mirror for 2 to 3 minutes right after I brush my teeth."

- **Perceptual:** using a sensory experience to stimulate the new behavior. "When I see it is nine o'clock on my watch, I will go find a mirror and look compassionately at myself for 2 to 3 minutes."

The neat thing about cues is that you can take them with you anywhere, and they can trigger your desired behavior even in novel situations. In general, the more ways you practice new lifestyle strategies, the more automatic and natural they will become. The reverse is also true. If you don't practice mindfulness or positivity behaviors regularly, it will be much more difficult to use them to offset a downward depression spiral.

JUST IN CASE: POSITIVITY AS PROTECTION AGAINST RELAPSE

Depression researchers have known for decades that a lack of positive, reinforcing daily activities is a key risk factor for developing a depression (Carvahlo and Hopko 2011; Lewinsohn and Libet 1972). Research has shown that these behavioral deficits typically precede the development of a depressed mood. In other words, before you ever feel depressed, you are already in the process of decreased engagement in behaviors that produce positive emotions and increased engagement with depression-producing behaviors.

Now, the concept of positivity provides us with a very clear explanation of how this works and what intervention is needed to reverse the downward spiral of depression. Indeed, one well-respected treatment for depression, called *behavior activation therapy* (Martell and Addis 2004), focuses almost exclusively on helping depressed patients identify and engage in pleasant and reinforcing behaviors on a daily basis. From a neuroscience perspective, this form of treatment attempts to strengthen the reward-anticipating circuitry of the brain by scheduling activities that produce hedonic and eudaimonic rewards.

Neuroscience studies demonstrate that downward-spiraling systems like depression hinge on the capacity of negative emotions to narrow the scope of attention and cognition (Schmitz, De Rosa, and Anderson 2009). Put simply, our attention becomes narrowly focused on negative thoughts, feelings, memories, and sensations. We can't see these private experiences for what they are because we are over-identified with them. In turn, this leads us to engage in behaviors that create, amplify, and maintain a downward depression spiral.

Whereas negative spirals narrow attention and cognition, positive spirals broaden attention and create more expansive forms of awareness, which in turn lead to a wider than usual access to sensory information and ideas. And the probability of spontaneously engaging in new positive emotion–producing behaviors increases (Frederickson and Branigan 2005). Thinking becomes broader and more flexible, leading to an increased likelihood of *metacognitive shifts* of perspective. Think of a metacognitive shift as a sudden large change of perspective—the kind that can turn the meaning of a life setback from a downer into an opportunity for personal growth (Schmitz, DeRosa, and Anderson 2009).

When life gives you an unexpected challenge, you are at a choice point: You can use positivity lifestyle strategies to offset the stress, or you can fall into a familiar but unworkable pattern of emotional and behavioral avoidance behaviors. Andy's example demonstrates how situational stresses beyond our control can lead us to abandon positive emotion–producing lifestyle behaviors and subsequently trigger a relapse into depression.

ANDY'S STORY

Andy, a forty-one-year-old married man with three children, works as a branch manager at a local bank. He started having problems with depression at age twenty-five, when his father died suddenly of a heart attack. They had been very close, and Andy held him up as a role model. His father was very ambitious and driven at work, and he taught Andy to excel by outlasting his competitors on the job. As a result, Andy arrived at work before everyone else and left after everyone else. This created quite a bit of tension in his marriage because his wife felt he was always preoccupied with work. He tended to get irritable with his children when his job stress was high. He had also developed a smoking habit, which his wife really disliked.

ACT helped Andy see that his depression was a signal that he was expending too much energy in his work life, to the detriment of other important areas of life. He felt unhealthy, he had trouble relaxing and playing, and his relationships weren't going well. Andy made and kept a promise to limit his work hours and schedule fun activities with his wife and children at least three times weekly. He also used his mindfulness skills to help him stay present during these activities, rather than thinking about work issues. Over a six-week period, Andy noticed that his sense of vitality was steadily increasing. He and his wife began talking about taking a long road trip with their children, which would require Andy to take an extended vacation. Andy was enthusiastic about this idea and put in for a three-week vacation that would occur in six months, when his kids were out of school. At the urging of his wife, Andy also made a choice to quit smoking and, with the aid of his family doctor, set a quit date. Andy was on the path out of depression and into vital living!

Four months later, Andy was informed that his bank had been purchased by a much larger regional bank and that he was being laid off with only one month of severance pay. Andy was devastated. He felt betrayed and was extremely angry about the way he'd been treated. Buying his father's messages about work, Andy ruminated for hours on end about not being a success unless he could find a job with the same status as his previous one. However, job options at that level were extremely limited and he couldn't find a similar position. He stopped going out with his wife and children, and he started smoking again. Whenever his family tried to enlist Andy in some type of positive emotion–producing activity, he would snap at them and tell them to go have fun without him. His depression level steadily increased as the weeks went by without any job opportunities surfacing. Andy got hooked by his reactive mind's evaluation that he was a failure, that he had let his family down, and that life had treated him unfairly. Andy was back in the depression trap.

Building the Protective Shield

There is sometimes very little you can do to protect yourself from an unfortunate, life-altering event, such as the one Andy experienced. But there is a lot that you can do to help buffer the effect of that event, situation, or interaction on your mood. When these situations happen, you have a job to do: protect yourself from unknowingly generating a depression spiral. The most important thing to remember is that positive *and* negative emotion spirals obey the same basic principles. They are built from the ground up on a day-to-day basis, and the longer they persist, the longer they carry over their energy and influence from one day to another. So, you must be focused on countering the emotional force of a negative life event with the cumulative emotional force of strategies designed to produce positivity.

In Andy's case, he reverted back to the very strategies he had used after his father's death, and that had led to his depression in the first place: attaching to unworkable rules about his values, withdrawing from the people he loved, and breaking his promise to protect his health. While you can't predict every act of fate that will occur in life, and you certainly can't prepare for devastating losses, you can learn to anticipate life situations that might elevate your risk for depression.

IDENTIFY YOUR RISK SITUATIONS

One easy way to forecast depression-triggering situations is to look back on your depression history and identify events, situations, or interactions that have triggered past depressions. An *event* is a specific occurrence, like being fired from a job. A *situation* is an ongoing process that poses emotional challenges, such as having a child with severe behavior problems. An *interaction* is an emotionally challenging relationship between you and one or more people, such as a spouse, several family members, or friends. Take a moment now to reflect on this, and then write down potential depression risks in each category.

Risky Situations

Risky life events: _____

_____

_____

Risky life situations:_____

_____

_____

Risky interactions: _____

_____

_____

Further Exploration. What did you come up with in the way of depression risks? Were these primarily specific life events that could set you off, or are you more prone to being triggered by difficult interactions with people? Did you identify some life situations that would pose an ongoing risk to you? The key to staying on top of your situation is to make sure you anticipate the setbacks that life is going to offer you.

MONITOR DEPRESSIVE BEHAVIORS

Although being laid off was the triggering event for Andy's slide back into depression, he didn't become depressed again overnight. It took weeks for Andy's depressive behaviors to take hold, and this made it difficult for him to see what was happening. He didn't stop going out with his wife and children all at once; he started by begging off a few outings and slowly ended up stopping altogether. This is a key characteristic of a developing depression spiral: Each depressive response increases the intensity and downward force of the spiral a little bit. You can get stuck in this trap little by little without realizing what's going on.

To prevent this from happening, regularly take inventory of your depressive behaviors in the four major life domains—relationships, work/study, leisure/play, and health—using the Behavioral Risk and Vitality Assessment in chapter 2. (You can also download a fresh copy from http://www.newharbinger.com/38457.) Go ahead and review your previous responses to this inventory; then fill it out again and score it.

In the first row of the worksheet that follows, write today's date and record how you scored today in each category. Since the greatest risk for becoming depressed again occurs in the first year, we ask that you do this inventory once each month for the next year and record your scores on the worksheet. Post this worksheet in your home to serve as a reminder to do the inventory each month.

DEPRESSIVE BEHAVIORS MONITORING WORKSHEET

Date Inventoried	Relationships Score	Work/Study Score	Leisure/Play Score	Health Score
Today:				
Month 1:				
Month 2:				
Month 3:				
Month 4:				
Month 5:				
Month 6:				
Month 7:				
Month 8:				
Month 9:				
Month 10:				
Month 11:				
Month 12:				

Further Exploration. If you notice at any point in time that your scores in any area are going in the wrong direction, it's crucial that you spring into action. As the old saying goes: "A stitch in time saves nine." Ask yourself the following questions:

Has anything happened in my life recently that might be responsible for this higher score?

How have I been feeling during the last several weeks?

Is there anything that I'm avoiding dealing with in my life right now?

What might be out of balance in my life that I need to fix or address?

What does my wise mind have to say about the situation I'm in right now?

Am I drifting away from my positivity lifestyle? If so, what is missing and how can I restore it?

After carefully thinking through the answers to these questions, the next step is to implement the mindfulness and positivity strategies in your written prevention plan. In the next section, we are going to help you develop your plan.

CREATE A DEPRESSION PREVENTION PLAN

Andy's story illustrates something that occurs all too often: He stopped using mindfulness strategies that could generate a powerful positive emotion counterforce when he needed it the most. In his case, spending quality time with his wife and children—and being accepting, nonjudgmental, and detached in relation to his thoughts and feelings—would have helped widen his perspective on what he could and couldn't control in life. This likely would have buffered him from the stress of losing his job and lessened the likelihood that he would slide back into a depression.

In this case, Andy didn't have a written prevention plan in place that he could follow, and he was forced to wing it at the very time his emotional resources were the most depleted. That is not a good combination for protecting yourself against a relapse.

To avoid this pitfall, it's essential that you develop a depression prevention plan. This is a written description of the actions you'll take if you sense your depression is increasing, or if you score more than 3 points higher than your baseline score in any life domain during your monthly inventory. In the following worksheet, describe specific mindfulness strategies you will use in each area of life if you're getting more depressed. Ideally, the behaviors you come up with should produce positivity in you when you engage in them.

MY DEPRESSION PREVENTION PLAN

Life Domain	Specific Positivity or Mindfulness Strategies I Will Use
Relationships	
Work/Study	
Leisure/Play	
Health	

Further Exploration. Were you able to think of at least one specific positive emotion or mindfulness strategy that you could apply in each area of living? If you came up empty in one or more life areas, think about it some more, and then come back and try this exercise again. If you feel like you have a pretty well-developed prevention plan, post it in a conspicuous location in your home, perhaps on your refrigerator, on a mirror in the bedroom, by your computer, or on a toilet seat. Choose a place where you'll make visual contact with your plan daily. This will help you be vigilant for high-risk situations and prepare you to use mindfulness and positive emotion strategies in those situations. And, just as when you first acted on your depression, you need to follow through on these strategies regardless of your energy level or how you feel. If you keep at it, your prevention plan can quickly reverse a downward depression spiral.

ANDY'S JOURNEY TOWARD A VITAL LIFE

When Andy reflected on his situation, he realized that anything related to job seeking was a huge trigger for a downward depression spiral. He had trouble responding with self-compassion whenever he was turned down for a job, and he promised to begin practicing self-compassion phrases during daily walks. He realized he wasn't emotionally connecting with his wife and children, and was opting out of family activities that he valued and made him feel good inside. He made a promise to ask his wife out on an inexpensive date at least twice a week.

In the following weeks, Andy had a few more unsuccessful job interviews, but this time he had a plan and he followed through on it. He noticed that he was much less attached to his harsh, critical self-story when he was involved in activities with his wife and children. Granted, he was concerned about his family's financial security, but those concerns seemed to be balanced by the fact that he had a loving relationship with his wife and that he enjoyed being around for his children. Andy resolved to continue his job search, this time looking for jobs that were less competitive and would demand less of his time. He noticed that his depression, irritability, and sense of isolation were no longer the dominant experiences of each day; instead, he was able to enjoy spending quality time with his wife and playing dad for his kids. He eventually found a job that would support his new, more relaxed lifestyle—and it wasn't even in the banking industry. Andy was back on the path toward a life worth living!

A SNEAK PREVIEW OF YOUR FUTURE

This is the end of the book, but not the end of your life journey, so we'd like to offer a sneak preview of the path that lies before you. You've learned a lot of strategies that will be very helpful as you reengage in your life. You understand and accept that life has its many challenges—that there will be good times and there will be bad times. By accepting and participating in both the good and the bad, you will be able to experience both in a healthy way. You'll be able to show up and stay present in your life on a daily basis, and your stance of mindfulness will put you into direct contact with the immense richness and vitality life offers. Because you are in touch with your closely held values, you'll have a compass bearing to follow when things get difficult or confusing. You will persist in pursuing your dreams no matter what obstacles life puts in your way. You will be flexible enough to revise or abandon strategies that aren't working and to sense new opportunities that you may not have been aware of before. In short, you will be an unstoppable force in the world, free from self-defeating attachments and focused on what matters most. As fellow travelers, we wish you all the best and pray that you will have the rich and fulfilling life that you deserve.

IDEAS TO CULTIVATE

- Life is a marathon, not a sprint. You need to build a positive emotion lifestyle that will help you stockpile coping resources for dealing with the challenges that life has to offer.

- Positive emotion spirals work the same way depression spirals do, only in reverse. They help you spiral up rather than spiral down emotionally.

- Positive emotion spirals involve being mindful and in the present moment, seeing the growth potential in challenging life situations, and actively savoring positive life events as they occur.

- Positive emotion lifestyles should include a variety of behaviors in the life domains of relationships, work, play, and health.

- Lifestyle change involves setting specific goals, troubleshooting barriers, mentally rehearsing planned behaviors, regularly reviewing your results, and making changes based upon results.

- You don't have to live in fear of depression, but you do need to have a (hopefully written) plan for how you intend to respond if depression knocks on your door.

Accessing Further Treatment and Support Resources

Many people who complete a self-help book like this one decide that they would like to continue working to develop their mindfulness skills. This might be because the skills have really helped them and they want to learn more, or because they have not benefited from the program as much as they had hoped.

One thing we've learned over the years is that everyone's path to a depression-free life is different. Some people move faster; some people respond a little slower. Whatever your situation, here are some ways to access further help and foster support resources.

INTERNET-BASED TREATMENT PROGRAMS

With the seemingly endless expansion of the Internet, people now have access to all kinds of resources for better understanding depression and what to do about it. If you would like to bone up on your ACT skills, you can register to participate in an Internet treatment study conducted by Michael Levin, PhD, a well-known ACT researcher. To access the study website, go to http://usucbs.com/participate.html. Once there, you will go through a simple screening process that will determine which of several Internet treatment studies you might be eligible for.

Another well-known Internet-based treatment program for depression is called MoodGYM (https://moodgym.anu.edu.au). Originally developed in Australia in 2001, this self-guided program for depression uses a more traditional cognitive behavioral approach, meaning there will be less emphasis on mindfulness and more on correcting negative thinking, personal problem solving, and pleasant-activity scheduling.

MOBILE APPS

Mobile applications are accessible via most smartphones and have the advantage of being portable and accessible at any time. You can also use the reminder functions on your smartphone to prompt you to practice skills on a specific schedule. Although research is fairly preliminary on mobile apps, findings do show they can be quite helpful. Many of the mobile apps listed below have not been tested by researchers (although some have) to determine the extent to which they produce benefits or positive skill changes over time, but they are generally consistent with teaching the skills we know can improve people's lives. We think these apps could be quite helpful for you and are worth trying out.

General ACT Apps

These ACT apps are designed to teach you skills that can help with a wide range of challenges and goals:

- ACT Coach (iOS; free), https://itunes.apple.com/us/app/act-coach/id804247934?mt=8

- ACT Companion (iOS and Android; $15), http://www.actcompanion.com

Mindfulness Apps

There are several mindfulness applications out there, and most will probably be useful in helping you learn beneficial meditation skills. Here are some favorites we recommend:

- Stop, Breathe & Think (iOS and Android; free), http://stopbreathethink.org

- Mindfulness Coach (iOS; free), http://www.ptsd.va.gov/public/materials/apps/mobile app_mindfulness_coach.asp

- Headspace (iOS and Android; free for limited use and then paid subscription), https://www.headspace.com

Depression Apps

Mood Coach is a mobile app developed by the U. S. Department of Veterans Affairs for depression (iOS; free; https://itunes.apple.com/us/app/mood-coach/id1060947437?mt=8). It teaches behavioral activation, a treatment approach we describe in this book. Behavior activation helps depressed individuals learn how to reengage in their lives and improve their moods as a result.

ENLIST PROFESSIONAL HELP

If you feel you need more help than this book and other resources can provide, we recommend you seek some professional help, either from a therapist or a health care provider. If you've been working with a therapist to help your depression, you might want to take this book with you to your next appointment and together go over the structure of the program. When we use this program with depressed people, we organize therapy goals so that they correspond to the structure of the book. For example, the goal between sessions may be to complete the values compass work in chapter 5 and bring the results in for review and discussion. If you aren't currently working with a therapist but have had good results with one in the past, you might want to schedule several visits now to develop a plan for preventing a relapse.

Another important form of support involves discussing your situation with a health care professional, such as your family doctor, a nurse practitioner, or a physician's assistant. Every day, these people provide health care to patients experiencing depression. Your doctor might already be aware of your situation and may be prescribing antidepressants for you. Although most health professionals are very familiar with the use of antidepressant medications, they may not be familiar with the ACT approach. Either way, it will be to your advantage to initiate a discussion with your doctor about your goals in the ACT program. Medical professionals are usually very busy and may not have the time to get a full history of your depression and your use of ACT. You can facilitate the dialogue by giving your health care provider a copy of your depression prevention plan. This way, if you do start to backslide, your health care provider can review the plan and support you in following it. Often, this is all that is needed to keep another depression from developing, or to keep your current depression from worsening.

RALLY YOUR SOCIAL SUPPORT

Another important strategy to help you continue on your quest to transcend depression is to enlist the aid of a spouse or partner, friend, or family member. Ultimately, we live in an interpersonal world. It's hard to go anywhere or do anything without running into other humans. Even when approaching the very summit of Mount Everest, climbers often find themselves in a long string of people with the same goal in mind. Reaching the summit requires each individual to summon the will to persevere, but in most cases it also involves teamwork and compatible climbing partners. One way of keeping your momentum is to create a network of people who know what you are trying to do and are willing to support you as you carry this program forward in your life. *This is particularly true if you are still struggling with depression as you complete this book, even though you might have experienced some benefit. In this case, reaching out for additional help and support is essential.* Let's first take a look at what social support is, what it isn't, and the qualities to be on the lookout for as you seek people to be your supporters.

Look for Competent Social Support

Not all kinds of social support are created equal. Some forms of social support can actually be destructive, so it is important to know when you are receiving a healthy form of encouragement. We use the term *competent social support* to describe a healthy form of connection characterized by a nonjudgmental and empathic stance. It doesn't involve criticism, lecturing, giving advice, or comparing how you're doing with how that person (or anyone else) dealt with a similar problem. When you're struggling and your morale is sagging, the last thing you need is someone who criticizes you, lectures you, makes you feel like a failure, or tells you what to do.

The best social support is often provided by people who have a similar view of the world or share a common interest with you. For example, if you go to church, other members of the congregation probably share many of your religious or spiritual views. If you take a yoga class or go on a meditation retreat, you'll probably be surrounded by people who are interested in acceptance and mindfulness as a way of living. Even something as simple as a reading group or a gardening club can help you connect with kindred souls.

Find a Vitality Partner

Normally, people value their privacy and are reluctant to share their deepest, darkest secrets with others. One of the most powerful forms of social support is having a person you can share your most private feelings and yearnings with. This person might be a very close friend, a sponsor in a self-help group, a spouse, or life partner. This person can help you stay focused on your true north in your quest to live a vital, valued life; hence the term *vitality partner*.

To help you stay accountable, this person will need to know about your struggle with depression and how you intend to use the ACT approach to create a vital life. In most cases, people who are likely candidates to be your vitality partner will already know you've been depressed. If he or she is not familiar with the ACT approach, that's okay; you may have to educate your vitality partner about the essentials of the ACT model. A natural result of this process of education is that he or she might get interested in using ACT as well! This is a great outcome because you can then support each other in your joint quests toward vital living.

Take a few minutes to develop a short list of people you know who might qualify as a vitality partner. Think about each candidate and ask yourself, "Is this person likely to be emotionally supportive and nonjudgmental? Can this person motivate me?" If the answer is yes, you have a very good candidate for your vitality partner. If you hesitated for a moment, look at the basis for hesitating. You might not want to bother this person, for example, thinking he or she is very busy and might not have the time to support you. That is a legitimate reason to pause, and maybe you will or won't initiate a contact. If you hesitated because you are unsure if this person can remain nonjudgmental or can avoid telling you what to do, that is a red flag. Move on to the next person on your list.

Next, it is important to be clear about what kind of positive support you would like your vitality partner to engage in. For example, you might ask him or her to call you on Saturday mornings and ask how your ten-minute morning mindfulness practice is going and what you've been learning from it. If one or more support requests seem vague, go back and rewrite them in more specific terms: what you would like your vitality partner to do, and when and how often you would like the person to do it.

Now that you've identified a potential vitality partner and have developed a list of specific support activities, it is time to meet with this person and discuss your request. The best way to follow through with this is to develop it as a behavioral intention, as recommended in the previous chapter. If you frame this request as something you intend to do in a very specific way, it's more likely that you'll do it. Complete the brief statement of intention below as a way of making this commitment to yourself.

MY VITALITY PARTNER

I intend to meet with _____ [potential vitality

partner] on _____ [date], at _____ [location]. I intend to

ask my vitality partner if he or she would be willing to help me by engaging in the following support behaviors

[for example, check in with me weekly about my goal to be more self-compassionate and less self-critical; send

me regular text messages encouraging me to keep pursuing my goals]: _____

_____

_____

Acknowledgments

We want thank Catharine Meyers for her undying support of us in our journey to become authors; Vicraj Gill for her monumental insights and suggestions that made this book far better than it was to start with; and Marisa Solís for her out-of-this-world copyediting skills and her knack for practicing compassionate firmness with us!

References

Alloy, L. B., L. Y. Abramson, W. G. Whitehouse, M. E. Hogan, C. Panzarella, and D. T. Rose. 2006. "Prospective Incidence of First Onsets and Recurrences of Depression in Individuals at High and Low Cognitive Risk for Depression." *Journal of Abnormal Psychology* 115: 145–156.

Andrews-Hanna, J. 2012. "The Brain's Default Network and Its Adaptive Role in Internal Mentation." *The Neuroscientist* 18: 251–270.

Arch, J. J., K. B. Wolitzky-Taylor, G. H. Eifert, and M. G. Craske. 2012. "Longitudinal Treatment Mediation of Traditional Cognitive Behavioral Therapy and Acceptance and Commitment Therapy for Anxiety Disorders." *Behaviour Research and Therapy* 50: 469–478.

Baer, R. A., G. T. Smith, E. Lykins, D. Button, J. Krietemeyer, S. Sauer, et al. 2008. "Construct Validity of the Five Facet Mindfulness Questionnaire in Meditating and Nonmeditating Samples." *Assessment* 15: 329–342.

Baer, R. A., G. T. Smith, J. Hopkins, J. Krietemeyer, and L. Toney. 2006. "Using Self-Report Assessment Methods to Explore Facets of Mindfulness." *Assessment* 13: 27–45.

Barnhofer, T., C. Crane., E. Hargus, M. Amarasinghe, R. Winder, and J. M. Williams. 2009. "Mindfulness-Based Cognitive Therapy as a Treatment for Chronic Depression: A Preliminary Study." *Behavior Research and Therapy* 47: 366–373.

Baumeister, R., E. Bratslavsky, M. Muraven, and D. Tice. 1998. "Ego Depletion: Is the Active Self a Limited Resource?" *Journal of Personality and Social Psychology* 74: 1252–1265.

Bihari, J., and E. Mullan. 2014. "Relating Mindfully: A Qualitative Exploration of Changes in Relationships Through Mindfulness-Based Cognitive Therapy." *Mindfulness* 5: 46–59.

Blarrina, M., C. Luciano, T. Cardenas, J. Suarez-Falcon, and K. Strosahl. 2016. "An Effectiveness Study of Focused Acceptance and Commitment Therapy for Emotional Disorders." Manuscript under review.

Bohlmeijer, E., P. ten Klooster, M. Fledderus, M. Veehof, and R. Baer. 2011. "Psychometric Properties of the Five Facet Mindfulness Questionnaire in Depressed Adults and Development of a Short Form." *Assessment* 18: 308–320.

Brewer, J., P. Worhunsky, J. Gray, Y. Tang, J. Weber, and H. Kober. 2011. "Meditation Experience Is Associated with Differences in Default Mode Network Activity and Connectivity." *Proceedings of the National Academy of Sciences USA* 108: 20254–20259.

Bryant, F., Chadwick, E., and Kluwe, D. 2011. "Understanding the Processes that Regulate Positive Emotional Experience: Unsolved Problems and Future Directions for Theory and Research on Savoring." *International Journal of Well-Being* 1: 107-126.

Buckner, R., J. Andrews-Hanna, and D. Schacter. 2008. "The Brain's Default Network: Anatomy, Function, and Relevance to Disease." *Annals of the New York Academy of Science* 1124: 1–38.

Campbell-Sills, L., D. H. Barlow, T. A. Brown, and S. G. Hofmann. 2006. "Acceptability and Suppression of Negative Emotion in Anxiety and Mood Disorders." *Emotion* 6: 587–595.

Cape, J., C. Whittington, M. Buszewicz, P. Wallace, and L. Underwood. 2010. "Brief Psychological Therapies for Anxiety and Depression in Primary Care: Meta-Analysis and Meta-Regression." *BMC Medicine* 8: 38.

Carlson, R. 1997. *Don't Sweat the Small Stuff—And It's All Small Stuff: Simple Ways to Keep the Little Things from Taking Over Your Life.* New York: Hyperion.

Carvalho, J., and D. Hopko. 2011. "Behavioral Theory of Depression: Reinforcement as a Mediating Variable Between Avoidance and Depression." *Journal of Behavior Therapy and Experimental Psychiatry* 42: 154–162.

Chambers, R., Gullone, E., and Allen, N. 2009. "Mindful Emotion Regulation: An Integrative Review." *Clinical Psychology Review* 29: 560-572.

Chavez, R., and T. Heatherton. 2014. "Multimodal Fronto-Striatal Connectivity Underlies Individual Differences in Self-Esteem." *Social Cognitive and Affective Neuroscience* 10: 364–370.

Chödrön, P. 2012. *Living Beautifully with Uncertainty and Change.* Boston: Shambhala Publications.

Cohn, M., B. Frederickson, S. Brown, J. Mikels, and A. Conway. 2009. "Happiness Unpacked: Positive Emotions Increase Life Satisfaction by Building Resilience." *Emotion* 9: 361–368.

Covey, S. 1989. *The Seven Habits of Highly Effective People: Powerful Lessons on Personal Change.* New York: Simon and Schuster.

Dalai Lama, K. Lhundrub, and J. Cabezon. 2011. *Meditation on the Nature of Mind.* Boston: Wisdom Publications.

Dalgleish, T., and J. Yiend. 2006. "The Effects of Suppressing a Negative Autobiographical Memory on Concurrent Intrusions and Subsequent Autobiographical Recall in Dysphoria." *Journal of Abnormal Psychology* 115: 467–473.

Davidson, R., and S. Begley. 2012 *The Emotional Life of Your Brain: How Its Unique Patterns Affect the Way You Think, Feel and Live—And How You Can Change Them.* London, UK: Hudson Street Press.

Deshmukh, V. D. 2006. "Neuroscience of Meditation." *Scientific World Journal* 16: 2239–2253.

Dong, M., H. W. Giles, V. J. Felitti, S. R. Dube, J. E. Williams, D. P. Champman, and R. F. Anda. 2004. "Insights into Causal Pathways for Ischemic Heart Disease: Adverse Childhood Experiences Study." *Circulation: Journal of the American Heart Association* 110: 1761–1766.

Eisendrath, S., E. Gillung, K. Delucchi, Z. Segal, J. Nelson, L. McInnes, D. Mathalon, and M. Feldman. 2016. "A Randomized Controlled Trial of Mindfulness-Based Cognitive Therapy for Treatment-Resistant Depression." *Psychotherapy and Psychosomatics* 85: 99–110.

Farb, N., A. Anderson, H. Mayberg, J. Bean, D. McKeon, and Z. Segal. 2010. "Minding One's Emotions: Mindfulness Training Alters the Neural Expression of Sadness." *Emotion* 10: 25–33.

Felitti, V., R. Anda, D. Nordenberg, D. Williamson, A. Spitz, V. Edwards, M. Koss, and J. Marks. 1998. "Relationship of Childhood Abuse and Household Dysfunction to Many of the Leading Causes of Death in Adults: The Adverse Childhood Experiences (ACE) Study." *American Journal of Preventive Medicine* 14: 245–258.

Fennell, M. J. V. 2004. "Depression, Low Self-Esteem, and Mindfulness." *Behaviour Research and Therapy* 42: 1053–1067.

Fields, H., G. Hjemstad, E. Margolis, and S. Nicola. 2007. "Ventral Tegmental Area Neurons in Learned Appetitive Behavior and Positive Reinforcement." *Annual Review of Neuroscience* 30: 289–316.

Finucane, A., and S. W. Mercer. 2006. "An Exploratory Mixed Methods Study of the Acceptability and Effectiveness of Mindfulness-Based Cognitive Therapy for Patients with Active Depression and Anxiety in Primary Care." *BMC Psychiatry* 6: 14.

Fledderus, M., E. Bohlmeijer, M. Pieterse, and K. Schreurs. 2012. "Acceptance and Commitment Therapy as Guided Self-Help for Psychological Distress and Positive Mental Health: A Randomized Controlled Trial." *Psychological Medicine* 42: 485–495.

Forman, E., J. Chapman, J. Herbert, E. Goetter, E. Yuen, and E. Moitra. 2012. "Using Session-by-Session Measurement to Compare Mechanisms of Action for Acceptance and Commitment Therapy and Cognitive Therapy." *Behavior Therapy* 43: 341–354.

Fox, M., A. Snyder, J. Vincent, M. Corbetta, D. Van Essen, and M. Raichle. 2005. "The Human Brain Is Intrinsically Organized into Dynamic, Anti-Correlated Functional Networks." *Proceedings of the National Academy of Sciences USA* 102: 9673–9678.

Frederickson, B., and C. Branigan. 2005. "Positive Emotions Broaden the Scope of Attention and Thought-Action Repertoires." *Cognition & Emotion* 19: 313–332.

Frederickson, B., and M. Losada. 2005. "Positive Affect and the Complex Dynamics of Human Flourishing." *American Psychologist* 60: 678–686.

Frederickson, B., M. Cohn, K. Coffey, and J. Pek. 2008. "Open Hearts Build Lives: Positive Emotions, Induced Through Loving Kindness Meditations, Build Consequential Personal Resources." *Journal of Personality and Social Psychology* 95: 1045–1162.

Fugelsang, J., and K. Dunbar. 2004. "A Cognitive Neuroscience Framework for Understanding Causal Reasoning and the Law." *Philosophical Transactions of The Royal Society of London.* Series B 359: 1749–1754.

Galliet, M., R. Baumeister, C. Dewall, J. Maner, E. Plant, and D. Tice. 2007. "Self-Control Relies on Glucose as a Limited Energy Source: Willpower Is More Than a Metaphor." *Journal of Personality and Social Psychology* 92: 325–336.

Garland, E., B. Frederickson, A. Kring, D. Johnson, P. Meyer, and D. Penn. 2010. "Upward Spirals of Positive Emotions Counter Downward Spirals of Negativity: Insights from the Broaden-and-Build Theory and Affective Neuroscience on the Treatment of Emotion Dysfunctions and Deficits in Psychopathology." *Clinical Psychology Review* 30: 849–864.

Garland, E., S. Gaylord, and B. Frederickson. 2011. *Mindfulness* 2: 59-67.

Gazzola, V., and C. Keysers. 2009. "The Observation and Execution of Actions Share Motor and Somatosensory Voxels in All Tested Subjects: Single Subject Analysis of Unsmoothed fMRI Data." *Cerebral Cortex* 19: 1239–1255.

Goldin, P., and J. Gross. 2010. "Effect of Mindfulness Meditation Training on the Neural Bases of Emotion Regulation in Social Anxiety Disorder." *Emotion* 10: 83–91.

Grant, B. F., D. A. Dawson, F. S. Stinson, S. P. Chou, M. C. Dufour, and R. P. Pickering. 2004. "The 12-Month Prevalence and Trends in DSM-IV Alcohol Abuse and Dependence: United States, 1991–92 and 2001." *Drug and Alcohol Dependence* 74: 223–234.

Haggard, P. 2008. "Human Volition: Towards a Neuroscience of Will." *Nature Reviews: Neuroscience* 9: 934–946.

Hankey, A. 2006. "Studies of Advanced Stages of Meditation in the Tibetan Buddhist and Vedic Traditions I: A Comparison of General Changes." *Complementary and Alternative Medicine* 3: 513–521.

Hayes, L., C. Boyd, and J. Sewell. 2011. "Acceptance and Commitment Therapy for the Treatment of Adolescent Depression: A Pilot Study in a Psychiatric Outpatient Setting." *Mindfulness* 2: 86–94.

Hayes, S., and S. Smith. 2005. *Get Out of Your Mind and into Your Life: The New Acceptance and Commitment Therapy.* Oakland, CA: New Harbinger Publications.

Hayes, S., D. Barnes-Holmes, and B. Roche, eds. 2001. *Relational Frame Theory: A Post-Skinnerian Account of Human Language and Cognition.* New York: Plenum Press.

Hayes, S., K. D. Strosahl, and K. G. Wilson. 2011. *Acceptance and Commitment Therapy: An Experiential Approach to Behavior Change.* New York: Guilford Press.

Holzel, B., M. Carmody, C. Vangel, S. Congleton, T. Yerramesetti, H. Gard, and S. Lazar. 2011. "Mindfulness Practice Leads to Increases in Regional Brain Gray Matter Density." *Psychiatry Research: Neuro-imaging* 191: 36-43.

Hughes, B., and J. Beer. 2013. "Protecting the Self: The Effect of Social-Evaluative Threat on Neural Representations of Self." *Journal of Cognitive Neuroscience* 25: 613–622.

Joorman, J., and W. Vanderlind. 2014. "Emotion Regulation in Depression: The Role of Biased Cognition and Reduced Cognitive Control." *Clinical Psychological Science* 2: 402–421.

Kabat-Zinn, J. 2005. *Coming to Our Senses: Healing Ourselves and the World Through Mindfulness.* New York: Hyperion.

Kelly, M. A. R., J. E. Roberts, and J. A. Ciesla. 2005. "Sudden Gains in Cognitive Behavioral Treatment for Depression: When Do They Occur and Do They Matter?" *Behaviour Research and Therapy* 4: 703–714.

Kessler, R. C., P. Berglund, O. Demler, R. Jin, K. R. Merikangas, and E. E. Walters. 2005. "Lifetime Prevalence and Age-of-Onset Distributions of DSM-IV Disorders in the National Comorbidity Survey Replication." *Archives of General Psychiatry* 62: 593–602.

Khin, N. A., Y. F. Chen, Y. Yang, P Yang, and T. P. Laughren. 2011. "Exploratory Analyses of Efficacy Data from Major Depressive Disorder Trials Submitted to the US Food and Drug Administration in Support of New Drug Applications." *Journal of Clinical Psychiatry* 72: 464–472.

Kirsch, I. 2014. "Antidepressants and the Placebo Effect." *Zeitschrift für Psychologie* 222: 128–134.

Kirwan, B., S. Ashby, and M. Nash. 2014. "Remembering and Imagining Differentially Engage the Hippocampus: A Multivariate fMRI Investigation." *Cognitive Neuroscience* 5: 177–185.

Kohtala, A., R. Lappalainen, L. Savonen, E. Timo, and A. Tolvanen. 2015. "A Four-Session Acceptance And Commitment Therapy Based Intervention for Depressive Symptoms Delivered by Masters Degree Level Psychology Students: A Preliminary Study." *Behavioural and Cognitive Psychotherapy* 43: 360–373.

Lappalainen, P., A. Granlund, S. Siltanen, S. Ahonen, M. Vitikainen, A. Tolvanen, and R. Lappalainen. 2014. "ACT Internet-Based vs Face-to-Face? A Randomized Controlled Trial of Two Ways to Deliver Acceptance and Commitment Therapy for Depressive Symptoms: An 18-Month Follow-Up." *Behaviour Research and Therapy* 61: 43–54.

Last, J. M. 1988. *Dictionary of Epidemiology*. Oxford, UK: Oxford University Press.

Leary, M., E. Tate, C. Adams, A. Batts, J. Hancock. 2007. "Self-Compassion and Reactions to Unpleasant Self-Relevant Events: The Implications of Treating Oneself Kindly." *Journal of Personality and Social Psychology* 92: 887–904.

Levenson, D., E. Stoll, S. Kindy, and R. Davidson. 2014. "A Mind You Can Count On: Validating Breath Counting as a Behavioral Measure of Mindfulness." *Frontiers of Psychology: Consciousness* 120: 1–10.

Lewinsohn, P., and J. Libet. 1972. "Pleasant Events, Activity Schedules and Depression." *Journal of Abnormal Psychology* 79: 291-295.

Libet, B., C. Gleason, E. Wright, and D. Pearl. 1983. "Time of Conscious Intention to Act in Relation to Onset of Cerebral Activity (Readiness-Potential): The Unconscious Initiation of a Freely Voluntary Act." *Brain Journal of Neurology* 106: 623–642.

Lundgren, T., J. B. Luoma, J. Dahl, K. Strosahl, P. Robinson, and L. Melin. 2012. "The Bull's-Eye Values Survey: A Psychometric Evaluation." *Cognitive and Behavioral Practice* 19: 518–526.

Lutz, A., J. Brefczynski-Lewis, T. Johnstone, and R. Davidson. 2008. "Regulation of the Neural Circuitry of Emotion by Compassion Meditation: Effects of Meditative Expertise." *PLoS One* 3: e1897. doi:10.1371/journal.pone.0001897.

Lutz, A., H. A. Slagter, B. N. Rawling, D. A. Francis, L. L. Greischar, and R. J. Davidson. 2009. "Mental Training Enhances Stability of Attention by Reducing Cortical Noise." *Journal of Neuroscience* 29: 418–427.

Lutz, W., N. Stulz, and K. Kock. 2009. "Patterns of Early Change and Their Relationship to Outcome and Follow-up Among Patients with Major Depressive Disorders." *Journal of Affective Disorders* 118: 60–68.

Marchetti I., E. Koster, and R. De Raedt. 2012. "Mind Wandering Heightens the Accessibility of Negative Relative to Positive Thought." *Consciousness and Cognition* 21: 1517–1525.

Marchetti, G. 2014. "Attention and Working Memory: Two Basic Mechanisms for Constructing Temporal Experiences." *Frontiers in Psychology* 5: 1–15.

Martell, C, and M. Addis. 2004. *Overcoming Depression One Step at a Time: The New Behavioral Activation Approach to Getting Your Life Back*. Oakland, CA: New Harbinger Publications.

Marcks, B. A., and D. W. Woods. 2005. "A Comparison of Thought Suppression to an Acceptance-Based Technique in the Management of Personal Intrusive Thoughts: A Controlled Evaluation." *Behaviour Research and Therapy* 43: 433–445.

Mynors-Wallis, L. M., D. H. Gath, A. Day, and F. Baker. 2000. "Randomised Controlled Trial of Problem Solving Treatment, Antidepressant Medication, and Combined Treatment for Major Depression in Primary Care." *British Medical Journal* 320: 26–30.

Neff, K. D. 2003. "Development and Validation of a Scale to Measure Self-Compassion." *Self and Identity* 2: 223–250.

Neff, K. D. 2016. "The Self Compassion Scale Is a Valid and Theoretically Coherent Measure of Self Compassion." *Mindfulness* 7: 264–274.

Neff, K., Y. Hsieh, and K. Dejitterat. 2005. "Self-Compassion, Achievement Goals, and Coping with Academic Failure." *Self and Identity* 2: 223–250.

Neff, K. D., S. S. Rude, and K. Kirkpatrick. 2007. "An Examination of Self-Compassion in Relation to Positive Psychological Functioning and Personality Traits." *Journal of Research in Personality* 41: 908–916.

Niemiec, C., K. Brown, T. Kashdan, P. Cozzolino, W. Breen, C. Levesque, and R. Ryan. 2010. "Being Present in the Face of Existential Threat: The Role of Trait Mindfulness in Reducing Defensive Responses to Mortality Salience." *Journal of Personality and Social Psychology* 99: 344–365.

Nolen-Hoeksema, S. 2000. "The Role of Rumination in Depressive Disorders and Mixed Anxiety/Depressive Symptoms." *Journal of Abnormal Psychology* 109: 504–511.

Paykel, E. S. 2006. "Cognitive Therapy in Relapse Prevention in Depression." *International Journal of Neuropsychopharmacology* 10: 131–136.

Peters, J. 2011. "The Role of the Medial Orbitofrontal Cortex in Intertemporal Choice: Prospection or Valuation?" *The Journal of Neuroscience* 31: 5889–5890.

Phan, K., T. Wager, S. Taylor, and I. Liberson. 2002. "Functional Neuroanatomy of Emotion: A Meta-Analysis of Emotion Activation Studies in PET and fMRI." *Neuroimage* 16: 331–348.

Quirk, G., and J. Beer. 2006. "Prefrontal Involvement in the Regulation of Emotion: Convergence of Rat and Human Studies." *Current Opinions in Neurobiology* 16: 723–727.

Quoidbach, J., E. V. Berry, M. Hansenne, and M. Mikolajczak. 2010. "Positive Emotion Regulation and Wellbeing: Comparing the Impact of Eight Savoring and Dampening Strategies." *Personality and Individual Differences* 49: 368–373.

Raes, F. 2010. "Rumination and Worry as Mediators of the Relationship Between Self-Compassion and Depression and Anxiety." *Personality and Individual Differences* 48: 757–761.

Raes, F., E. Pommier, K. Neff, and D. Van Gucht. 2011. "Construction and Factorial Validation of a Short Form of the Self-Compassion Scale. *Clinical Psychology & Psychotherapy* 18: 250–255.

Raichle, M., A. MacLeod, A. Snyder, W. Powers, D. Gusnard, and G. Shulman. 2001. "A Default Mode of Brain Function." *Proceedings of the National Academy of Sciences USA* 98: 676–682.

Sambataro, F., N. Donata Wolf, P. Guisti, N. Vasic, and R. Wolf. 2013. "Default Mode Network in Depression: A Pathway to Impaired Affective Cognition?" *Clinical Neuropsychiatry* 10: 212–216.

SAMHSA: Substance Abuse and Mental Health Services Administration. 2013. *Results from the 2012 National Survey on Drug Use and Health: Mental Health Findings*, NSDUH Series H-47, HHS Publication No. (SMA) 13–4805. Rockville, MD: Substance Abuse and Mental Health Services Administration.

Schaefer, C. 2006. *Grandmothers Counsel the World: Women Elders Offer Their Vision for Our Planet.* Boston: Trumpeter.

Schlegel, A., P. Kohler, S. Fogelson, A. Prescott, K. Dedeepya, and P. Ulric Tse. 2013. "Network Structure and Dynamics of the Mental Workspace." *Proceedings of the National Academy of Science* 110: 16277–16282.

Schmitz, T., E. De Rosa, and A. Anderson. 2009. "Opposing of Affective State Valence on Visual Cortical Encoding." *The Journal of Neuroscience* 29: 7199–7207.

Schotte, C. K., B. van den Bossche, D. de Doncker, S. Claes, and P. Cosyns. 2006. "A Biopsychosocial Model as a Guide for Psychoeducation and Treatment of Depression." *Depression and Anxiety* 23: 312–324.

Schuyler B., T. Kral, J. Jacquart, C. Burghy, H. Weng, D. Perlman, et al. 2014. "Temporal Dynamics of Emotional Responding: Amygdala Recovery Predicts Emotional Traits." *Social Cognitive and Affective Neuroscience* 9: 176–181.

Segal, Z. V., J. M. G. Williams, and J. D. Teasdale. 2002. *Mindfulness-Based Cognitive Therapy for Depression: A New Approach to Preventing Relapse.* New York: Guilford Press.

Shackman, A., T. Salomons, H. Slagter, A. Fox, J. Winter, and R. Davidson. 2011. "The Integration of Negative Affect, Pain and Cognitive Control in the Cingulate Cortex." *Nature Reviews: Neuroscience* 12: 154–167.

Shafir, R., R. Thiruchselvam, S. Gaurav, J. Gross, and G. Sheppes. 2016. "Neural Processing of Emotional-Intensity Predicts Emotion Regulation Choice." *Social Cognitive and Affective Neuroscience* 11. doi:10.1093/scan/nsw114.

Sheppes, G., W. Brady, and A. Samson. 2014. "In (Visual) Search for a New Distraction: The Efficiency of a Novel Attentional Deployment versus Semantic Meaning Regulation Strategies." *Frontiers in Psychology* 5: 346.

Shiota, M., and R. Levensen. 2012. "Turn Down the Volume or Change the Channel?: Emotional Effects of Detached versus Positive Reappraisal." *Journal of Personality and Social Psychology* 103: 416–429.

Singh, M., and I. Gotlib. 2014. "The Neuroscience of Depression: Implications for Assessment and Intervention." *Behaviour Research and Therapy* 62: 60–73.

Sirois, F., R. Kittner, and J. Hirsch. 2014. "Self-Compassion, Affect and Health Promoting Behaviors." *Health Psychology* 34: 661–669.

Sirois, F., D. Molnar, and J. Hirsch. 2015. "Self-Compassion, Stress, and Coping in the Context of Chronic Illness." *Self and Identity* 14: 334–347.

Smallwood, R., J. Potter, and D. Robin. 2016. "Neurophysiological Mechanisms in Acceptance and Commitment Therapy in Opioid-Addicted Patients with Chronic Pain." *Psychiatry Research: Neuroimaging* 250: 12–14.

Smith, R., and J. Ascough. 2016. *Promoting Emotional Resilience: Cognitive-Affective Stress Management Training*. New York: Guilford Press.

Somerville, L., W. Kelley, and T. Heatherton. 2010. "Self-Esteem Modulates Medial Prefrontal Cortical Responses to Evaluative Social Feedback." *Cerebral Cortex* 20: 3005–3013.

Spreng, R., J. Sepulcre, G. Turner, W. Stevens, and D. L. Schacter. 2013. "Intrinsic Architecture Underlying the Relations Among the Default, Dorsal Attention, and Frontoparietal Control Networks of the Human Brain. *Journal of Cognitive Neuroscience* 25: 74–86.

Strosahl, K., and P. Robinson. 2014. *In This Moment: Five Steps to Transcending Stress Using Mindfulness and Neuroscience*. Oakland, CA: New Harbinger Publications.

Sundquist, J., A. Lilja, K. Palmer, A. Memon, X. Wang, L. Johansson, and K. Sundquist. 2015. "Mindfulness Group Therapy in Primary Care Patients with Depression, Anxiety and Stress and Adjustment Disorders: Randomised Controlled Trial." *British Journal of Psychiatry* 206: 128–135.

Tang, Y., and M. I. Posner. 2009. "Attention Training and Attention State Training." *Trends in Cognitive Neuroscience* 13: 222–227.

Teasdale, J. D., Z. V. Segal, J. M. Williams, V. A. Ridgeway, J. M. Soulsby, and M. A. Lau. 2000. "Prevention of Relapse/Recurrence in Major Depression by Mindfulness-Based Cognitive Therapy." *Journal of Consulting and Clinical Psychology* 68: 615–623.

Teasdale, J., M. Pope, R. Moore, S. Williams, and S. Zegal. 2002. "Metacognitive Awareness and Prevention of Relapse in Depression: Empirical Evidence." *Journal of Consulting and Clinical Psychology* 70: 275–287.

Teper, R., and M. Inzlicht. 2012. "Meditation, Mindfulness and Executive Control: The Importance of Emotional Acceptance and Brain-Based Performance Monitoring." *Social Cognitive and Affective Neuroscience* 8: 85–92.

Wagner, D., J. Haxby, and T. Heatherton. 2012. "The Representation of Self and Person Knowledge in the Medial Prefrontal Cortex." *Wiley Interdisciplinary Reviews: Cognitive Science* 3: 451–470.

Wakefield, J. C., M. F. Schmitz, M. B. First, and A. V. Horwitz. 2007. "Extending the Bereavement Exclusion for Major Depression to Other Losses: Evidence from the National Comorbidity Survey." *Archives of General Psychiatry* 64: 433–440.

Weng, H., A. Fox, A. Shackman, D. Stodola, J. Caldwell, M. Olson, G. Rogers, and R. Davidson. 2013. "Compassion Training Alters Altruism and Neural Responses to Suffering." *Psychological Science* 24: 1171–1180.

Whitaker, R. 2010. *Anatomy of an Epidemic: Magic Bullets, Psychiatric Drugs and the Astonishing Rise of Mental Illness.* New York: Broadway Books.

Williams, J. M. 2008. "Mindfulness, Depression and Modes of Mind. *Cognitive Research and Therapy* 32: 721–733.

Williams, J. 2010. "Mindfulness and Psychological Process." *Emotion* 10: 1–7.

Williams, J. M. G., J. D. Teasdale, Z. V. Segal, and J. Soulsby. 2000. "Mindfulness-Based Cognitive Therapy Reduces Overgeneral Autobiographical Memory in Formerly Depressed Patients." *Journal of Abnormal Psychology* 109: 150–155.

Williams, M. G., J. D. Teasdale, Z. V. Segal, and J. Kabat-Zinn. 2007. *The Mindful Way Through Depression: Freeing Yourself from Chronic Unhappiness.* New York: Guilford Press.

Wolff, P., and A. Barbey. 2015. "Causal Reasoning with Forces." *Frontiers of Human Neuroscience* 9: 1–21.

Zettle, R. D., and J. Rains. 1989. "Group Cognitive and Contextual Therapies in Treatment of Depression." *Journal of Clinical Psychology* 45: 438–445.

Zettle, R. D., and S. C. Hayes. 1987. "Component and Process Analysis of Cognitive Therapy." *Psychological Reports* 61: 939–953.

Zettle, R. D., J. C. Rains, and S. C. Hayes. 2011. "Processes of Change in Acceptance and Commitment Therapy and Cognitive Therapy for Depression: A Mediational Reanalysis of Zettle and Rains (1989)." *Behavior Modification* 35: 265–283.

Kirk D. Strosahl, PhD, is cofounder of acceptance and commitment therapy (ACT), a cognitive behavioral approach that has gained widespread adoption in the mental health and substance-abuse communities. He is coauthor of *Brief Interventions for Radical Change* and *In This Moment: Five Steps to Transcending Stress Using Mindfulness and Neuroscience*. Strosahl provides training and consultation services for Mountainview Consulting Group, Inc. He is a pioneer in the movement to bring behavioral health services into primary care. He resides in Portland, OR.

Patricia J. Robinson, PhD, is director of training and program evaluation at Mountainview Consulting Group, Inc., a firm that assists health care systems with integrating behavioral health services into primary care settings. She is coauthor of *Real Behavior Change in Primary Care* and *The Mindfulness and Acceptance Workbook for Depression*. After exploring primary care psychology as a researcher, she devoted her efforts to its dissemination in rural America, urban public health departments, and military medical treatment facilities. Robinson resides in Portland, OR.

Foreword writer **Steven C. Hayes, PhD**, is Nevada Foundation Professor and director of clinical training in the department of psychology at the University of Nevada, Reno. An author of forty-one books and nearly 600 scientific articles, his career has focused on analysis of the nature of human language and cognition, and its application to the understanding and alleviation of human suffering and promotion of human prosperity. His work has received several awards, including the Impact of Science on Application Award from the Society for the Advancement of Behavior Analysis, and the Lifetime Achievement Award from the Association for Behavioral and Cognitive Therapies.

FROM OUR PUBLISHER—

As the publisher at New Harbinger and a clinical psychologist since 1978, I know that emotional problems are best helped with evidence-based therapies. These are the treatments derived from scientific research (randomized controlled trials) that show what works. Whether these treatments are delivered by trained clinicians or found in a self-help book, they are designed to provide you with proven strategies to overcome your problem.

Therapies that aren't evidence-based—whether offered by clinicians or in books—are much less likely to help. In fact, therapies that aren't guided by science may not help you at all. That's why this New Harbinger book is based on scientific evidence that the treatment can relieve emotional pain.

This is important: if this book isn't enough, and you need the help of a skilled therapist, use the following resources to find a clinician trained in the evidence-based protocols appropriate for your problem. And if you need more support—a community that understands what you're going through and can show you ways to cope—resources for that are provided below, as well.

Real help is available for the problems you have been struggling with. The skills you can learn from evidence-based therapies will change your life.

Matthew McKay, PhD
Publisher, New Harbinger Publications

If you need a therapist, the following organization can help you find a therapist trained in acceptance and commitment therapy (ACT).

Association for Contextual Behavioral Science (ACBS)
please visit www.contextualscience.org and click on Find an ACT Therapist.

For additional support for patients, family, and friends, please contact the following:

Anxiety and Depression Association of American (ADAA)
Please visit www.adaa.org

National Suicide Prevention Lifeline
Call 24 hours a day 1-800-273-TALK (8255) or visit www.suicidepreventionlifeline.org

Depression and Bipolar Support Alliance (DBSA)
Visit www.dbsalliance.org

National Alliance on Mental Illness (NAMI)
please visit www.nami.org

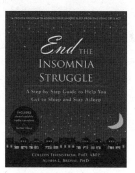
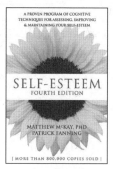

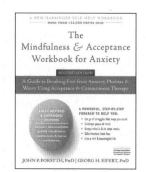

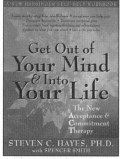

Register your **new harbinger** titles for additional benefits!

When you register your **new harbinger** title—purchased in any format, from any source—you get access to benefits like the following:

- Downloadable accessories like printable worksheets and extra content

- Instructional videos and audio files

- Information about updates, corrections, and new editions

Not every title has accessories, but we're adding new material all the time.

Access free accessories in 3 easy steps:

1. Sign in at NewHarbinger.com (or **register** to create an account).

2. Click on **register a book**. Search for your title and click the **register** button when it appears.

3. Click on the **book cover or title** to go to its details page. Click on **accessories** to view and access files.

That's all there is to it!

If you need help, visit:

NewHarbinger.com/accessories

new harbinger
CELEBRATING
40 YEARS